DISCARD

Out of a Clear Blue Sky

First Edition
1971

TENNESSEE'S FIRST LADIES AND THEIR HUSBANDS

Inscribed
For Clinch Powell Regional Library
With Best Wishes
By The Author
Nancy Wooten Walker

NANCY WOOTEN WALKER
Cleveland, Tennessee

Nancy   Wooten   Walker

Contents

(Contents Continued on Next Page)

Contents (Continued)

Gov. Winfield Dunn.

Acknowledgements

Writing a book is one thing; writing about Tennessee Governors and their Ladies is something else again. When I first approached this subject, First Ladies in Tennessee Mansion, I found that very little was known about any of the wives of the governors.

Approximately two hundred letters were sent to descendants of the governors and the ladies' families and Out of a Clear Blue Sky got under way.

If there are doubts that nothing remarkable has expired to have anything written about these sixty-three women and forty-four men—you can read for the first time of these pioneer women who came on horseback, flat boat, covered wagons to the Tennessee Country to the First Ladies who now drive Cadillacs, play golf, ride in airplanes, and live in the Governor's Mansion.

The intent of this book is to present the content of letters to me on the subject of "Tennessee Governors and Ladies from 1796 to 1971."

I am indebted to so many who have contributed to this book, which made my researches possible.

I am grateful to A.O. DeLozier, a past Superintendent of Tennessee schools and an ex College Professor, who has been a source of inestimable help and encouragement to complete this as a future reference for every school child as well as the adult lovers of Tennessee history.

I wish to express sincerest thanks to those descendants from whose storehouse of memory, scrapbooks and diaries came much of the information for this book:

Mrs. H. W. Feeman, Dr. and Mrs. W. H. Masterson, Mrs. Lowell Sevier Hays, Melba Hargis, Mrs. John Serrill Deal, Miss Zella Armstrong Southern Families (Sevier), Ann Campbell, Mr. and Mrs. A. H. Russell, Concord, Tenn., Mr. and Mrs. Bivens, Mrs. Lloyd T. Householder Sr., Ellen A. W. Campbell, Margaret Campbell, Lebanon, Tenn., Mrs. Laura McAlister Bathriek, Mrs. Prentice Cooper, Louise Harle, State R. D.A.R., Della Knox Jarnigan, Ann Knox, Wooten's History of Bradley County, Betty Horner, Jane Gaut Smith, Virginia Bradford Johns, Mrs. Herbert Carroll, Atty. Allen Trousdale and Mrs. Guild, Dr. Van Houston Stickley, Miss Eliza Moore, W. H. Hitchcock, Dr. Burk Nelson, Mrs. Donald Nelson, Librarian John Hall Hodges, Sewanee, Tenn., Mrs. Joe Bowman, Franklin, Tenn., Robbie Cannon Morton, Mrs. Vanhoosier, Allie Van Horn, Elizabeth Buchanan Worly, Mrs. Broadis Maples, Dr. and Mrs. Madison Dill, Murfreesboro, Dr. Leland Crabb, George Peabody College, Dr. Macie Southall, Mary Hall, Dudley Porter, Mrs. Albert S. Marks, Clarksville, Confederate Veteran, Vol. Jan. 1906 pp. 18 and 20, Helen Hawkins Morford, State R. D.A.R., Mary Hawkins Edward, Clerk and Master Ida Mebane, Huntingdon, Tenn., Alonzo Hawkins, Atty. and Mrs. Julian Bate Mastin, Mrs. Richard Gilliam, Huntsville, Ala., Helen Wooten Maywhort, Librarian McCallie School, Mrs. Hillsman Taylor, Memphis, Mrs. Ben Taylor, Mrs. Jay Pouder, Johnson City, Tenn. Betsy Wooten U.C. Librarian, Rev. and Mrs. James Ransom, Mrs. Earl Ransom, Louise Buchanan Webb, Murfreesboro, Mrs. J. B. Thorogood, and Miss Clara Williams, Winchester, Tenn., Opal Sharp, Cleveland, Tenn., Atty. Frank Kelley, Jasper, Tenn., Helen Zucarella, Pulaski, Tenn., Mrs. Millie Wilson Farrell, Nashville, Tenn., Mrs. Mabel Woltz, James Knox papers in Library of Congress, Judge Harry Phillips, Mrs. Netha Munford Fowler, Notable Men in Tenn., by W. Spears (1880), Mrs. A. B. Herron, Brentwood, Tenn., Mrs. J.B. Moore, Brentwood, (Brown) Mr. Sam Fleming, Nashville, Tenn., Atty. Neil S. Brown III, Nashville, Mrs. Margaret Johnson Bartlett, Greenville, Tenn., Georgia Harris Cox, Mrs. Will Turner, Virginia Travis Chapman, Travis Jackson, Cleveland, Tenn., Old Times in Tenn., by Joe Conn Guild, Holston Conference, RN Price Vol. III, Mrs. James F. Brownlow, Knoxville, Tenn., Mrs. Dorothy Cable May, Jefferson City, Tenn., Andy Weddington, Margaret Butler, Pulaski, Tenn., Confederate Vet. Vol 3 p. 242, Mrs. Frank Spoon, Elizabeth Fillauer, Mrs. Will Fillauer, Mrs. Neil S. Varnell, Mrs. A. M. Bryant, Burr Harrison, Mary Ramsey Evans, Susie Ramsey Brown, Ida Leach Browning, Mrs. John Stockard, Mrs. Buford Ellington, Mary Cheek, Mrs. John Cheek, Laura McAlister Bathrick, Gov. Jim Nance McCord, Mrs. Nell Rye Nolan, Miss Mary Leach, Mrs. Irā Shires, Anna Bell Clement, Miss Lucy Clemenson, Gov. Mansion Sec., Mr. and Mrs. Wm. Senter, Senter School, Chattanooga, Mrs. Ethel Senter Manly, Mrs. Harvey Templeton, Winchester, Freda Kenner, Atty. Denton Marks, Mrs. John Marks, Mrs. Nora Capel, Mr. and Mrs. Thomas Hooker, Lookout Mt., Mrs. Mary Patterson Phillips, Memphis, Tenn., Ruth Cox

Butler, Robert L. Taylor, Memphis, Tenn., Mrs. Stacy Grayson, Mrs. William I. Reiley, Mrs. Wylie Perry, Halls, Tenn., Miss Elizabeth Pritchard, Mrs. Winfield Dunn, First Lady, Mrs. Judith H. Custer, Secy. to Gov., Mrs. George Thorogood, Mrs. Edgar Lambert, Mrs. Charles Kerley, Elizabeth Roberts Uffleman, Cleo Shambaugh Gervin, Nancy and Dorothy Foster, Misses Louise and Kathryn Keith, Mrs. John K. Maddin, Vicky Hardwick Rymer, Dean Mable Meacham, Austin Peay College, Amaryilis Peay Armstrong, Margaret Blount, Mrs. F. W. Boechman, Dr. Macie Southall, Mrs. Roy B. Smith State U.D.C. Pres., Prentice Price, Mrs. James Arnold, Georgie Blackburn, Helen Qualls, Monterey, Tenn., Mary Price Smith, Maude Whiteside, Mrs. Spencer Barham, Agnes English, Franklin, Tenn., Mrs. Dewain Peterson, Winchester, Anna B. Hall Kyle, Lottie McCall, Miss Emily Mosley, Winchester, Mrs. Jane Stokely Jones, Newport, Mrs. Edward Hurd, Mrs. Jaunella Hooper Carpenter, Mrs. Ben W. Hooper (First Lady), Mrs. Lou Boteggi, Nashville, Tenn., Nancy Kelley Hunt, Hendersonville, Tenn., Jenny and Pati Walker, Frances Baine, Cleveland, Tenn., Prof. Roy Lillard (President of East Tenn. Historica Society), Mrs. Granville Ridley, Christine Meadows Reynolds (deceased), Elizabeth McGowan, Collierville, Tenn., Miss Nannie Lee Hicks, Knoxville, Mrs. Bryan Williams, Paris, Tenn., Intelligencer, Frank Hardwick II, L. J. Sheeley, Paris, Tenn., Sue Hardwick, Mrs. John Horton, Vanderbilt, Nashville, Mrs. Adeline Horton Beasley, W. B. Wooten Sr., Martha W. Foster, Mrs. Marquis Triplett, Johnson City, Mrs. Pat Randolph, Gayle McLain, Margaret Williamson, Joe Rymer, Congressman J. B. and Mrs. Frazier, Mrs. Bethel Brown, Keith Frazier Summers, Cleveland, Mississippi, Charles Rymer, Brenda Hall, Mrs. Nichols, Karen Masters and Stanfields Studio, Betty Sharp, Miss Ruth Chambers, Mrs. Aaron Brown, Mrs. Mangese of Cleveland Public Library, Dr. and Mrs. Charles C. Walker. Mrs. Elizabeth Cate Manly for editing the Manuscript and unselfish use of her time and car, and who out of the rich generosity of her spirit, gave criticism and encouragement fortifying me warmly in the struggle that invariably comes with giving birth to a book.

9

A Backward Look

Tennessee was first of all a settlement where lived several tribes of Indians. The Chickamaugas lived near where Chattanooga now stands; the Creeks lower down on the Tennessee river partly in Alabama; the Cherokees, who were the most warlike of all inhabited the mountains of the east with Kentucky on one side and Georgia on the other. The Chickasaws lived near Memphis. The Uches lived near Nashville.

These Indians lived in this vast wilderness filled with wild animals and dense forests.

When the white hunters of Virginia and North Carolina heard of this vast wilderness filled with deer and buffalo, some of them ventured into the dangerous and disputed territory.

William Bean, of Virginia, made the first settlement on the Watauga River, building his log cabin at the mouth of Boone's Creek. His family moved into it in 1769. Here his son Russel Bean was born, who was the first known white child to be born in Tennessee.

This was the beginning of Tennessee History. The Indians used a road called "The Great Trace" in their expeditions. This road ran through East Tennessee and connected the Southwest and the North.

The title to the land which is now Tennessee was in dispute for a long time. King Charles II, of Great Britain claimed all territory on the North American Continent which was settled by his subjects. He gave away large tracts of land, sometimes to individuals and sometimes to corporations and companies. He maintained no one could get land from the Indians except himself.

North Carolina was granted to a company of distinguished Englishmen, and this land included Tennessee. The English adopted the policy of building forts. The first fort built in East Tennessee was Fort Loudon in 1756.

Hostilities between the white men and the Indians began when upon returning home from Virginia, the Cherokees saw some horses running at large and thinking they were wild,

11

caught them. The owners thought they were horse thieves and killed some of the Indians. In revenge the Indians killed all the whites they could find. They besieged Fort Loudon, killing all except one officer and twenty men who lived to tell of the butchery.

By the year 1768 many pioneers began emigrating from older settlements to the Tennessee country where they could get plenty of land cheap. The real hardship and danger they had to undergo to hold their lands was the greatest price they paid.

Pioneers from Virginia and North Carolina began to rear their cabins along the Holston and Watauga rivers and by 1770 a substantial settlement was in progress.

Although nominally within the province of North Carolina, the settlers south of the Holston and along the Watauga were practically without any form of government. Responding to that dominant trait of the Anglo-Saxon race for self government, these sturdy pioneers in 1772 met in convention on the Watauga, where the city of Elizabethton is today and formed the "Watauga Association". This was the first seat of government in Tennessee and continued until August of 1776, when upon petition by the people of Watauga, the territory was annexed to the state of North Carolina and known as "Washington District" into a county of the same name, assigning to it the boundaries of the whole present State of Tennessee.

Two years later in 1778, Jonesborough (now Jonesboro), the first town in Tennessee, was established as the first seat of government of Washington County.

By an act of the Legislature of North Carolina in June, 1784, the territory embraced in Washington District was ceded to the United States subject to acceptance within two years. The Wataugans were indignant at being cast off without being consulted and were apprehensive of their state of affairs during that time. Representatives of three of the four counties in "Washington District" assembled at Jonesboro on August 23, 1784.

These forty representatives elected John Sevier as their president and formed an association for laying out a new state and provide for another convention to form a constitution and start a new government. The new state was called Franklin in honor of Benjamin Franklin, and John Sevier was elected Governor. This was the first legislative Assembly in what is now Tennessee, and Greenville became its capital.

12

In November of 1784, North Carolina General Assembly repealed the act of cession and assumed jurisdiction over the Western Territory, which caused a conflict of the governmental authority. The people began to fall away from the Franklin Government and depend on the state of North Carolina. In March 1778, Sevier's term had expired and the State of Franklin was dead. In 1789, John Sevier was the first Congressman elected from the Mississippi Valley.

Two years later in 1790, it became the Territory of the United States South of the Ohio River, continuing as such until June 1, 1796 when Tennessee was admitted as the sixteenth state in the Union.

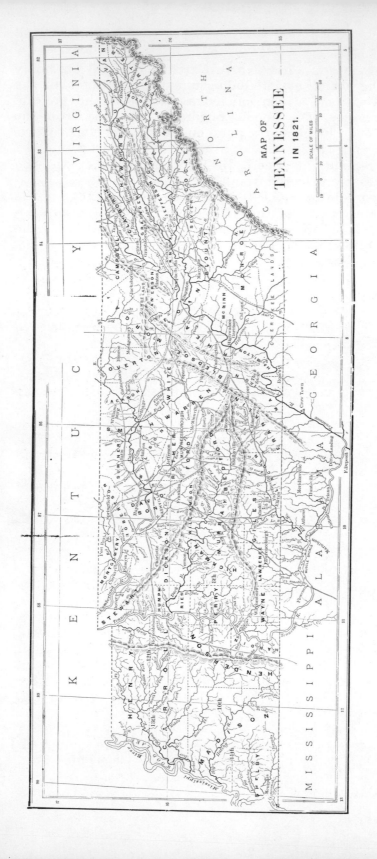

MAP OF
TENNESSEE
IN 1821.

SCALE OF MILES

A Forward Look

More than any other person in Tennessee the Governor is responsible for the operation of the State government. Through the departments responsible to him he must see to it that the laws are enforced, that the taxes are collected, that public money is wisely spent.

The General Assembly has the sole power to pass the laws, the members of the Assembly look to the Governor to recommend legislation. If the Governor thinks the laws it passes are unwise, he can veto them.

Courts alone have the power to try cases and interpret the laws. The Governor appoints Judges and Chancellors to fill vacancies caused by death or by resignation.

The Constitution of Tennessee makes the Governor Commander in Chief of the Army, Navy and Militia of the state, and the federal law makes him Commander in Chief of the National Guard.

The Governor is the state leader of his political party. Therefore, he has a strong voice in shaping his party's National policies. He has the power to pardon people convicted of crimes or to commute their sentences.

A spokesman to the nation for the people of his state and is also an agent and employee of the people. He must protect legitimate interests of the people as a whole and of many groups, labor, management, farmers and businessmen, people from cities and people from counties.

A man does not have to go into politics unless he wants to and he will never find himself elected Governor of the state unless he has some sort of taste for the task, but when he· does move into the Governor's Mansion he has to have someone, some woman to be hostess for all the grand and important social functions that a Governor is obliged to give. Usually the task falls on the Governor's wife and she is expected to turn herself into a grand lady and a social leader over night, when perhaps she has not the least taste or talent in the world for such a life.

So it is a matter of luck when the Governor's lady of the State happens to fit her post eminently well. She cannot be elected in the way her husband is; we could elect her Governor if we wanted to, but we cannot elect her Governor's wife. She just goes along.

Yet for all of that, there have been famous Tennessee Governor's wives, some have been important persons on their own account and others have risen to the occasion and become brilliant hostesses and leaders of the social life of the State Capitol. Some are remembered for this and some for that, but a surprising number of them have been remembered in the past history of Tennessee in name only.

It is the hope of the Author that the readers of "OUT OF A CLEAR BLUE SKY," will gain a new appreciation for the value of wives, mothers, daughters, and women who have played a part in the lives of Tennessee Governors.

The Governor, his wife and family live in the Governor's Mansion in Nashville, Tennessee.

The first First Lady did not live in the Governor's Mansion at all, or even in Nashville. It was then Nashborough, a celebrated French Lick or Great Salt Lick and one of the eight stations or forts of the Cumberland in 1779.

The Capitol land of Tennessee was purchased in 1843, by the City of Nashville. Legend is that Judge Campbell acquired it in 1811 as a part payment for a cow and a rifle.

The cornerstone of Nashville Capitol was laid in 1845 and the final stone put in place in the tower in 1855. The first architect died during the construction, and his funeral was held in the Hall, and he was buried in a vault in the walls of the building.

The capitols of the State of Tennessee have been: Greenville of the state of Franklin, Rogersville of the Southwest Territory, Knoxville - 1792 until 1811, and again in 1817. Moving westward we find the capitol located at Murfreesboro from 1819 to 1825, in which year a resolution was adopted to remove the seat of government to Nashville, where sessions of the Legislature had already been held in 1812, 1813, and 1815. On April 8, 1826, Governor Carroll, in a proclamation, declared Nashville the capitol of the State from May 1 of that year, although it was not until October 7, 1843 that the Legislature passed an act establishing Nashville as the permanent seat of government.

There was no Governor's Mansion until 1907, among Governor Malcolm R. Patterson's progressive accomplishments was the purchase of an official residence for the Governor. The residence was authorized and purchased one-half block from the Capitol.

Governor Hooper, who was the second Governor and family to occupy the Mansion, gave a description of it as follows.

"This building had been constructed on a rather expensive scale and very ornate, inside and out, but it had been wisely unloaded on the state for an executive mansion, when all the fine houses in that neighborhood began to be converted into boarding houses. This happened about the time that the salutary exodus of well-to-do people to rural suburbs set in."

"This old Governor's Mansion had no grounds whatever around it, unless one should be daring enough to denominate about fifteen feet of hopeless, smoked choked lawn as grounds."

Mary Russell Gardner of Union City, Tennessee married Governor Patterson during his term as Tennessee Governor and was the first First Lady to live in the Mansion. However, Mary Gardner was not the first, First Governor's Lady in Tennessee.

CAPITOL, NASHVILLE, TENNESSEE

First Capital of the State of Franklin.

Sarah Hawkins Sevier
B. 1746 — M. 1761 — D. 1780

Buried Amid a Midnight Storm

The first First Lady of the State Maker, John Sevier of Franklin, was Sarah Hawkins Sevier. She was born in 1746 in Shenandoah County, Virginia and married John Sevier in 1761.

Sarah was a wisp of a girl, her golden blonde hair with flecks of the sun giving golden tints, pulled back but soft around her high forehead, a soft curl above her left eye and four curls from the crown of her head falling around her right shoulder, a dress of woven yarns in a brown, yellowish color made by using copperice and maple bark in the dye which she had watched and helped her mother, Sarah Marlin Hawkins make.

Her father, Joseph Hawkins, had established a trading post in a stockade or fort on the frontier of what was then Fredrick County, Virginia. The newly-weds were living there when at the break of dawn the Indians attacked. The sixteen year old bridegroom and the older men of the fort galloped away after them, taking all the ammunition with them. Sarah and her two young brothers at once set about melting lead in the open fireplace to mould enough bullets to last until they returned.

Her grandfather, Richard Marlin, left all his property at his death to his son-in-law, Joseph Hawkins. Here on this land near Peak Mountains, Sarah grew up with her three brothers, Benjamin, Joseph, Samuel; and her four sisters, Rebecca, who became the mother of David Crockett, Mary, Rachel, and Elizabeth.

John Sevier was the son of Joanna Goad and Valentine Sevier, Sr. John was their oldest and most distinguished son. Before coming to the Tennessee Country, the Seviers lived at Tool House Farm, an unusual house of five large rooms with eighteen inch thick walls, two stories high. The cooking, weaving and other household operations were carried on in separate buildings on the place.

John Sevier age 19 purchased land in Virginia and laid off the town of New Market, Va. in 1768. He lived there and prospered as a merchant in the town he built. He had accumulated a fortune when he was attracted by the stories told of life in the mountains. He came in 1770 to visit his brother, Valentine, who had already located in the Tennessee Country. At his first glimpse of East Tennessee, he remarked, "Surely the Lord never made a more beautiful place."

He was more charmed on seeing than hearing. It so fired his interests and although he returned to Sarah and the children, he never again called New Market home. He made the hazardous trip again in 1772, stopping at a horse race at Old Field on the Watauga. He brought goods to sell on both trips. On this visit he was chosen as one of five original commissioners of the Watauga Association.

In the winter of 1773, a caravan of four-horse-team wagons moved out the road from New Market, threading their way through forests of snow-covered trees. They descended into the wilderness of the mountains, and after three long months and a three hundred mile trek they landed in the Holston Settlement on the North shore of the Holston river. On Christmas Day, the weary band of travelers, which included John Sevier's parents, arrived in the Keywood Settlement - Sarah, with the baby Valentine, III and six other children - Joseph, John, James, Elizabeth, Sarah Hawkins and Mary Ann. The day was cold and snow lay thick on the ground that stretched up the hillside to the cabin that was to be the first home of the first First Lady in the Tennessee Country.

The logs were chinked with clay with a roof of split boards held on with wooden pegs. Inside the cabin, the floor was made of split logs, smooth on one side and called puncheon floors. There was one window and one single wooden door on wooden hinges. There was a huge fireplace with big logs where Sarah soon had her pots suspended over the fire and a large skillet on the coals of the hearth with corn pone baking. The family of nine had to eat after the long journey.

The beds were built against the walls with bear skin rug covers, slab tables and benches to eat and sit on. The children went about hanging their capes and hoods on the pegs around the walls.

John Sevier, the blue-eyed, handsome, vivacious young cavalier from Virginia, was immensely popular though he had been at Watauga only a year when he attended the great council at Sycamore Shoals. He was a gentleman by birth, the son of a Huguenot. He possessed more education than the average leader and corresponded on equal terms with Madison, Franklin and other statesmen. He had an erect military carriage and commanding presence with refined manners and great natural dignity, ready tact and generous hospitality to friends and the back woodsmen. He was made Colonel of the Militia.

In 1776, Richard was born, and the Settlements were much exposed to Indian hostilities. The most dangerous of them all was headed by Oconostata, crawling like a snake in the grass to storm Fort Lee. Nancy Ward had warned the white men at Watauga, "Be prepared!"

The fort was crowded with women and children, but there were only forty men with James Roberson in command and John Sevier, Lieutenant. In confusion the fort gates were shut before all had gained admittance, one being Catherine Sherril, who scaled the palisades into the arms of John Sevier, who saw her plight and called, "Jump, my Bonnie Kate, jump!"

John Sevier entertained friends often at his Mount Pleasant home. For three days duration, Sarah and the servants prepared food for Colonel Richard Henderson, Colonel John Williams, and Colonel David Hart while they and Sevier discussed the precarious situation that faced the Watauga and Holston settlers with no protection from North Carolina from the frequent Indian raids.

In 1776 the Seviers moved to the north bank of the Watauga, three miles from Elizabethton, a city he helped to build. In 1811-1815, John Sevier took his seat in Congress from Washington District. He became Governor of the State of Franklin with Greenville as capital and David Campbell as Judge of Superior Court.

The State of Franklin, lost star in our flag, was to rise and fall in 1778. The year 1779 was a troublesome year with the Tories, and the men were afraid to leave their families. One of the wives of a Tory, whom Sarah and Mr. Sevier had furnished the necessities of life while her husband was aiding the Tories, overheard a conversation at her door concerning a plot to murder John Sevier. On pretext for food, she came to see Sarah Sevier, and while standing with her apron held out to ask for a quart of meal, she related the message to Sarah as they neared the smokehouse for a piece of meat also. Sarah, in turn, relayed the message in time to avoid the plot. She often stood the test of taking care of business affairs. She was noted for the gracious hospitality which included taking into her home General McDowell and his family and others driven from their homes by the British and Tories.

Early in the 1780's, John Sevier was building new mills north of Nolichucky near Jonesboro. News came of a large party of Indians on the warpath, and it became urgent to get his family to the fort in Nolichucky. Sarah had given birth to her tenth child, Nancy. They reached the fort safely, but Sarah died early one morning and was buried that night. As the Indian attack was expected at any time, soon after dark the men slipped out of the fort into the nearby forest and dug her grave. Before midnight the burial took place; this was considered the safest time as the Indians generally attacked at dawn. Sevier declared that all of the children must be present to show their respect for their mother, even the new-born baby. So, there in the heart of the forest, in darkness, gloom, and pouring down rain amid flashes of lightning and claps of thunder, John Sevier laid to eternal rest Sarah Hawkins Sevier.

Sarah's grave was leveled off and covered with brush and leaves, lest the Indians discover it and desecrate it. One of the little girls, Ann, related in later life her rememberance of the age of eight, "She wore mitts to the funeral and was so frightened of the storm that she fell down on her way home and was carried back to the fort by two young ladies who had accompanied them to the burial.

Sarah Hawkins Sevier will be remembered for This or That as stated on her stone now on the Court House Lawn in Knoxville, Tennessee:

"Sarah Hawkins Sevier, Daughter of Joseph and Sarah Marlin Hawkins, born in Shenandoah County, Virginia, 1746, died in Washington County, 1780. She had an unusual education and great strength of character. She married at fifteen and was for nineteen creative, formative years of Sevier's life the greatest single factor in his spectacular rise to fame and fortune. A wise, capable, understanding wife and mother who commanded her husband's fast advances; made the hazardous journey down the Shenandoah Valley in 1773 with seven children under eleven years of age. The mother of ten, giving five fighting sons to the protection and building of Tennessee. Finally giving her life during an Indian uprising."

Mary Granger Blount

B. — M. 1778 — D. 1802

A Deserved Friend of the Indians

Mary Grainger Blount was the beautiful daughter of Mr. and Mrs. Kaleb Grainger of Wilmington, North Carolina, living near the sea in the Cape Fear region. They were land owners, a prominent family. Kaleb Grainger had been a merchant; he died sometime before Mary and William Blount, destined to be Territorial Governor of the Territory Southwest of the Ohio, were married February 12, 1778.

William was the eldest son of Barbara Gray and Jacob Blount of Craven County, North Carolina. Jacob was moderately wealthy,. The grandfather, Thomas Blount, third son of Sir Walter Blount of Saddington, Worcestershire, England, came to America in 1664, settling in the Isle of Wight County, Virginia.

William Blount grew to manhood in spacious Blount Mansion, and joined his father and brothers in many enterprises — they were slave holders, dealing in cotton, tobacco, tar, pitch, turpentine, loaning money and running a corn mill.

They were a close-lived family. The children were tutored at home by the parents; William was a lad of fifteen before he had a teacher in the home in 1764. They were active in the Episcopal Church.

On December 11, 1776, William Blount was named Paymaster of the North Carolina Battalion of the Continental Troops. In 1777 he was busy in Army duties and private land purchases with his father. He often found time to turn his horse down the Road to Wilmington, where lived the widow Grainger, her son, William, and the vivacious, dark-haired Mary.

Mrs. Grainger was a stubborn little woman with a mind of her own; yet, she was unable to cope with settling Kaleb Grainger's estate. She welcomed William Blount, the merchant, and his excellent business advice, but William was interested in the heiress of "The Estate", Mary, whom he had nicknamed "Molsey".

Mary thought William with his courtly graces a very handsome man. With pressing war duties, he thought the best plan was a marriage with Mary early in the new year.

The newlyweds started housekeeping at "Piney Grove". William had received the farm at Martinburg from his grandfather, Thomas Blount.

By the year 1780, Blount's mind and thought turned from politics to an oncoming military happening. He had lost $300,000 of the soldiers' payroll at Camden on the disastrous day of August 16, 1780, for which he was accountable.

Mary was expecting her second child, and William Blount was to come home and help care for the oldest son and assist in his fatherly duties.

In the meantime, Mary's brother, William, had died, and Mrs. Grainger came to live with the lively family, their apprentices and wards in 1788. In 1789 the third son, Richard Blackridge, was added to the family.

In the fall of 1783, William visited his half brother, Wylie, at Princeton University. He also became a governor of Tennessee in 1809.

In these years, William was busy with the new federal government, but being a loving family man found time to visit Mary and the children. While home they broke the monotony by going to Greenville, North Carolina, where they attended Episcopal services. He and Mary often visited the theater, dances and musicals at New Bern, N.C. and went to Washington to the races.

After the close of the Revolutionary War, William Blount served several terms in the State Legislature. He was a member of the Confederation Congress.

He went to visit the Washingtons at Mount Vernon in the fall of 1787. Although sick with chills and fever, he dressed in his Philadelphia broadcloth and Nankeen with his body servant in toe cloth and milled drab and drove to the Potomac.

He was so charmed with the noted Washington household, he said in a letter to his brother, John Gray, "I verily believe he is as awful as God." Later, when he heard Washington was to visit the South, he remarked, "I want that Molsey and the children should see him, for certainly such another man will not again appear in their day."

Whatever Washington thought of William Blount on that visit must have been acceptable to the President, for in 1790 he appointed him as Territorial Governor of the South West.

William came south and spent several weeks at William Cobb's home. An emigrant from North Carolina, he was no stranger to comfort and taste nor unaccustomed to what in that day was called style.

Like the old Carolina and the Virginia gentlemen, he entertained elegantly, without ceremony and without grudging. The house was a nine room log house with large fireplaces and pine mantels in every room. Here the first government was organized west of the Alleghenies and became the capitol of the new commonwealth.

Time came to move the large and well equipped household. Mary Blount, shedding copious tears, was reluctant to leave her luxurious Wilmington home; she was not as enthusiastic as her husband but finally consented to move to the new territory. The Cobb House was her first home and that of her two sons, also Wylie Blount, who was to be his brother's secretary. The two girls, Mary and Ann, had remained in North Carolina with their aunt.

Here she heard the singing of the Watauga and the Holston as they hurried down the stairway of the out cropping rocks of the hills toward the distant valley of the Tennessee River. Here, too, was one of the earliest gardens of apple, plum, pear, cherry and quince trees, with vegetables and surrounded by shrubs, flowers and many herbs.

In 1792 they left the relative comforts of Cobb House at Rocky Mount for Knoxville. Their home was a large log house on a knoll by the river, called Barbara Hill, because Barbara Blount was born while they lived here. She was one of the first of five coeds to graduate from what is now the University of Tennessee.

All the while living here with the pigs rooting in the streets of Knoxville, Mary was anxious for luxurious Blount Mansion to be completed. She lived in holy terror of kidnapping or murder of her children by these savage Indians. They called the Mansion "The Snow House with the glass eyes." Soon, with the help of Blount slaves, the first two story house of sawed lumber west of the Allegheny Mountains was finished. Mary, supervising the slaves, soon had the yard surrounding the Mansion the most attractive in Knoxville.

The early American home was placed in the center of the extensive grounds, which extended to the Tennessee River, in terraces, and there old fashioned flowers bloomed in profusion. The garden at the rear was laid out in rectangular beds where the vegetables and fruits grew. In front of the Mansion was the brick terrace surrounded by a picket fence, a yard full of old fashioned flowers, and a vine covered gate.

Mary in her new Mansion had made it a place of family warmth and gaiety, while the Governor enjoyed his wife and children and planned for their prominence and future wealth.

Many of the friendly Indian chiefs paid frequent visits to the new Capital building (which was an office building in their back yard). Mrs. Blount became much interested in the Indians and used her address and persuasion to induce the chiefs to restrain the young warriors from further aggression upon the frontier people; with these she was a desired favorite. She was an accomplished lady and did much to soften and refine the manners of the first inhabitants of Knoxville. Under her administration, a grace and charm was given to the society of the place, and she was adored by poor and wealthy.

In 1796, the territory had become the State of Tennessee, and Governor William Blount became a United States Senator. The next year, while visiting in Raleigh, N.C., Mary fell from her carriage and suffered a badly fractured arm. Through August and September, William stayed with her at the home of Colonel Ben Williams.

Despite the Blount Conspiracy and Eastern disgrace and financial ruin, the ex-Governor and Senator's manner of living was elaborate as ever, and he far outshone that of Governor Sevier's modest menage. William Blount was in ill health with chills and fever. While his loyalty insisted on the superiority of Tennessee's climate, he had lost thirty pounds, and his failing eyesight now compelled him to wear spectacles. Doctor Fourneir lived in the Mansion to minister to the ailing politician—longing for his "Molsey", also an invalid, ailing and absent from home.

The year 1799 was a political doldrum for ex-Governor Blount personally. Plagued by ill health, he devoted his time to his business and family. Now Mary was recovered; she and her mother had joined the household at the Mansion where the activity of the seven Blount children filled the house.

He and Mary went to Philadelphia; they were a handsome couple, moving with grace, charm, and pleasure at plays, balls, dinners and receptions. Despite the tragedy and danger of a miscarriage, Mary Blount entered into all social life of Philadelphia and Washington where her graces grew and drew grudging admiration.

In March they came home; public functions became fewer, and fewer. The girls, Ann and Mary Louisa, were interested in the young men of Knoxville, especially Henry Toole and

Pleasant Miller. William was still under Dr. Garrick and Richard was soon to follow. Mary was busy with the social rounds of the older four and the three younger children.

Knoxville suffered several epidemics and on March 11, 1799, Mrs. Grainger died of a malarial disease—Mary and two of the children were bedfast—William, the oldest was seriously ill—Governor Blount waiting on him in the cold house became ill with chills, a severe cold and fever. Even with bleeding, blistering and poultices, on March 21, 1800 he lost the battle for life; he soon drew his last breath in his Blount Mansion bedroom.

The unexpected death was a complete shock to Mary, still bedfast; Wylie Blount was in Nashville. The funeral was in Knoxville at the First Presbyterian Churchyard, then known as the Presbyterian Meeting House, attended by his children, John Sevier and other friends.

Wylie came from Nashville; the children were made his wards. He then took over their education and with John Gray Blount's help tried to salvage what little was left of William's ruined estate.

Mary Grainger lingered two years, until jaundice caused her death in 1802. She is also buried in First Presbyterian Churchyard in Knoxville.

Mary Grainger and Governor Blount, dispensed, for that age, a real hospitality. The Blount Mansion was a rendevous for society, wit, and political affairs. The Governor, with his charming courtly manner and his beautiful and gracious Mary, were the center upon which all social life of the Knoxville capital turned.

28

Blount Mansion from an old print.

Blount Mansion, as it looks today. Knoxville, Tenn.

The room which gave
birth to the state of
Tennessee in 1796.

Blount Mansion
upstairs bedroom.

The Children's room
Blount Mansion.

The French doll
in the
Blount Mansion.

The First Presbyterian cemetery. Here are the graves of William and Mary Grainger Blount.

Nancy Walker with granddaughters Jenny and Pati on a
research tour 1967

Rocky Mount

Rocky Mount was built by William Cobb in 1770, two years before the formation of the Watauga Association and six years before the Declaration of Independence. In the years that followed, this two-story log house bore silent witness to much of Tennessee's history.

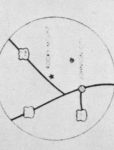

Rocky Mount was the first home of Mary Grainger Blount.

Catherine Sherill Sevier

B. 1754 — M. 1780 — D. 1836
First Lady—Six Times

It is not surprising, after the death of Sarah Hawkins in January of 1780, that the tall, handsome widower with ten children began casting a romantic eye for another "This or That", choosing Catherine Sherrill, whom he had christened "Bonnie Kate" during the Indian attack at Fort Lee, for his second spouse.

On August 14, 1780, his friend Joseph Wilson of Sevier County performing the ceremony, "Bonnie Kate" became Mrs. John Sevier.

Miss Zella Armstrong said, "That the life of John Sevier and 'Bonnie Kate' was as full of romance and thrill from their wedding day on as one would find in any novel."

"Bonnie Kate" proved her courage at the very beginning of her marriage at the age of twenty-six to become the step-mother of ten children from Joseph, age eighteen, to Nancy, a few months old.

In the few months between her wedding day and the Battle of King's Mountain, she made the homespun suits which her thirty-six year old husband and three sons, Joseph, John and James were to wear to battle.

Someone complimented her on this. She replied, "If all of Governor Sevier's ten children were boys, all old enough to go to battle, I could have outfitted them all."

Catherine, with the piercing blue eyes, Roman nose and raven hair, was credited as being the handsomest young lady of her day, at least in the Watauga settlement. She could outrun, outjump, walk more erectly and ride more gracefully than any other female in the Mountains.

The Sam Sherrills came from Yadkin County, North Carolina in 1773 before the Seviers moved here, but Catherine had never seen John Sevier until she leaped the palisades into his arms at Fort Lee. "The savages almost upon her, firing and shooting arrows which she said, 'Fell like hail, it was leap or die, for I will not die captive.' "

Her grandfather was Adam Sherrill who moved to North Carolina in 1747; her father, Sam, who had become a wealthy man and soon bought land and built the home, "Daisy Field", on the Nolichucky in Tennessee. His children were Catherine, Adam, Sam, Susan, George, John, Uriah, and William.

"Bonnie Kate", on more than one occasion, saved Sevier's life in turn for the day he called, "Jump, my Bonnie Kate, jump."

His escape from Morgantown, North Carolina authorities was of Madam Sevier's planning. When she heard of his plight through Colonel Love, she immediately sent his brother, Joseph, son John, and five others who spent the night with her brother, Uriah, who went along as bondsman for John Sevier.

Joseph told him his horse was ready for him and he must go. They escaped the sheriff, and the case was dropped by his enemy, Tipton.

Sevier's return was made a happy occasion and celebration at his Mount Pleasant home; his neighbors and friends gathered far and near to do honor to the hero who had protected his country. John Sevier had the servants turn the horses into the cornfields and for a week a jubilee was held. Mrs. Sevier and the visiting ladies helped with serving turkey, bear meat and refreshments for the crowd. Catherine dispensed unstinted hospitality.

Among the guests was an old fiddler named Black, who played as the Ex-Governor of the State of Franklin and "Bonnie Kate" led off the country dances to such tunes as the "White Cockade" and the "Flower of Edenburg".

John Sevier delighted in making both young and old happy.

They were the parents of eight children in 1792. These were: Ruth, who learned the Indian language and was a great help to her father in his dealings with the Redmen; the others were Catherine, George, Samuel, Polly, Eliza, Robert, and Joanna Goade.

The family had moved to Plum Grove, and in 1790 John Sevier went to New York where he was sworn in at the First Congress of the United States.

By 1796, there were eleven counties in the Tennessee Country. Governor William Blount of the Southwest Territory, called a meeting of the representatives of these counties at Knoxville, Tennessee on January 11, 1796. In all, there were fifty-five men and delegates that flooded the five inns and taverns of Knoxville. By February these men drew up a constitution; it was copied from that of North Carolina, with a few changes; the principles applied were of English origin. The new state was called Tennessee, and on March 28, 1796, the new Legislature announced that John Sevier was elected Governor and Tennessee was admitted to the Union as the sixteenth state on June 1, 1796.

Catherine Sherrill Sevier became the first First Lady of the new State of Tennessee.

During the Governor's term (1796-1801) and again in 1803-1809, they lived in Knoxville. He built a log cabin at Marble Springs, about six miles from Knoxville, where he could go at times to entertain in the good old country fashion. The home resembled a hamlet; the principal apartment was a reception room which occupied the whole of one cabin and was elegantly furnished. The puncheon floor was partly covered by an imported carpet, 12' X 15', the first known rug in the State of Tennessee. It never made its appearance except to honor some distinguished guest. The guest had no sooner left than it was dusted and rolled up and boxed by two servants, Jeff and Suzy.

During the French Revolution, the exiled Prince of Bourbon, who later became the King of France and his brother came to America on a visit. They were sent by President Washington through the new Tennessee Territory, where they were guests of "Bonnie Kate" and Governor Sevier.

The name Sevier was originally Xavier. St. Francis Xavier, born in 1506, was the ancestor of the exiled Prince of Bourbon and was also John Sevier's.

In the large log home in Knoxville it was more formal for holding dinners and teas. The James Park home in Knoxville is of outstanding interest because it was intended by John Sevier as his Knoxville residence; the foundation, a little above the basement was built by him. He did not have sufficient funds to complete the mansion, and in 1812 it was sold to James Parks.

John Sevier, writing in his diary, states, "Sent money to Knoxville store keeper, where 'Bonnie Kate' had borrowed to purchase a large beef from an Indian." She could not resist bargains even though she carried no money with her.

He also describes a "curious dream" while living at Marble Springs, his father living one hundred and twenty miles away. "Tuesday, January 10, 1804 - I dreamed my father came descending in the air in what appeared at first to be a cloud; as it came nearer, it assumed the appearance of one of the finest rigged vessels I had ever seen; the sail, rope, and everything of the apparatus appeared richer and of superior quality to anything I had ever seen. He came out of the vessel when it halted or alighted and told me that on Friday before New Year's Day, he had to set out to the Great High Court."

"I asked him if there was any news where he had been. He answered that nothing existed there but the utmost peace and friendship; that he had heard much conversation respecting the quarrel between Judge Andrew Jackson and myself."

"I then asked him if it was possible that the affair had reached so far, to which he replied that long before he arrived, the news was there and also every other transaction that had taken place in Tennessee. I then asked him what was said and he told me that Jackson was viewed by all as a very improper person for judge and a very wicked, base man and said 'I have it in charge to intimate you, either in a dream or some other mode that you have nothing to fear provided you act a prudent part, for they are all your friends.' "

"On his saying 'by a dream', I began to think I was dreaming and immediately awakened— On Saturday, January 14, I was informed by major Doherty of Jefferson that my father was dead (born in London, England in 1702 and died December 30, 1803)."

John Sevier's son said, "My father never made a profession of religion, but he gave three acres of land to build a Baptist Church in the town of New Market, Virginia in Shenandoah County. Sarah Hawkins, his first wife, was baptized in the Anglican Church of Virginia, which was never active in Tennessee. John Sevier engaged the Presbyterian ministers, the best educated Americans of their day, to give academic education to his children. He and Catherine Sherrill attended protestant denominations. He also attended Catholic Mass; he was a Mason."

In 1809, Governor Sevier left the governorship after serving six terms. The growth and prosperity of the State had been wonderful. Treaties had been made with the Indians; farms cleared; roads opened; bridges built; churches and schoolhouses built; new counties formed; towns laid out and occupied; stores, shops and post offices opened; more and better homes built; free navigation on the rivers. Preachers and teachers, as well as lawyers, were coming into Tennessee. Silk dresses, leghorn bonnets, ruffled shirt fronts, and beaver hats were seen in the Capital City of Knoxville.

John Sevier was elected to Tennessee Senate and for two terms was a United States Congressman. He remained in office from 1811 until his death September 24, 1815.

After his death "Bonnie Kate" went to Overton County where young and old met and enjoyed her hospitality.

When someone would comment on her graceful run with the fleetness of a doe, she often remarked, "I feel ready to have another such race and leap over the pickets to enjoy another such introduction."

Her grandson-in-law, Putman Tennessee Historian, said of her, "I have seen Catherine Sherrill in advanced age, tall in stature, erect in person, stately in walk with piercing blue eyes, raven locks, a Roman nose and firmness unmistakable in every feature; she was able to teach her children in health and usefulness of nerve and action; none could with equal grace and facility, placing a hand upon the mane of a spirited horse and standing by his side seat himself upon his back or saddle."

"She had the appearance and used the language of independence, haughtiness and authority, and she never entirely laid these aside. Yet her pride was not offensive nor her words or demeanor intended heedlessly to wound."

She reverenced her husband and instilled the same sentiment of his children. Their eight children survived until maturity. She also raised four grandchildren of Elizabeth Sevier's, a stepdaughter, after her death. Several nieces and nephews were reared by "Bonnie Kate" also.

In 1836 at the age of eighty-two, she went to Alabama to live with her son, Dr. Samuel Sevier. "Bonnie Kate" fell ill and died three months later on October 7, 1836.

Her granddaughter, Mrs. Simpson, said, "In her last days she became a wisp of a woman with white hair. As her aged body became unable to keep up with her still strong spirit and will power, she had two large negro men servants whom she had taken to Alabama, who carried her, packsaddle style when necessary, anywhere she wished to go, ran her errands and enabled her to have a sense of usefullness and participation in things to the last."

Monument on Knox Court House Lawn of John Sevier, also nearby are small markers to his wives, Sarah and Bonnie Kate.

Marble Springs Home of John Sevier.

The stick chimney of pioneer days of the Knox County farm home.

The Sevier-Park House, Walnut Street, Knoxville, Tenn., begun by John Sevier while he was governor. was not able to finish it and sold to James Park.

Ann Campbell Roane

B. 1749 — M. 1788 — D. 1799

Wife of Governor Archibald Roane

Ann Campbell Roane became new first Lady of Tennessee when Archibald Roane became Governor in 1801. The State Constitution stated, "A governor could not serve more than three consecutive terms." John Sevier had to step down for the young lawyer, Roane, born in Derry Township, Lancaster, Pennsylvania; the son of Margaret Walker and Andrew Roane, a weaver by trade, who emigrated from Ireland in 1739.

Ann, the fair, brunette daughter of Mary Hamilton and David Campbell of Abingdon, Virginia, was one of their thirteen children. Her sisters were Marsha, Sarah, Margaret (who married her cousin, David Campbell, who erected a Block House in Tennessee, widely known as Campbell Station in Knox County.)

Margaret was a very religious person and very conspicuous for her many traits of character. She died in 1799 at the age of fifty-one. Mary married before the family moved to "Royal Oaks" in Abingdon, Virginia, which was called "Wolf Hills" at this time, a little hamlet with two taverns.

The brothers were Lieutenant John Campbell, well educated, accompanied Dr. Thomas Walker in 1765 and bought for his father the farm "Royal Oaks", near the head of the Holston River. In 1766 he, Arthur, and Margaret moved to "Royal Oaks" and made improvements and in 1771 the parents and other children—James, William, David, Robert, Patrick, another daughter and Ann came to this place.

Here Ann became the bride of Archibald Roane in 1788. He was first a teacher at Liberty Hall Academy at Rockbridge, Virginia, and later he was Judge of the Supreme Court of Tennessee.

Before marriage, he was with General George Washington when he crossed the Delaware on Christmas night in 1776, also at the surrender of Yorktown in the Revolutionary War.

He came to the Tennessee Country about the same time as Andrew Jackson—two men so distinguished in the state and nation in later years.

Archibald Roane, John Sevier, Andrew Outlaw, David Campbell, and Joseph Hamilton were the men requested to draw up a representation of their situation and earnest desire to be in the Federal Union. Roane was the thoughtful, cultivated scholar, rather than a forceful man of action. He was at one time the instructor of Hugh L. White of Knoxville, Tennessee, a candidate for President of the United States in 1836.

An incident related by R. N. Price "Holston Methodism": "On one occasion Judge Roane was passing the home of Madam Russell in East Tennessee and stopped for a short visit. She received him with all her true dignity and urbanity in entertaining guests for which she was noted. On his leaving, she said 'Judge, it has been long since we met, we may not meet again—we have been preserved and blessed. It is fitting that we acknowledge our Heavenly Father and His providence. Will you pray with us before you leave?' "

"The Judge, who was a worthy member of the Episcopal Church, immediately clapped his hand on his pocket and finding it empty, replied, 'Indeed, Madam Russell, I would do so with great pleasure, but I have forgotten my Prayer Book.' "

" 'Well, then Judge,' said she, 'If you will join me, I will try to pray without a Prayer Book.' "

"The Judge was too polite to refuse if he had been otherwise disposed. So they both knelt and solemn, fervent prayer was offered."

During Governor Roane's administration, Jackson County was organized. At this time, two committees were appointed by the Legislature to prepare a State Seal design and contract for the manufacture of the seal, which was made by William and Matthew Atkinson of Knoxville and first used by Governor Roane on April 24, 1802. This was the first and only Seal of the State, and Governor Roane issued an order to pay the Atkinson brothers $100.00 in full compensation for making the Great Seal of the State, with a press to work the same.

Governor Roane was a trustee of Greenville College, which was founded by Reverend Hezikiah Balch. It was chartered in 1794 before Tennessee became a state. Greenville, Blount, and Washington Colleges became the first three incorporated colleges of Tennessee.

During his administration as Governor from 1801 until 1803, there was a continual growth and prosperity in the

The David Campbell home at Concord, Tenn., near the "Grassy Valley" home of his sister Anne Roane.

state; it was during his administration that the State was divided into three congressional districts, Mero, Washington, and Hamilton.

When he and Ann were first married, they moved a short distance north of Concord Road in Knox County. In this home Ann became the mother of nine children, the five boys were Dr. James Roane, Archibald, Jr., David, William, and Andrew. Their girls were Laura, Margaret, Mary, and Ann Roane.

Andrew's son, Judge William Roane of Oxford, Mississippi, married a Miss Minnie Martin of Lebanon, Tennessee.

When he left the Gubernatorial chair, Governor Roane retired to his country estate, "Grassy Valley" in Knox County, where he died at the age of sixty on January 18, 1819. His grave in Pleasant Forrest Cemetery near Campbell's Station was unmarked for one hundred years until the state erected a monument June, 1918.

At "Grassy Valley" farm home we have delightful glimpses of Ann carrying on her country chores, such as overseeing the skimming of milk in the early morning hours, sewing by candlelight by her fireside, caring for her many flowers, and attending Episcopal services with the family on Sundays. . . . . . As a First Lady entertaining many notable men, such as Andrew Jackson, Wylie Blount, the notable Scotch kinsmen, the many David Campbells, James King, Captain John Crozier, Samuel and Nathan Cowan, James White, the Chisholms, the Stones, the Dunlaps and many others with grace and charm unending.

When Governor Archibald Roane's term had expired in 1803, he again campaigned with John Sevier. It was a hot struggle, personally and politically with the two men.

Soon after Roane became Governor, the Major General of the Militia died. The candidates for office were the bitter enemies, John Sevier and Andrew Jackson. Sevier was over twenty years older than Jackson, who had little experience in the militia field. Yet, the tie was seventeen to seventeen between the two men. Jackson was the dear friend of Archibald Roane, who cast his vote for Jackson and in this way sent him to his military career, finally leading to the presidency of the United States.

In the campaign, the majority of the people were still friends of Sevier, and they unanimously elected John Sevier Governor again in 1803. He left the Governorship in 1809. Tennessee had over two hundred sixty thousand people, including the Indians and whites. The Indian boundaries had been made. The Great Revival had started the religious movement in Tennessee. Inhabitants had moved from East Tennessee to Middle Tennessee, and other emigrants had found their way to the Cumberland Settlements.

Wylie Blount, a half-brother of William Blount, of Montgomery County became Governor of Tennessee in 1809.

Lucinda Baker Blount

B. 1750 — M.   — D. 1830

Wife of Governor Wylie Blount

Willie Blount came to Tennessee in 1790 as Secretary to his half-brother, William Blount, Territorial Governor of the Southwest Territory. Willie (pronounced Wyley) was born on April 18, 1768 at Blount Hall, Cravens County, North Carolina, the son of Jacob Blount and his second wife, Mrs. Hannah Salter Baker Blount. He had two full brothers. His three older half-brothers, William, John Gray, and Thomas Blount, engaged in extensive speculation of Western lands. There were eleven children in all of Jacob Blount, who first married Barbara Gray.

He studied at Princeton and Columbia Colleges and read law with Judge John Sitgraves in New Bern, North Carolina. After William became Territorial Governor, he came with Mary Grainger and her two sons to live with his brother at the William Cobb House at Rocky Mount.

Arriving in Knoxville in 1792, he quickly became identified with the growing frontier, making the most of his opportunities, associating with notable men who exercised powerful and lasting influence in public affairs such as Andrew Jackson, John Sevier, John White, Samuel Doak, and Archibald Roane.

These were soldiers, orators, statesmen, educators and ministers. He was elected as one of three Judges in 1796, but he refused to serve. Soon after 1802 (after the death of William and Mary Grainger Blount) he became the ward of their children and moved from Knoxville to Montgomery County, where the Blounts had large land holdings, and on a large plantation he established his home.

He had married Lucinda Baker, daughter of Major John Baker (born in 1750 - died in 1830) and his wife Ann Norfleet Baker of Bertie County, North Carolina. They were the parents of two daughters, Eliza Ann (who became the wife of Dr. John Dabney) and Lucinda, whose husband was John Dortch.

Lucinda Blount was the mother of Wylie Blount Dortch, who married Medora, a daughter of Sarah Burrus and Governor Aaron V. Brown. Medora Brown had a daughter, Laura, who became the wife of William King McAlister and were the parents of Hill McAlister, who married Louise Jackson of Belle Meade, Nashville. He was Governor of Tennessee in 1933-1937.

Lucinda Baker Blount was the great, great, great grandmother of Laura McAlister Bathrick and Louise McCAlister Love of Fort Lauderdale, Florida.

From the time Governor Wylie Blount came into office in 1809-1815, he was confronted by Indian problems which were complicated by white aggression and red resistance. Some of these Indians were not friendly to Tennesseans and stirred to fury by anti-Americans.

It was an exciting time in history. Tennessee population had grown to 300,000 by 1814. The Bank of the State of Tennessee was established in Knoxville with branches at Clarksville, Columbia, Jonesboro, and Nashville.

During this year, there was an earthquake in Tennessee, and Reelfoot Lake was formed. Wylie Blount was a great friend of Andrew Jackson. During the War of 1812, he tendered to the United States two thousand, five hundred volunteers, and it is from these that Tennessee gained its name, "The Volunteer State".

Governor Blount pledged his personal credit to equal three regiments, which went to General Jackson at New Orleans.

He was also active in the Creek War, raising the tremendous sum (at that time) of $300,000. Troops were raised in both East and Middle Tennessee. The war closed in 1812, with the Treaty of Ghent in 1814, and General Andrew Jackson put the finishing touches on it by his victory at New Orleans January 8, 1815.

At the expiration of his term of office, Blount and Lucinda with their family returned to the Plantation Home near Clarksville.

His quiet home life was not destined to last, and Lucinda lived in the political atmosphere as Wylie resumed the duties in the Legislature. They returned to Knoxville in 1817, but no records show they lived at Blount Mansion.

In 1827 he was induced to become a candidate for Governor but was defeated by Sam Houston. In 1834, he was Montgomery County's representative to the State Convention. This Constitutional Convention was his "Swan Song" to politics.

At his home, "Bakerdon", he wrote religious subjects and a digest of the Constitutions of the United States and Tennessee which was still incomplete at his death on September 10, 1835. A marble staff was erected in Clarksville in 1878 with Governor James Porter officiating, saying, "Let this monument be a witness to all ages to come of our reverence for the character of a great and good man."

Lucinda Blount will be remembered as an elegant, accomplished woman, with a charming mind and dignity of manner in which she was the beloved wife, mother and First Lady of Tennessee.

William Blount, Governor in and over Territory of the United States, South of the River Ohio.

To David Henley Esquire Agent for the department of War)

Pay to William Rickard temporary Pay-master to the Troops in the territory of the United States aforesaid, three hundred and nineteen dollars out of the money in your hands appropriated for the pay of the Army, for the pay of a company of Infantry of the Third Sub Legion of the United States command-ed by Lieutenant William Rickard, for the month of December 1793, agreeably to pay Roll and your Report thereon of the 28th Instant, taking his Receipt to be accountable for the same to the accountant of the department of War, for which this shall be your warrant, Given at Knoxville under my hand and seal this 30th Day of October 1794 —

Wm BLOUNT

By the Governor
Willie Blount. Pro Secretary.

Countersigned
David Henley Agent

This manuscript from the collection of Mrs. Alice Warner Milton is a warrant authorized by Gov. William Blount to David Henley, agent for the Department of War, and also shows the signature of Willie Blount, secretary. It is dated Oct. 30, 1794.

Hannah Cooper McMinn

B. 1760 — M. 1785 — D. 1811

Wife of Governor Joseph McMinn

The Quaker, Joseph McMinn, was born in West Marlborough Township, Chester County, Pennsylvania on June 27, 1758. He was the fifth of ten children of Robert and Sarah Harlan McMinn. The parents of Joseph provided education to son Joseph by seeing that he availed himself of educational offerings of the time. As a member of the Friend's Church, he was taught not to believe in violence and war, although the church allowed each member to decide for himself whether he should engage in warfare.

As a young man, Joseph did not enter the Revolutionary War in the struggle for freedom. Soon after the close of the War he left the well-laid-out and governed Philadelphia for the venturous trek into the Mountains, settling in Hawkins County, Tennessee. It was then Sullivan County.

It was May 9, 1785 that Joseph married Hannah Cooper. Hannah was the daughter of Rowena and James Cooper. She was born near Pequea Church, Chester County, Pennsylvania on June 20, 1760. The Coopers moved from Chester County, Pennsylvania to Rowan County, North Carolina in the early 1760's and then to Carter Valley in Hawkins County in 1779. Rowena Cooper survived her husband, James, who died in 1782 while it was still Sullivan County.

Hannah Cooper McMinn came with her parents to the Tennessee Country when she was about nineteen years of age. The family lived in the extreme northern part of Hawkins County near the Virginia line. Her home, "New Market", was in the present town limits of Mt. Carmel. The home that they lived in was gone by 1850. Hannah was one of eight children; her sisters were Margaret, who married Edward Waterson; Ann, who married Thomas Larkin; Sarah, who became the wife of Aaron Wells; and the other sister who married Michael Dougherty. She had three brothers, James (the Revolutionary War pensioner); Robert, and John Cooper.

Soon after the State of Franklin had been established and a Constitution had been adopted in 1785, the first Franklin

Legislature had met at Greenville, and John Sevier had been elected Governor. The newlyweds, Joseph and Hannah, bought a farm near the site of "Oak Well" close to New Market. Here, they settled down to the typical life of the pioneer. Interspersed with his farming pursuits were various types of service in the local militia as Sergeant and later Commander General.

Many mornings in the new settlement the McMinns would awaken to see their backyard full of pigs rooting in the ground and twenty to thirty painted Indians sharpening their axes on their grindstone.

Hannah was a Presbyterian in faith as were all the Coopers, but Joseph, having grown up among the Quakers, possessed the simplicity of character, honesty of purpose and industry for which the Quakers were noted. It was said to be no uncommon thing for Hannah Cooper in her long linsey dress and split bonnet to be seen working beside Joseph hoeing corn or vegetables in their fields.

Hannah and Joseph had only one child, Jane McMinn, born August 27, 1787 in Hawkins County. Hannah Cooper McMinn died February 27, 1811 in Hawkins County, with the exact location of her grave being unknown. Her death was ascribed to "inward inflammation". No portrait of Hannah McMinn is known. A portrait of Governor McMinn painted in Philadelphia is in the Tennessee State Library Building in Nashville, Tennessee.

Jane was married twice, first to Hugh Campbell (born in Donegal, Ireland in 1762) on May 9, 1804 in Hawkins County, Rogersville. He died of cholera morbus. She then married the second time on November 20, 1808 at Rogersville, Tennessee, James Taylor Gaines (born in Culpepper County, Virginia in 1775). They had no children. Jane preceded him in death by six years. He died February of 1821. Jane died January 27, 1815, the same year her father became Governor of Tennessee, in the month of September. She died of a cold plague of three days duration, thought to have been the first case of influenza in Tennessee. This epidemic which raged with violence in different parts of the state, carrying with it frequent death, was described by Dr. Felix Robertson of Nashville as an Epidemic Catarrah or influenza. He said, "From experience, early and free blood letting is the only cure." The McMinns of Bradley County, Tennessee are descendants of Joseph McMinn's brother, John. There are no living descendants of Joseph.

53

The site "New Market" is the present site of Mt. Carmel, as previously stated, in Hawkins County, then in the country and now has a State Historical Marker.

Rebecca Kinkead McMinn

B. 1793 — M. 1812 — D. 1815

Wife of Governor Joseph McMinn

Joseph McMinn was honest, friendly, not a scholar, but a man with good common "horse" sense. He dressed in the plainest of clothes, was good looking, a good mixer, and popular with people and politicians of his day.

In 1790, when the future Tennessee became a Federal Territory, William Blount appointed Joseph McMinn to a county office, which marked his advent into politics that continued until the time of his death. He held many different offices; was a member of the Territorial Legislature of 1794; and in 1796 was a member of the Committee that framed the Constitution of Tennessee.

He practiced kindness to his Red Brother, the Cherokees. He was an agent for the Cherokees from 1822 until 1824, near Calhoun, Tennessee on the Hiwassee River. He had held many different offices when he became Governor in 1815. Hannah Cooper had been dead six years when he became Governor; he had married his second wife, Rebecca Kinkead, on January 5, 1812 in Hawkins County.

Rebecca was born October 7, 1793 in Carter's Valley in Hawkins County, Territory of the United States south of the Ohio River. She was the daughter of Mary Williams and David Kinkead. David was born in 1758 and died in 1828. Mary Williams, her mother, was born in 1769 and married David Kinkead in 1788, and she died in 1822. The Kinkeads were Presbyterians.

Rebecca had no children. She died January 11, 1815, about two weeks before Jane McMinn died. Rebecca died at New Market of a nervous fever of twenty-nine days in duration. She is buried in an unmarked grave near the old Kinkead home, high in Carter's Valley near the Virginia line. The cemetery is near the place where two railroads cross.

When Joseph McMinn wrote in 1818, ordering the sale of his household goods at "New Market", he asked that "the two cotton counterpoints woven by my dear, departed Rebecca not be sold unless the agent could get upwards of $15 each". This was contained in a letter from Joseph

McMinn to James T. Gaines and Robert McMinn, Knoxville, April of 1818.

Governor McMinn was interested in Indian lands for white settlement, improving Tennessee educational status and in making the Tennessee rivers navigable for transportation. While he was Governor, treaties were made with the Cherokees, giving up all their lands except the "Cherokee District".

Despite a crowded public life, he maintained a reputable hostelry after retirement; guests found him affable, kind, and communicative. McMinn County and McMinnville, Tennessee are named for him.

On August 4, 1816, during his term as Governor, Joseph McMinn married his third wife, Nancy Glasgow Williams (forty-five years old) at South West Point in Roane County, Tennessee. The Knoxville Register gives "Saturday 10 August 1816, married on Sunday, the 4th inst., Joseph McMinn, Esq. Governor of Tennessee to Mrs. Nancy Glasgow Williams, of Kingston, Roane County, Tennessee."

Nancy Glasgow Williams McMinn

B. 1791 — M. 1816 — D. 1857

Wife of Governor Joseph McMinn

Nancy Glasgow was born in Dobbs County, North Carolina the part which became Glasgow County named for her father in 1791; name was changed to Green County in 1799, when it became known publicly that Glasgow was involved in land frauds.

Nancy's father James Glasgow, Secretary of the State of North Carolina in 1777-1778, died February 1820, his wife Pherobe Glasgow survived him.

Nancy first married Wiloughby Williams of North Carolina, as a distinguished officer in the Revolution, he served as Commander of Issues, he fought and was wounded in the battle of Cow Pens.

There were four sons: James Glasgow, Wiloughby born 1798, married Nancy Nichols and Rebecca Branch. Robert born 1802, married Susan Branch, Christopher married Jane Nichols.

Nancy was a sister to Elizabeth Glasgow who married Martin Donelson Anderson.

Official business frequently occasioned Joseph McMinn from home, as recorded in Governor McMinn's Bible records, his married life with Nancy was not a happy one, so Nancy left him.

Joseph McMinn and Nancy made a separation agreement on October 9, 1821. A bill of divorcement was presented to the Tennessee House of Representatives soon after October 16, 1821.

From a typed copy in the State Archives, Nashville, Tenn. three weeks after Governor McMinn retired, Representative William Brady of Rutherford County presented the petition of Joseph McMinn, praying to be divorced from his wife Nancy — as follows:

October 16, 1821

To the Honorable Legislature of the State of Tennessee, the undersigned petitioner, humbly begs leave to represent, that his wife Nancy McMinn has been absent for nearly eight months and has on other occasions absented herself for shorter periods without causes known to your petitioner and has on present occasion declared in the presence of a highly respected witness her determination, never more to return to live with her said husband under any pretense whatsoever.

Your petitioner therefore does humbly conceive that a separation has actually taken place between the parties, that no alternative now remains, so likely to promote their future happiness, as the interference of your honorable body, by dissolving the obligation of their marriage contract in legal form.

The foregoing is most respectfully submitted by Joseph McMinn.

Murfreesboro Tennessee, State Capitol of Tennessee
16 October, 1821

The first business conducted by House of Representatives October 1821 concerned the following item:

"Mr. Felix Grundy presented a memorial of Nancy McMinn praying that application of her husband Joseph McMinn for a divorce may be referred to the judicial tribunals of the country."

"It was ordered that said petition lie on the table."

Fortunately a typed copy of Mr. McMinn's memorial discloses that there is truth in the adage that both sides should be heard. If Mrs. McMinn had relied solely upon political influence among the membership of the legislature she could not have been more fortunate in the selection of the person who introduced her memorial. Felix Grundy was undoubtedly the ablest member of the House of Representatives and the peer of any member of the Senate.

Let the reader judge "The Merchant of Venice," "Look up on this picture and upon that."

The memorial of Nancy McMinn respectfully represents that within a few days past she has been advised that a petition has been presented to your honorable body, by her husband Joseph McMinn praying for, to divorce him from your memorial wife—

Averse as she is to appearing in defense before your body unprepared to support such defense at present, by other means, than her own solemn statements on oath, yet in support of her character and justice to herself, your memorialist (with extreme reluctance) is compelled to remonstrate against the passage of law, prayed for by her husband—

58

If your memorialist is properly advised the means of obtaining the necessary evidence in such cases if not altogether beyond the power of your body) is often so removed as not to be reached, and thus it is the party praying for divorce may often succeed by false statement and no one present can contradict, where as the proof produced received is open Judicial way and were both parties cited and authorized to appear before an enquirer's court, it would very frequently and clearly by good testimony, appear that the party complaining is in truth and fact the offender, but for his or her first and continued aggressions, no possible cause would have existed in their consequences leading to measures so truly unpleasant to all who unfortunately became involved in them.

Your memorialist solemly denies that the difference at present existing between herself and her husband and she is advised, produced in his said petition was ever commenced or continued by improper conduct on her part or forgetfulness of the nature of her obligations as his wife, she did submit and act as become her and she is unconscious of any act of hers, that could have merited the ill treatment in all instances and upon all occasions heaped on her aged and defenceless head by the man who called her his wife. (She was 51)

From the first relations, the conduct of Mr. McMinn has been every thing else, but what it ought to have been. It would be painful to your memorialist to particularize, nor does she before your Honorable body deem it material. It was in consequence of his conduct and treatment of your memorialist that she now lives apart from him, depends for peace and content on the kindness of her friends, whose protection she has been forced to claim: She only claims from her husband, that after thus destroying (perhaps forever) her peace, he may not be permitted before your honorable body (by trial altogether 'exparte') to rob her character and thus leave her destitute of all that to her is desirable on earth.

If Mr. McMinn charges your Memorialist with acts inconsistent with marriage vows she begs that in defense of her reputation and those who are by nature intimately concerned therein, she may have time and opportunity to answer and with the confidence of innocence she hopes to refute; and to show if necessary (and she is permitted to do so) that himself is alone to blame and but for his own unmanly treatment your Memorialist would not have been compelled to appear in her own defense. With difference to the better judgment of your honorable body, your Memorialist submits that the courts of the country are open to Mr. McMinn and fully competent to give him redress if in truth he has cause for complaint.

It is there from the nature of their powers, their habits of doing business and the time allowed over matter of fact, may be made to appear before a discriminating Judge and in the presence of the parties concerned, before such a tribunal your Memorialist will confront Mr. McMinn or before your honorable body if permitted and hopes to show innocence.

But your Memorialist does here and again enter into her solemn protest against the course now pursued by her husband tending to condemn her, unheard and in presence and before the highest authority known to the laws of her state, thereby endeavoring to prestated (or to say at least) strongly and greatly injuring the character of your Memorialist.

Relying firmly on her innocence and the high and disinterested feeling of the Honorable Body, she addressed.

Your Memorialist prays that Mr. McMinn is referred to the Constitutional Tribunals of Justice for redress of pretended wrongs or if future proceedings he had before your Honorable Body, your petitioner be heard with such evidence as she can address.   Nancy McMinn
Sworn to and subscribed before me
29th day of October 1821
H. Call, Justice of Peace
Davidson County, Tenn.

Ordered that said petition lie on table.

On October 31, the bill to divorce Joseph McMinn from his wife Nancy, passed first reading as matter of routine.
Three days later
The House took up and proceeded to consider a bill to divorce Joseph McMinn from his wife Nancy.

And the question being stated, "Shall the said bill pass the second time?" It was determined in the negative:

Aye   19
Noes 20

By narrow squeak the House of Representatives did offer an "interference" that did not tend to promote the future happiness of the Quaker Ex-Governor as prayed for in his petition.

Ex-Governor McMinn's chagrin and humiliation was probably intensified if he ever read the satirical thrust contributed by the Knoxville Register for November 20, 1821.

One newspaper correspondent on learning that the Legislature had denied the requested divorce wrote;

"This is an unpardonable cruelty, when considered how great.a favorite he is with the ladies----both married and unmarried and how unreasonable his present wife is, in expecting him, at the early age of sixty-five to quit the fashionable gallantries and dissipations of a man of genteel habits and dignified sentiments.

"Nor let it be thought I speak to disparage .our venerable Chief Magistrate.

Socrates married a Scold, The Grecian Hero Menaleus a Courtesan, Moses an Ethiopean, Then why refuse to Governor A-SQUAW?"

Nancy Glasgow Williams McMinn, a leader of fashion in her lovely brown velvet gowns with matching hat and plumes lived in Nashville where she died at age of eighty-six on June 27, 1857.

After his retirement from the gubernatorial chair, Gov. McMinn purchased a farm near Calhoun, Tenn. on the Hiwassee River about ten miles above Cleveland. Here he died November 17, 1824 and is buried where the Cherokee Agency was located.

Miss Louise Harle, a foster great granddaughter tells of an unusual happening as handed down through the Knox family; "Governor McMinn was a pious old gentleman, he gathered the family and servants at night for scripture reading and prayer----one night one of the negroes fell asleep and snored in the midst of prayer, the Governor stopped and said, "Wake up the damned Negro over there" and continued his prayer.

Adella Knox Jarnigan, Irene Corn, Jane Knox Smith, and Betty Knox Horner of Cleveland are also descendants of McMinn.

His Bible records read, "He was afflicted with dropsy, and suffered a great deal." The Governor while writing at his desk fell back stricken with dropsy of the heart . . . . and his faithful body servant Dave was the only person present.

Joseph McMinn's will was probated in Hawkins County, will book I page 349 et seq.

Will of Joseph McMinn dated 6, November 1824;

"Now residing at the Cherokee Agency; mentions separation agreement made 9 October between Nancy and myself in the presence of Hon. John Williams of Knox County, which I now confirm; Sister Jane Kinkead (daughter of Mary and David Kinkead); my marriage with Rebecca, sister of said Jane; Jane's brother and sisters; Rebecca McMinn Long (daughter of John and Nancy Kinkead of Kentucky) residue of estate to the sons and daughters of my brothers and sisters; my niece Hetty McMinn Morrison whom I have adopted, I have given land at New Canton, her husband Robert Morrison; $300 dollars to McMinn Academy at Rogersville; Sarah Gaines daughter of James Gaines esq., Hannah Cooper Larkins, Nancy Williams daughter of James Glasgow Williams; (these three received silver spoons, Wiloughby Williams son of said James H. Williams a superfine fur hat; Mrs. Mary Rogers wife of Joseph Rogers of Rogersville. Richard Mitchell my spear cane; Stockley D. Mitchell my desk; Joseph McMinn Looney a horse; Friends John Williams of Knox County, and Orville C. Bradley esq. of Hawkins County executers.

James Cowan, James Bridges, John L. McCarthy, James G. Williams, William Cowan, James Mitchell, witnesses.

(The names of witnesses shows that this will was written at the Cherokee Agency near Calhoun, Tennessee.)

Cecelia Bradford Carroll

B. 1785 — M. 1813 — D.

Wife of Governor William H. Carroll

Nashville city limits were along the river bluff and obtained from Judge McNairy near Capitol Hill and most of life was found around the square. The Nashville Inn had been built in 1783 at the corner of Market Street and in June 1825 was the scene of the Governor and Mrs. William H. Carroll's Ball.

Cecelia Bradford Carroll received her guests dressed in a yellow satin embroidered dress, with flounce gathered back and sides at the hips, falling in folds to her ankles, a tight bodice, short sleeves trimmed in lace, a low neck with a u neckline, bertha also trimmed in lace, her only ornament a filmy handkerchief, and the halo band with her hair piled high, curls circling her ears and forehead.

General LaFayette, George LaFayette, General Andrew Jackson and party had arrived in a carriage drawn by four handsome gray horses to the Governor's Ball.

Doctor Phillip Lindsley delivered the address of welcome on a dias at the end of the hall of Nashville Inn where guests and the elderly ladies were seated.

They entered the Ballroom with General LaFayette escorting Rachel Jackson, Governor Carroll with Mrs. Shelby, General Jackson with Mrs. Prestly and Ceeclia Carroll. George LaFayette with Mrs. Stewart and Mrs. McNairy and Dr. Shelby with Mrs. Mennick. Mrs. Martin and Mrs. Andrew McEwin danced the first set. Miss Susan Trimble (sister of Mrs. Neil S. Brown), Miss Elizabeth Williams, Mrs. McIvery were also dancing in the first set.

Among the guests at the Ball was James K. Polk who had again found his Spanish Donna.

Cecelia Bradford had married William Carroll in 1813. He was an interesting man with steel blue eyes, fastidiously groomed figure. He had become rich and ruthless, a man who made and unmade Senators.

He was born near Philadelphia on his father's farm, Thomas Carroll was a Revolutionary soldier. He and his wife, Mary Montgomery, had nine children of whom William was the oldest. William had to help support a number of brothers and sisters and could expect but little in the way of property in inheritance. His education was limited. He had a small amount of instruction in grammar, bookkeeping, surveying, and some of the first principles in Mathematics.

For eighteen years on his father's farm he learned the value of hard work, economy and industry. The Carrolls emigrated to Nashville, Tennessee in 1810.

William was twenty-two years old when he begain working for a Mercantile establishment under a wide awake employer where he learned business procedure that served him well, both himself and his adopted Tennessee.

By attending to business and with the confidence of the wealthy merchant who encouraged him to yearn for greener pastures, he soon established a nail factory and domestic store in the town of Nashville, then with a population of 1,100 people.

He proved himself a good business manager. By 1818 he had constructed a steam boat, the first such vessel to reach Nashville. A sight so novel that it attracted crowds of spectators. It was named "The General Jackson."

General Carroll may well be termed the "Father of Steam Navigation in Tennessee. The boat was built in Pittsburgh at a cost of $16,000 and reported at Louisville on her first voyage down stream of the Cumberland March 13, 1818, six days from Pittsburgh. It was not until March 11, 1819 that it reached Nashville, the home port. Previous to that time, low water on Harpeth Shoals halted the boat there. Yet it reached Harpeth Island in twenty one days and six hours."

The new Orleans Gazette on February 18, 1818, published the misadventure on the Southern waters of General Carroll.

"General Carroll of Tennessee, who was second in command to General Jackson during the invasion in Tennessee in 1814-1815, arrived in town with his family on board the Steamship Buffalo, yesterday. The General had embarked for the place on board a barge loaded with tobacco and cotton which in descending the Ohio, struck a sawyer (near Smithland, Ky.) and was instantly severed and sank. The General loosing sight of his own danger in his anxiety to save his family consisting of his wife, child, and sister, placed them on a plank and swimming himself with great exertions brought them safe to land, four men belonging to the barge were drowned.

After wandering, wet and cold some time along shore,

they arrived at a small cottage, and the following day were taken up by the Steam boat Buffalo." (Nashville Whig and Adviser, Mar. 7, 1818).

When he was twenty-five he married Cecelia Bradford, the daughter of Henry Bradford of Fauquier County, Virginia and Elizabeth Payne Blackmore whom had married near Nashville in 1785.

William H. Carroll was intelligent and industrious. He was chosen captain of Volunteer Co., organized in Nashville. He won honors in Military services, and Brigadier inspector in March of 1812 with Andrew Jackson.

After the war, his fame was next to Andrew Jackson.

In 1821 he ventured into politics and was inaugurated Governor of State of Tennessee in Hall of Representatives at Murfreesboro, October 1, 1821, then the seat of government.

He was a resident of Davidson County at the time. He promoted more progressive legislation than any other period of time in the history of Tennessee.

He was ultimately responsible for initiating such far-reaching movements as resulted in the enactment of laws providing for a system of public education, internal improvements, revision of the penal code, and the erection of a penitentiary.

William Carroll died March 22, 1844 and is buried in the Old Cemetery, Nashville, Tennessee.

Cecelia was born 1885 in the first brick house built in Middle Tennessee. It was on a splendid estate which was cultivated in cotton and maize. The Henry Bradfords lived not too far from the home of Andrew Jackson.

Cecelia was the granddaughter of Josiah Payne II of Virginia. She was also a cousin of Dolly Paine Madison.

Her paternal grandparents were Mary Morgan and William Bradford, and her great grandmother Mary Marr Kingcarl, a widow from Scotland, married the great grandfather John Bradford of King George (Fauquier County) Virginia.

Mrs. Carroll's grandfather was a brother to Alexander Bradford and the grandparent of Miss Virginia Johns of Nashville, whose mother, Mary Bradford was one of the Heroines of Nashville during the Battle of Nashville, in the War Between the States.

Miss Virginia Bradford Johns said, "Cecelia grew up with her half sister, Molly Blackmore and four brothers Drostly, Lieutenant Larkin Bradford, killed at the battle of Talahassie, Ira who married a Miss Simpson. Henry became a Doctor and married a Miss Turner and died at Pine Bluff, Arkansas.

Cecelia had one full sister, Sophia Bradford who married George Grant of Pittsburgh, Pennsylvania. Her son, Henry Grant, born in Philadelphia, Penn. 1856, was a compiler of Genealogy during 1830's.

Her father and grandfather William, both were distinguished men in the Revolutionary War. The father's grave is covered with four inch marble slabs in the Bradford plot near Hendersonville, Tennessee.

William Carroll entered politics in 1821. He was governor for twelve years, 1821-1827, and 1829-1835.

His first advice to the people: "To start using a little common sense, to manage their own affairs, by taking less and working more, spending less and paying their debts and to quit spending money on Foreign goods, and give up the idea of luck, and political office holders to attend to their affairs." He advocated a good system of internal improvement, easier transportation. Changed mode of cruel and brutal hot iron branding for criminal whippings and hard labor in workhouses and Penitentiary. He established a hospital for insane in Nashville.

"It is said outside John Sevier no other governor ever exercised such an influence over the people and Legislature and Carroll's administration marked an Epoch that was almost Revolutionary in results."

Eliza Allen Houston

B. 1809 — M. 1829 — D. 1865

Wife of Governor Sam Houston

When Eliza Allen of Gallatin, Tennessee became the First Lady of Tennessee, the first wife of Sam Houston, twice elected Governor in 1827 and 1829, Nashville was the back woods state with five thousand people and one thousand negro slaves.

Eliza Allen's parents, John and Letitia Saunders Allen, were people of prominence and social significance in Sumner County. They were friends of the Governor, a six-foot, six-inch, well-proportioned man—commanding and gallant-dressed for the public in his bell crowned black beaver hat, standing collar, patent leather shoes, a military stock ruffled shirt, black trousers, gathered at the waist with legs full, the same size from seat to ankle, his broad shoulders draped with a "gorgeous red hunting shirt—silk socks lavishly embroidered and his patent leather pumps set off by silver buckles."

He rode a dapple gray in his campaign for Governor; he was often a visitor at the Allen home.

One day out of a clear blue sky, the Governor discovered that the little blonde girl, Eliza, had grown up into a very beautiful lady.

"There were two classes of people pursuing Sam Houston all his life: artists and women."

But above all the women he had known, Sam desired Eliza, and meant to win her. Members of the Allen family were not indifferent to his
were not indifferent to his many visits to the plantation, although Eliza was bewildered to find Houston, a man of years who had been a sort of grown-up confidant and comrade, changed to the role of suitor, with fire in his wooing.

Sam was born on March 2, 1793, in Rockbridge County, Virginia. Soon after the death of his father, Sam Houston, Sr., Elizabeth Paxton Houston and her nine children: Paxton, Robert, James, John, Sam, William, Mary and Elizabeth, in her four hourse team wagon came over the mountain country to Blount County for better opportunity for her sons and daughters. Blount County was the extreme frontier in the year 1807, when she settled near relatives on land previously purchased by her late husband.

Elizabeth Paxton Houston was from a well-to-do family, when she first married Sam Houston, Sr.; they owned land that could be seen for miles from the front veranda of their home.

She was a strict Presbyterian mother—walking, she and the nine children covered many miles over unpaved roads as they attended services twice a week, spring, autumn and winter, at the little country church at Baker's Creek.

Sam, fifteen years of age, was a book lover; he preferred to lie under a tree and read while the other brothers worked the farm and did the family chores. He finally ran away from home. Carrying his copy of the Illiad with him; he lived for a time with the Cherokee Indian, John Jolly at Jolly Island near Dayton, Tennessee.

On his return home he taught school in a little log school house near Maryville, Tennessee. In a few years he was an Indian agent; he served in the Creek War. He became Adjutant General of Tennessee, Prosecuting Attorney and a Congressman from Nashville.

In 1827 he became Governor and was re-elected in 1829. Mr. and Mrs. John Allen, attended the Inaugural Ball at Nashville, rode in the family coach with a Negro driver. Eliza and her small brother, B. F. Allen, with her father and mother rode in the coach, while the two older brothers rode horseback.

At the Ball, Eliza, in her pale blue tulle over a blue pettycoat, danced every dance, including two with the new Governor, the thirty-six year old bachelor.

In her estimate, he was her Demagog, her soldier and Statesman; the tallest and handsomest man she had ever met. He seemed eager to do the slightest wish of the beautiful Eliza, soft, charming, slim, with hands showing long slender fingers that were not used for much except embroidering samplers. Eliza was not interested in reading, just herself, often told she was truly beautiful. A lovely girl of eighteen, she cared little for the responsibility of life.

Walking with Eliza on a bright moonlight night, the newly elected Governor said, "Eliza, you would make me the happiest man on earth by consenting to be my wife."

Eliza was so astounded at the proposal—He took her silence for a tendency to display her emotions. "Eliza, let us go and ask Mr. Allen's blessing." He did not take her in his arms as he desired, but merely kissed her lily white hand.

Colonel Allen readily replied, "It has been the hope of Mrs. Allen and myself that you and Eliza would find happiness in each other."

Alone, Governor Houston swept Eliza in his arms with a first passionate kiss for the blushing girl which astonished and frightened her.

Letitia Saunders Allen considered it indecent to discuss marriage with Eliza; so they spent endless hours together receiving guests, talking about how to manage servants, the kind of clothes a Governor's wife should wear, how to entertain the Governor's friends and the right use of her linens and silver.

One gift—Rachel Jackson's silver service had been given by the recently bereaved Andrew Jackson, who could not stay for the wedding. He was on his way to Washington to become President of the United States.

His beloved Rachel had exclaimed, when her husband's glories of the White House were told to her, "I had rather be a door keeper in the House of God than live in that place." In less than an hour after the remark, Rachel was dead. Now her silver service was a bride's gift.

Eliza thought after all being a Tennessee First Lady was a dignified honor to be bestowed on her.

A cold blustery snow lay on the ground, January 29, 1829. The home Allendale was aglow with the whale oil lamps and candlelight, the wedding gifts galore on display—Colonel Allen conducted his daughter down the great stairway to her place beside the Tennessee Governor in the spacious Ballroom with the colored string band of musicians playing the wedding march and the ceremony said by Dr. Hume, the Presbyterian minister of Nashville Aristocracy.

After a magnificent wedding supper at the Allen home, the bride slipped away from the table in tears into the arms of her old black mammy, Aunt Delsy, who tried to comfort the bride, "Everybody gets married and is happy about it."

The following day, the cold unsmiling bride was not taken directly to Houston's apartments in the Nashville Inn. They went for a few days visit to one of his cousins. Eliza, smiling and pleasant in company, gave no sign the Governor slept on a pallet on the floor while she enjoyed the comfort of the nice, warm featherbed.

For awhile she lived at Nashville Inn. When Houston

came home one night in April, 1829, he found her packed and she asked him to put her on the stage coach for Gallatin.

It is said, "As Houston watched her leave it was a moment he regretted, Eliza regretted a lifetime."

Eliza, home, pale, and weeping, led her parents to believe Houston thought her unfaithful, omitting details of their trouble.

Sam in his agony phrased a letter with simplicity of despair—"I do love Eliza---that she is the only earthly object dear to me, God will be my witness." Sam assured Colonel Allen he believed her virtuous, if mortal man had dared to charge his wife or say anything against her virtue, he would have killed him. He had treated her with affection, she was dear to him, "Eliza stands acquitted of me; she was cold to me and I thought she did not love me; you can realize how unhappy I was to be married to a woman who did not love me."

He hoped once more he and Eliza could be happy and the Allens forget the past. John Allen did not let Eliza see the letter. To the Allens, private life of the family was expected to remain private, and to the present day it has remained so.

Eliza was a Presbyterian in faith but attended church with the family taking no special part in church work and after the fiasco was reluctant to move in circles as before. She later married Dr. Elmore Douglas. His wife had been killed by lightening, leaving ten children. Eliza became the mother of two children, Harriet Louise, born September 2, 1843, died September 26, 1853. The son, William Douglas, born June 3, 1848, died February 25, 1849. They are buried with the Allens and Douglases in the old Gallatin cemetery.

Eliza died on March 3, 1862, during the years of the war when markers were hard to buy. Her grand-niece, Mrs. Guild, of Gallatin, later placed a stone at her grave.

Attorney Allen Guild of Gallatin is a great nephew of Eliza Allen and said his grandfather, B. F. Allen, said his sister's affair was never mentioned in his home.

Ten days after Eliza went home, Sam resigned as Governor, burned his bridges, walking with his friends, Dr. Shelby and Sheriff Wiloughby Williams, he took his departure at Nashville's Steam Boat Landing.

On Governor Sam Houston's last visit to Tennessee, before his departure for Texas, "Aunt Dilsy, was busy about her cabin near the big house when Marse Sam suddenly appeared, frightening the Negress almost out of her wits. Winning her confidence with a piece of silver, Houston persuaded Dilsy to call her Mistress to the cabin; he concealed himself and thus harbored by a slave is said to have gazed upon the face and heard the voice of his wife for the last time."

Eliza, once the high-spirited socialite, who reluctantly avoided people, was said on one occasion, to have disguised herself and talked with Houston on one of his visits to Nashville, but it was too late for a reconciliation.

Diana Rogers Gentry Houston

The Indian Wife of Governor Sam Houston

Sam Houston went from Nashville to what is now eastern Oklahoma, where he was received warmly in the home of John Jolly, the Indian Chief with whom he had lived as a boy at Jolly Island.

Jolly called him, "Sam Son," made him a citizen of the Cherokee Tribe, and he soon became active in Indian affairs, running a frontier store near Fort Gibson.

One, especially, had the power to disturb him. She was tall with a graceful carriage, slender, with her sleekly braided hair, her small moccasins beaded in flower designs, and her white doeskin dress close fitted to her slender hips and waist. He knew her as, "Tiana Rogers."

Sam remembered Tiana as a ten year old, half naked sprite, a half-sister to his chums, John and James Rogers, sons of old Hedgeman Rogers, who had confined his two wives, Elizabeth and Jennie Due to one wigwam. Jennie was Tiana's mother.

In the meantime, since Houston had last seen Tiana, she had been married to David Gentry, a blacksmith—his whereabouts dead or a "divided blanket."

But Tiana was free, a widow in her late twenties, a beautiful girl; moreover, she was socially eligible to become the wife of the adopted son of the supreme chief.

The Rogers were of a distinguished tribal lineage, their name and their strain of Caucasian blood, coming by tradition from a British Officer of the Revolution.

They were related to the Black Coats, the Bushyheads, the Rattlingourds, the little Terrapin and most of the principal families on the Arkansa, including that of Oolookeka.

Tiana's half-brother, Captain John Rogers, succeeded Oolokeka as first chief and his grandson, William Charles Rogers, was the last chief of the Cherokee Nation. William Rogers of Beverly Hills was Tiana's great-great-nephew.

In the summer of 1830, Sam Houston left his foster father's lodge for one of his own, with Tiana to cheer the hearth.

The Cherokees considered Sam and Tiana as man and wife. There was peace and tranquility at the Wigwam Neosha, where Sam Houston established his dwelling place, near the Neosha River; he bought and built a large log house, put out an apple orchard.

There they lived in style, transacting his affairs and entertaining his friends. There was no concealment. Tiana was his wife, her barbaric beauty a part of the solace he had found as he said, "Amid the lights and shadows of the forest life."

In August of the dark year a letter came from Tennessee to Neosho. In September, Sam Houston climbed the slope to Baker's Creek in Blount County to the porticoed house on the hillside. There he wept at the bedside of a "heroine," his mother, Elizabeth Payston Houston, who pressed his hand that wore the ring with a motto "HONOR" engraved in it, and then died.

In October, Sam Houston was back to the wigwam; he told Tiana that he was going East on business and might be gone sometime.

He settled up his domestic affairs with finality. Diana, may have known from the first, the Tribal marriage would end if Sam Houston ever resumed public life in the states and she would not then be a part of his life.

He left her the Neosha wigwam with the orchards and surrounding meadows, the herds of cattle and horses and two slaves—Thus Sam Houston bade adieu to Diana, his Indian Princess—Texas needed him and he needed Texas.

San Jacinto Day in Texas came and was observed with a great celebration and ball. With this victory of Americans over the Mexicans, Texas became Independent, with Sam Houston as President, and now a free man.

Eliza Allen had been divorced, Mrs. Houston was represented by council, but there was no charge of abandonment.

Houston was asked by John Regean, "Why did you leave Eliza Allen?" "That is an absolute secret," replied Sam, "and will remain so."

Diana died of pneumonia, although much courted after Sam left for Texas, for she was well-to-do and tradition is, "still handsome," although she did not remarry. In the National cemetery at Fort Gibson is a stone with this legend: "Sacred to the memory of Tathilhina, Cherokee wife of General Sam Houston, Liberator of Texas." She died at Wilson Creek in the year 1838. She was removed to Ft. Gibson on May 30, 1905

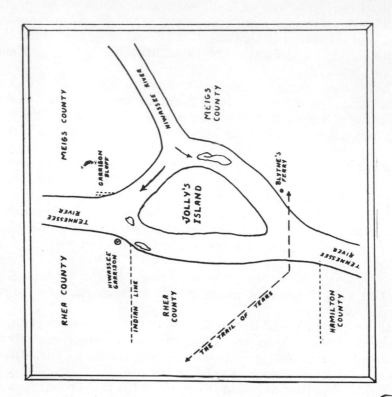

John Jolly, uncle of Tiana Rogers Houston.

Sam Houston School House on John McCulloch's farm near Maryville, Tennessee

The Three wives of
Sam Houston from the
Governor's and Wive's
Doll collection of
Nancy Walker.

The Sam Houston House in Huntsville, Texas.

Margaret Moffet Lea, third wife of Governor Sam Houston.

Margaret Moffatt Lea Houston

B. 1820 — M. 1840 — D. 1867

"My Heart Embraces You"

A small girl of grace and beauty with brown hair with a band of golden ringlets circling her temples like a halo, Margaret Moffatt Lea stood on the Pier as a steamer docked at New Orleans.

The Baptist minister John and Nancy Lea's daughter attending Convent Catholic School, had heard of the Great Texas hero, Sam Houston, who would come to New Orleans, slipped away from school to see the Hero.

Margaret Lea gazed at the great man with tears in her eyes as he hobbled up the gang plank, haggard and wounded after the battle of San Jacinto. Houston did not see her or know what happiness in the future was to be his with this lovely talented, blue eyed Margaret Lea.

She heard of him at different times through the years. Later he was President of Texas and her sister, Emily Bledsoe, teased her about her wild Texas man.

Still later, Houston was a guest at the Bledsoe home; he was interested in blooded horses, which Mr. Bledsoe raised. The sisters planned a meeting in the Rose Garden with Margaret dressed in a rose sprigged dress, carrying a basket of red ripe strawberries.

From this meeting a courtship ensued, although her mother and Emily thought he was too old for her. Mrs. Lea was skeptical about Texas being a suitable place for Margaret to live.

Nancy Lea and her son-in-law, Mr. Bledsoe, went to visit Houston and to purchase some Texas land. In April, 1840, Margaret wrote her mother that she had made herself a blue cotton dress, a purple mohair silk, and a white satin wedding dress.

Margaret and Governor Houston were married at the home of her eldest brother, Henry Lea, in Marion, Perry county, Alabama on May 9, 1840.

After the ceremony her girl friends sang an original ode to the tune of the Old Oaken Bucket. It celebrated the Bridegroom's fame. The last Stanza is:

"Our Washington's name has been hallowed in story,
A founder of freedom's retreat in the west.
Another has risen to share his glory,
The Texean Patriot—Our honored guest."

On their honeymoon they went from Mobile by boat to New Orleans, transferred to the New York to Galveston, Texas.

In July the Houstons were living in their two room house at Cedar Point near Galveston Bay with a lean-to and a separate shed for the servants.

Nancy Lea had given some pieces of furniture to augment pieces Margaret had bought—brought by oxcart from Galveston; their bed mattress was filled with Spanish moss.

Margaret sang sweetly, played the piano, harp, and guitar; now she had only the guitar, the piano was on its way.

She liked housekeeping with the ex-Governor, helping to make a house a home, but by 1841 Margaret was suffering from malaria and illness caused by her Texas diet.

Letters were exchanged while Houston was away from home frequently: "My Love: I do surely hope that you will hear no more slander of me; it is the malice of the world to abuse me and really were not that they should reach my beloved Margaret, I would not care one picayune but that you should be distressed is inexpressible wretchedness to me."

"My dear: do be satisfied, and now in your feeble health, be cheerful, for that is all important to you; and my dear if you hear the truth you never shall hear of my being on a spree.

My heart embraces you.
Thine ever Truly-
Houston."

Margaret had influenced her husband to quit drinking, gambling, swearing; everything except chewing tobacco. At the age of fifty-four he made a profession of faith—he even joined the Baptist church. When the minister said, as he baptized him in a creek, "Sam, this water has washed away your sins," Sam replied, "God have mercy on the fish." His son said later, "After father joined the church he did not use intoxicants of any kind."

In a letter to Nancy, affectionately called Nannie— "Familiar acquaintance with the word of God is worth more then all the wisdom of the schools."

And to the oldest Samuel he once wrote: "Youth—to point of young manhood. Through out this stage of life you must walk erect, truthfully and fear not. Be just. Try my son, to seek God while you are young."

They were the parents of eight children: Samuel Jr., Nancy, married a Morrow, Margaret Lea (Williams), Mary, Nettie Power, Andrew Jackson, William and Temple.

Sam Houston, Margaret and the young son, Sam Jr., made the long trip to the Hermitage on June 25, 1845, thirty minutes too late for the blessing of Andrew Jackson on his little son, Sam Houston knelt and laid his head on his old friend's chest.

In 1846 the late President of Texas was a Senator in Congress in Washington, D. C. Early in the spring of 1846, Dr. Ashbel Smith removed from Margaret Lea Houston a breast cancer. Sam rushed home to find her recuperating nicely.

After a bout with the Missouri Compromise in Congress, Sam returned home again to straighten out his inefficient farm manager. Margaret's ward, Virginia Thorne, had eloped with the overseer and Margaret was disabled with a broken ankle and pregnant with the fifth child, praying that this child would be a son. This prayer was answered on June 21, 1854; a son who was named Andrew Jackson.

In late June, 1858, after many letters to Margaret— anxious to get home to see the new son, William Rogers, born May 26, which Margaret came through safely again; she was thirty-eight and Sam was sixty-five.

In 1841 to 1844, Sam Houston served his second term as President of Texas. As First Lady of the Executive Mansion in Austin, Texas, Margaret managed gay parties. Later they sent Sam Jr. to Allen Military Academy. Margaret taught the girls music and Latin at home, even with her attacks of asthma and always expecting another pregnancy she found time for reading her Bible and her children's education.

She was overjoyed when her husband retired from the Presidency to be back at their Plantation home in Huntsville, Texas. Her husband bought her a great yellow coach to travel to her former home "Raven Hill" which she disliked because of its isolation.

For himself Houston erected of square logs in the side yard, a place of his own where he could whittle and scatter his pipe ashes to his heart's content. He had a pine table, a great oak chair with a rawhide bottom. His walls were lined with shelves of books; his law library, old classical and standard literature, Nelson's Cause and Cure of Infidelity.

In 1861, Houston refused to swear allegiance to the Confederacy. Yet his son, Sam, had joined the Second Texas Confederate Infantry, although his father did not know it. The boys passed and called a greeting to General Houston who was sitting on a balcony of the City Hotel. He started to tell the boys some things a young soldier should know, but a bystander made a sneering remark. Sam threw down his cane and spoke, "One swallow could not make a summer and one victory would not win a war. Fame would see badges of sorrow in their places, but these boys went to battle with his blessing—His prayer would follow them, that they be brave, trust in God and fear not."

His son had been told, "Houston is not a name in the Confederacy that will be a favorite!"

Sam arrived at Cedar Point, found Margaret in tears over young Sam.

At one time after the battle of Shiloh, Sam appeared at the gate where his mother, working in her yard, spoke and came forward to speak to the wounded soldier, who said, "Ma, I don't believe you know me."

In 1863 at the Fall of Vicksburg, Margaret wrote her husband: "Temple, the baby, talks a great deal about you; he grows more and more interesting. Nannie is visiting her Aunt Emily Antoinette Bledsoe at Independence. Sam Jr. after many delays has crossed the Rio Grande in high spirits."

"Mrs. McGray's funeral was held yesterday and brother O'Brien preached a fine sermon—Mr. Seat preached tonight on the prophesies and the Confederate Government. I do hope he will have better luck in predicting than he has heretofore."

"I do hope, my love, you will soon recover your health and be able to return home, but do not worry or hurry on account of any anxiety about us—I must ask a favor to get another supply of James Whitcomb's Remedy for asthma.

Thy devoted wife, Margaret L"

P. S. "Maggie sends her love in which all unite—I hope soon to get a letter from you written with a bad pen and muddy ink."

He did not write; he came home to the Steamboat House with a quite miserable cold; with pneumonia—On July 25, 1863, the family gathered around the bed, Margaret read from the Bible, "In my Father's House are many Mansions."

Nettie Houston Bringhurst said, General Sam Houston was buried during a rainstorm in the little cemetery upon which he used to look from his great oak where he sat and whittled. His coffin was made by the ship's carpenter of the "Harriet Lane," one of the Union Soldier prisioners of War for whose comfort General Houston had interceded. A simple stone bearing only his name and date of his birth and death was replaced later by a larger monument.

After her husband's death Margaret Lea removed her family to Independence, Texas.

The Confederacy was crumbling and within a year they were hard pushed for cash. One day, the old slave, Joshua, who had been left at Huntsville, Texas, appeared riding a mule and laid a heavy leather pouch at his mistress' feet.

It contained two thousand dollars in U. S. gold and silver, a fortune in the Confederacy in 1864. This represented Joshua's savings at extra work as a blacksmith. General Houston had always allowed his servants to keep their outside earnings.

Joshua said, "The money is yours." Margaret asked him to spend it on Christian education for his children. The loyal old servant did this and his son, Sam Houston, became President of the Sam Houston Normal School training for colored at Huntsville.

A yellow fever epidemic swept southern Texas in 1867; her mother suffered the disease, was nursed through by Margaret, who went out as a volunteer nurse, was stricken and died at Independence, Texas.

Mrs. Grace Longino, director of Sam Houston Shrine, in Huntsville, Texas, her staff and the citizens each year in April celebrate Margaret Houston's birthday. They dress in costumes of the Houston Period and host thousands of visitors to the Shrine of the man who once dreamed of becoming President of the United States.

All Houston's colorful episodes in life are depicted at the Shrine; the leopord vest he wore to Congress in 1846, shocking the elete of Washington, hangs in a case.

On the grounds is the home where the last two children, William and Temple, were born and the Steamboat house where Sam's final words, "Margaret----Texas," were spoken.

Mary Brandon Alexander Hall
Wife of Governor William Hall

On the sudden and dramatic resignation of Governor Sam Houston in 1829, William Hall of Sumner County, Speaker of the House, became the new Tennessee Governor. His wife finds herself a First Lady.

Mary Brandon Alexander Hall, called Polly, had come to the Tennessee country as a young girl with her parents Mary. Brandon and William Locke Alexander from Iredell County, North Carolina along with the Brandons. Her mother was born 1752 and died 1834. Her father was born in Cecil County, Maryland. He emigrated first to Mecklenburg County, North Carolina and then to Smith County, Tennessee, dying at the age of eighty-four in 1830 in Sumner County. He enlisted in 1775 in his brother-in-law's (Richard Brandon) Co. of Volunteer Spies against the Cherokee Indians. He lived at Rowen County, North Carolina during the Revolutionary War and served as Captain of troops.

Six members of the Alexander family were signers of the Mecklenburg Declaration of Independence in 1775.

Mary grew up with her brother Robert Alexander who married Nancy Cunnigham Sanders, William Locke Jr., and Jane Alexander who married Raymond Barry. Jane was known as the Cumberland beauty.

Mary and Jane lived in the days that land needed men to manage, and their plantations needed their ladies.

Mary married her faithful and affectionate William Hall who lived at "Locust Land Estate" on the old Hall plantation at Castalian Springs near Gallatin, Tennessee.

It was called "Bledsoe Lick" when William Hall came with his father Major William Hall, who had sold his possessions in Mecklenburg, North Carolina in 1779, and started to Kentucky. But being unable to get through the wilderness with his family, he stopped at New River, Virginia, and bought land. In 1784 he moved to Tennessee Country, bought land, and built a residence. He moved his family in January 1785 before Tennessee became a state.

It was August 2, 1787, that scouts reported Indians sulking about the neighborhood. Early next moring Major Hall began moving his family to Blesoe Lick Fort. The household goods were conveyed by sled. Mrs. Hall and the smaller children remained at home to assist with the packing and loading. The oldest girl went to the fort to set up their furniture. Three loads had been brought to the Fort. It was late in the afternoon, Major Hall, Mrs. Hall, three sons and a daughter with her husband Charles Morgan were about halfway from home and the Fort with the last load, when they were attacked by Indians who were in ambush for over a hundred yards on each side of the road. Uttering a war whoop, the savages sprang up into the settlers a deadly fire. Richard Hall, the eldest son, received a fatal shot and fell in the woods.

A short distance away, the horse Mrs. Hall was riding became frightened, dashing through the lines carrying her safely to the Fort. William, the future governor of Tennessee, twelve years old, was driving the sled. He dropped the lines and ran back to his younger brother and sister Prudence. His father ordered them to scatter to the woods while he and Charles Morgan covered the Indians' retreat. All three children reached the Fort safely. Morgan's body was pierced by thirteen bullets. Major Hall fell in the road mortally wounded; the Indians scalped him and taking his rifle and powder pouch, disappeared into the forest.

The untimely death of Major Hall was a loss greatly deplored by his fellow settlers. Later in the winter Charles Morgan was scalped close to the Hall home.

William Hall grew to manhood in the Castalian Springs community. At school his penmanship was considered the best in the neighborhood. He spent his hours working on the farm. In 1793, Governor William Blount engaged him to serve three months as a spy in search of Indian signs. It was during this period that Castalian Springs and other Tennessee settlements suffered a small pox epidemic.

William Hall, in his first-hand account of the Indian wars of 1787-1795 says, "I have suffered as much as any one could have suffered in the early settlement of this country. Having lost my father, Major William Hall, two brothers James and Richard, two brothers-in-law, Capt. Charles Morgan, a sister and her child by the Indians, besides one brother-in-law, twice severely wounded, but it is some satisfaction that I have not been driven from my heritage."

Governor William Hall's mother was Elizabeth Thankful

Doak, the daughter of Samuel Doak and Jane Mitchell who emigrated to America from Ireland circa 1804. Her grandfather was Samuel Doak from County Antrium, Province of Ulster, Ireland. Governor Hall's brothers were James, Richard and John. The sisters were Mary Morgan Cage, Thankful Morgan, and Sarah Lynum Anderson. The youngest sister was Prudence Hall.

Governor William Hall was a devoted friend of Andrew Jackson and Governor William Carroll. As speaker of the Senate he was an able and capable man. He served sixteen years in the Tennessee House of Representatives and Senate.

While he was busy as a politician, the First Lady Mary Alexander kept the home fires burning; it was necessary to make their own cloth, at which Mary was capable, and able to advise her servants to spin the thread and yarn at the flax and spinning wheels. Her dresses and clothing for her family as well as blankets, coverlets, quilts were made by her and the servants.

She lived in a time of history of Tennessee that the Block Houses had their dances and men drank whiskey from barrels, while the girls took snuff or smoked pipes. They cooked on an open fireplace, rendered lard, ground sausage, and made souse meat at hog killing time. They canned fruit, vegetables, and dried beans. All of these were the duties of the First Lady to supervise, as well as nurse the sick and teach the children to read and write.

The eight children of Governor William Hall and Mary Brandon Alexander were:

1. Martha Ann born the 25th of May, 1821 and died Oct. 4, 1852. She married Dr. B. R. Sharp.
2. Thankful Jane married M.W.H. Jenkins
3. Richard A. married Virginia C. Walsh. He was born Apr. 28, 1811 and died July 6, 1883.
4. Alexander
5. Mary B. (Nancy) married M. Cassady.
6. Robert P. was born March 28, 1823, and at the age of 6, died on June 25, 1829 while his father was Governor.
7. William Harrison was born Jan. 13, 1813.
8. John Alexander was born Dec. 24 1813. He married Nancy Babb, and then Sallie Mason.

Colonel William Harrison Hall fought in the Florida War. He married Katherine Barry first, and then Sarah Winseanna McDaniel, a great niece of Gen. James Winchester of "Craigfront." In 1845, they had a son William who married Mary Brandon Mentlo on December 14, 1874. He was educated in Sumner County and the Rural Academy at Castalian Springs. He was a farmer for twenty years. He became Assistant Cashier of the First National Bank of Gallatin, Tennessee in 1909. This William had a son William, and a daughter Sadie who became the wife of W. H. Witchcock in 1910. He is now President of the Bank and lives at the Mentlo place at Castalian Springs.

Governor William Hall, upon the resignation of Governor Sam Houston on April 16, 1829, succeeded to the governorship, serving until October 1, when he was succeeded by William Carroll.

He returned to Locust Acres with plants and flower seeds for Mary Alexander's flower garden, where at the farm home she would set out family dinners to the Kith and kin who worshipped at the Methodist Church on Sundays. Two years later he was elected to Congress, serving from 1831-1833.

In 1845, the seventy year old Governor wrote his friend William Martin, "Mrs. Hall is mending fast; she can get about on crutches and her broken limb appears but little shorter than the other."

He had lost the sight in one eye and seldom went far from home. In 1855, he became ill, which lasted for more than a year. During this time he gave frequent evidence of his trust in God, and his assurance of his acceptance of him. He died October 7, 1856.

Mary Hall, with stricken heart, was left a widow whose admirable traits characterized her as a woman of virtue, forgetful of self, a dignified lady with a heart full of sympathy for her family and friends. She was ever ready to share the honors and trust to which her husband was elevated.

Mr. John Hall Hodges, a University librarian at Sewanee, said of his great grandmother, "Polly Hall did not interest me as a child, as much as Grandmother Hodges with her stories of her father's Indian fighting and a heroic soldier Governor William Hall.

Governor William and Mary Brandon Alexander Hall home.

Leah Prior Perkins Cannon

B. 1797 — M. 1813 — D. 1816

Wife of Governor Newton Cannon

Leah Prior Perkins, the first wife of Governor Newton Cannon, was the daughter of William Perkins of Davidson County, Tennessee. She was almost sixteen years old when she married Newton Cannon on August 27, 1813.

She lived two years and seven months; she left a son, William Perkins Cannon, who fought in the Florida War. He later moved to Kentucky. The daughter, Leah America Cannon, became the wife of Thomas Fearn Perkins of Williamson County. She was the great-grandmother of Captain Thomas P. Henderson who died recently at Franklin, Tennessee at the age of eighty-three, one of eight Tennesseans who tried to kidnap Kaiser Wilhelm of Germany at the End of World War I.

The scheme was conceived by Col. Luke Lea, commanding officer of the 114th Field Artillery, Henderson, and six other Tennesseans. They planned to present the Kaiser to President Woodrow Wilson as a New Year's gift. One of the men was Larry MacPhail, later to become famous in professional basketball.

They went 300 miles from Paris to Luxemburg and bluffed their way inside the castle of a Dutch nobleman whom the Kaiser was visiting. They had been forced to abandon their kidnap plan because the bridge across a river they had to cross had been washed out. A ferry attendant refused to promise a return trip that night, and they feared they could not elude pursuing guards. The soldiers decided instead to try to convince the Kaiser that he should surrender to the Americans instead of the Dutch. They talked to the Dutch nobleman. He relayed their plea to the Kaiser, who turned them down. The incident came to light a few weeks later when the Kaiser protested officially and the men narrowly escaped court martial.

Henderson, on his return to Tennessee, practiced law. He managed the gubernatorial campaign of Austin Peay and became Democratic Chairman in 1928.

Living in Nashville, Thomas P. Henderson II is a descendant of Governor and Leah Perkins Cannon who had only a few years of life when she died in 1816.

Rachel Starnes Welborn Cannon

B. 1797 — M. 1818 — D. 1866

Wife of Governor Newton Cannon

Mrs. Leah Prior Perkins Cannon had been dead nineteen years when Newton Cannon became Governor in 1835, but there was a First Lady during his administration. His eldest daughter, Rachel Bostie, born of his second marriage tells in her diary of 1878 that she was the first child of Governor Cannon's wife, Rachel Starnes Welborn, daughter of General James Welborn of Yadkin County, North Carolina.

"Rachel was born June 6, 1797, and became the bride of Newton Cannon on August 26, 1818."

From this marriage there were six daughters and two sons: Newton and James Cannon, both dying during the War Between the States. The daughters were Rachel, who became the wife of L. C. Bostic, Ann, who became Mrs. McCullock, Mary, who married Macon Bryan, Adeline, who married Major Lewis Maney, and Marie who was born in 1837 while her father was Governor. She married John Davis Horton and died in Nashville, in 1915, the last surviving child of Rachel and Governor Cannon. She was the mother of Claiborne Horton, Mrs. J. M. Kile, and Mrs. H. W. Evans of Nashville, Tennessee.

Nancy Cannon died in early childhood in 1831 and was buried in the family plot near their home.

In Congress serving with General Newton Cannon was a Mr. Montford Stokes, later Governor of North Carolina, who was a warm friend of Newton Cannon—which friendship proved in after years the source of his second marriage in this way: "Mr. Stokes invited the widower Cannon to visit in his home on the Yadkin River in Wilkes County, in a joking manner he told him that he had both pretty nieces and daughters."

"On horse back attended by a servant, they stopped at the river to let the horses drink, hearing voices, Mr. Stoke's niece, Rachel Welborn, and her sister were strolling by the river bank. She stopped and greeted her uncle who introduced her to Mr. Cannon, the Congressman, and after a few pleasant remarks were exchanged, they parted. Rachel, going on her way home, was not conscious that cupid had shot a dart and the Congressman was resolving to extend his acquaintance with this very attractive girl or that this casual meeting had sealed her future destiny to someday become a First Lady of the State of Tennessee."

"Governor Cannon in 1839 retired to private life, resting from his labors as a public servant of the State. In his hospitable Mansion on Harpeth River near Franklin, he enjoyed meeting his friends around his table and fireside as well as large and liberal entertainment. My memory recalls the names of some of the familiar friends often in our home and happily greeted by my mother, Rachel, and her daughters. A few among our guests were Major David Graham, Comptroller of the State and later under President James K. Polk's administration, Register of the United States Treasury, Mr. Luke Lea, the faithful and accomplished Secretary of the State who afterward moved to Mississippi and became an eminent lawyer and judge.

Among the early investments of the life of Governor Cannon were the lands on which his Harpeth Home was built, in Williamson County. Here in his declining years he was comforted by Rachel until the age of sixty-one. He died in Nashville at seven o'clock p.m. on the 16th of September, 1841. Rachel survived him twenty-five years.

Rachel Cannon was a lady of gentle and winning manners. She possessed a face upon which beauty was written in unmistakable lines; tall, and gracefully formed, polished and elegant in the society of her day, proud of her husband, her eight children and two step-children. She carried out the duties of a First Lady with grace and charm from 1835 until 1839. She lived through the trying days of the Battle of Franklin during the War Between the States, and died in 1866." This daughter, Rebecca Cannon Bostic, and her husband lived in the Mansion, "EverBright," near Franklin. It was built in the late 1830's by John D. Bennet, a writer of a century ago. It tells of the splendid entertainment and the beauty of the garden of the lovely old house inherited by Jennie McEwing Cannon, grandmother of Mr. Sam Fleming, President of the Third National Bank in Nashville, Tennessee.

Governor Newton Cannon traced his family back to three brothers who came to America. One settled in North Carolina, one in Maryland, one in South Carolina. His father, Minos Cannon, was born in Maryland in 1757. He later moved to North Carolina and settled near Guilford Court House. He was a Revolutionary soldier, and he married Letitia Thompson of North Carolina.

In the year of 1761 he migrated to Tennessee Country with other families under the protection of fifty men. They got as far as the Cumberland Gap and turned back because of the Indians; he later made the permanent move.

The second time they got as far as the Old Fort on the Bluff—Nashborough, where they remained for some time. Mrs. Cannon, along with other women in the Fort moulded bullets while the menfolk fired at the Indian attackers through loopholes and cracks in the legs of the Fort.

On one such occasion the white defenders watched in surprise as a pig clumsily approached the Fort. Becoming suspicious, one of the men shot it, and a dead Indian rolled out of the pig hide.

The Cannon homestead with the weather boarding secured by square headed nails, is on the Nashville Pike, three miles north of College Grove. A State marker is at the entrance to the lane leading to the house.

The family cemetery is well cared for in the back yard of the present owners, Mr. and Mrs. Kelley Talliferro. Immense stones, some of the largest ever seen, compose the fence around the markers. Minos Cannon died in 1829; Letitia died January 11, 1832.

Newton Cannon started in business as a Saddler by trade, he later became a merchant. He took up surveying which he intended to adopt as a life profession. However, at about thirty years of age he became interested in politics and soon became a prominent man in the early history of Tennessee.

Unfortunately he and Andrew Jackson were bitter enemies. Once in a law suit, Cannon, many years Jackson's junior, offended him in some way; the fiery Jackson shouted, "Young man I will mark you." From that day on their paths never crossed without antagonism.

"Once at Clever Bottom, Jackson won every negro that Cannon owned and Mrs. Cannon had to borrow a cook from one of her neighbors."

"Their quarrels over horses, bitter as they were, were the least of it; they continued all their lives and letters still exist to show the depth of their animosity."

Governor Cannon's marker in the family cemetery reads: "In memory of Newton Cannon, born 22, May, 1781, Guilford Court House, N. C. Died Sept. 16, 1841 at Nashville, Tennessee." He served in the Legislature of Tennessee in 1811 and Congress of U. S. 1816-1820; in revising the Constitution in 1834; Governor 1835-1839. He held the commission of

Colonel in Creek War, fought at Talladega, and Tallahatchie. A man of stern integrity of character, of Republican simplicity of life, he enjoyed in a high degree the love of friends and confidence of his countrymen.

GRAVESTONE OF GOVERNOR N. CANNON.

courtesy of
Mrs. W. R. Morton, Franklin, Tenn.

GOVERNOR NEWTON CANNON HOME

Sarah Childress Polk

B. 1803 — M. 1824 — D. 1891

Wife of Governor James K. Polk

In 1839 James K. Polk carried the state of Tennessee for the Democrats, and was elected Governor. So Sarah Childress Polk left Washington D. C. for Nashville. "Where her house became the center of the fashionable elegance as well as the political diplomacy of Nashville's Capital."

At the First Presbyterian Church, on October 14, 1839, the inaugural ceremonies were opened with a prayer by the Reverend Howell of the Baptist Church.

Governor Polk gave his inaugural address to those in the well-filled pews. Included in them was his mother, Jane Knox Polk. The aisles were full, with people standing against the walls. The speech was pronounced by his hearers as, "The greatest ever to be delivered in the State of Tennessee."

At this time Nashville was only a temporary Capital; there was neither a government capital nor a Governor's Mansion. Sarah and Governor Polk lived in a five hundred dollar a year home on Cherry Street, West, lighted by whale oil lamps and candles.

Sarah was the daughter of Elizabeth Whitsett and Joel Childress. Mrs. Childress was the daughter of John Whitsett who came to Sumner County from North Carolina among the pioneers and located there before the Indian troubles of the frontier were settled. The Whitsetts were associated with the Browns, Haskeils, and Blackmores.

Joel Childress also came from North Carolina and first engaged as a merchant at Fox Springs, then a noted place; here he resided until Murfreesboro's first lots were sold and he then built the first house in Murfreesboro.

Joel Childress was the first postmaster in the town of Murfreesboro and held the appointment until his death in 1819.

Sarah was born September, 1803. Her father became a plantation owner with slaves, and was considered a rich man for those days. He allowed his children Anderson, John W., Susan, and Sarah every benefit to be derived from his fortunate circumstances.

He was able to dress his women folk in silks and velvets; Susan and Sarah were unusually good looking girls. They loved horse back riding with their brothers. They were sent to private school in Nashville.

James K. Polk, son of Jane Knox and Sam Polk, was alone in a classroom. He heard footsteps, "a lady and two young girls wearing velvet capes and silk dresses, he had hardly seen such elegance on Sundays." "They must be rich," he thought.

Jim was a shy fellow. He heard the mother say, "Sarah, have you forgotten this is a boy's school?" James K. arose and asked if he could help.

"The girls were to have lessons at four; we are looking for Mr. Black," Mrs. Childress replied.

James Knox's friend, Anderson Childress came up and introduced his mother and sisters. They chatted about "soon to go to Mrs. Abercombe's Private School in Nashville, where they would board with the Butlers, who had one of the few pianos in Tennessee."

James informed Sarah he was going to the University of North Carolina as a sophomore, which he attended from 1816 until 1818. He became the ranking scholar of his class.

In the meantime Sarah had been sent to the Moravian school in Salem, North Carolina. She came back able to sing as well as play instrumental music. Religion, discipline, culture and reading were stressed, which helped to mold her character.

When James K. Polk again met Sarah Childress, the slender girl with the Spanish Donna look, at Governor William Carroll's reception in Murfreesboro, he knew there was something like arrow darts in his heart. As time went on Mrs. Childress took a hand in the affair, and asked Sarah if she thought James Knox would be a son-in-law, to which Sarah replied in the affirmative.

On January 21, 1824, the nineteen year old Sarah became the bride of James Knox Polk in an elaborate wedding ceremony and reception, featuring a band of Negro musicians, and a seven course dinner as was typical of the festivities and merriment of the day.

Mr. Polk had recently entered public life, a member of the Tennessee Legislature, and in 1825 he was elected to Congress from Giles, Maury, Lincoln and Bedford Counties. He was one of Andrew Jackson's loyal followers. Tennesseans called him "Young Hickory."

Arriving in Washington, Sarah found it only a country village. They lived in a Boarding house among congenial Congressional friends, where they would take over a place with more than one parlor for common use.

They soon found themselves in the best society of Washington. They were in easy circumstances and Sarah rated high among the Congressional ladies for her polite manners, accomplishments, and sound judgment.

She was interested in all that related to James Knox, and took pains to inform herself on political affairs of the day. She read all the news and discourses relating to the interest of the United States.

Between sessions of Congress, they spent at their home in Columbia, Tennessee.

Living in Nashville, Mrs. Polk as First Lady of Tennessee in her native State , was representative of her husband's name and greatness; her calm, charming bearing was a source of constant praise.

She exerted a wide influence in Nashville Society into which she had been cast; she attracted even the hostile members of the Legislature and others with her winning gentle manners which were bred as part of her social qualities and fitted her for the Lady of the Chief Magistrate, Polk. She had her admirers among the rich, the poor for her benevolence and consistancy in her Presbyterian faith. She did not join the church until 1844, almost thirty-one years old at the time.

The Dark Horse candidate for President of the United States, the first such in the history of our country, James Knox Polk was the young est man at that time to become President.

At President Tyler's retiring dinner, Sarah held her own against Mrs. Tyler in her black velvet and plumes. On March 4th, during the President's inauguration, Sarah stood, watching, listening among the sea of umbrellas. But rain, she thought, was the Lord's doing and she could not complain. She attended both the five dollar and ten dollar inaugural Balls in her blue brocade ball gown while the President slipped off home, early to bed.

At the President's reception Sarah was seated on a sofa engaged in lively conversation with some ladies. She was wearing a maroon colored velvet dress with short sleeves and high neck, trimmed with very deep lace and a handsome pink headdress that really struck the eye of an observer.

Sarah Polk was the best dressed and best looking of

Washington society. She was fond of colors, especially purple.

In the White House she felt no hesitation. Dancing was stopped, no one called on Sundays on business. She even went so far as to stop serving refreshments at White House receptions—which she thought beneath the dignity of the Presidential Office. Neither did they ever attend the theater while he was President. She talked to her guests, a well-informed woman.

She served as Polk's confidential secretary, a position never before held by a woman. She was the first educated woman in the White House to really be a conversationalist.

She had cunningly sat in the background stitching her samplers and listened. No lady of the 1800's openly discussed politics. Polk later said, "None but Sarah knew so intimately my private affairs."

Neither did women receive very much publicity in the newspapers in Sarah Polk's day--yet her Presbyterian standards of no wine serving or dancing in the Mansion was noted in the Nashville Union, that, "even frivolous pastimes would respect Madam Sarah's wishes."

The Polks' money was vested in plantations; to them farms were factories expected to produce profit. Their slaves were valuable property not to be abused by the overseers who were paid good wages, and who were dismissed if undue harshness was administered to servants.

In 1849, the Polks, with cash in hand, removed to Nashville by way of New Orleans feated and feasted to the Polk Place.

They had purchased the house built in 1810, by Felix Grundy which was then a wooded area with ground cleared for vegetables and a flower garden. Beyond was a cedar thicket where the ten Grundy children were forbidden to play for fear the Indians might catch and scalp them.

The Grundy Mansion was remodeled and put in the most complete and elegant order and thereafter known as the Polk Place. It was a large house with imposing entrances, each with Greek facades, and tall fluted columns with pilasters on all four corners. The grounds were enclosed by an iron fence with heavy folding gates; the front gates were ornamented with anchors and surmounted by an eagle with out-stretched wings.

In the wide green lawns were many splendid shade trees with fountains and broad borders of flowers and shrubs. Sarah's garden was a refreshing sight to passers-by who stopped to enjoy the bright colors and fragrant odors. A block away they would say, "Mrs. Polk's Spice Pinks are blooming today."

They planned an European tour, James Knox Polk had engaged a courier who could interpret French and German to go with them, but unfortunately he contracted cholera on his way home.

James K. Polk wrote in his diary, "I generally go to the Presbyterian church with my wife though my opinion and predictions are in favor of the Methodist Church." "Attending church with my secretary, James Knox Walker, on that inclement, rainy Sunday, the text was Acts 17 - 31: Because he had appointed a day in which he will judge the world in righteousness by the man whom he hath ordained." Mr. Polk went on to say, "It awakened the reflections that I had lived fifty years and before fifty more I would be sleeping with my fathers."

Fulfilling a promise that he had made, James K. Polk was baptized June 9, 1849, by a Methodist minister. On June 15th, 1849, Polk died.

No man ever sought the happiness in private life with better prospects of finding it than James K. Polk. He had the society and companionship of a wife whose superior intellectual endowments combined with the choice graces and virtues of final excellence qualified her to shed luster upon public station or to influence contentment and happiness into the domestic circle.

Polk was a plain and simple man in manner, mild and forbearing, easy in conversation, respect for the Christian religion, a regular reader of the Bible and a constant attendant upon divine worship.

Sarah, the frail bride was now a forty-five year old widow—enclosed around her were James K. Polk's books, even his watch—keeping the vigil she was to keep for forty-three more years, leaving home only to attend church or a dinner at Belmont, with Adelica Hays Acklen as hostess, dressed in her black and lace widow's cap. She did not go out into the world but the world came to her. She received President and Mrs. Rutherford B. Hays, President and Mrs. Grover Cleveland, and even George Bancroft, age eighty-six called to see her. Every organization that convened in Nashville called on her.

Throughout widowhood she dressed in mourning in contrast to her early days of gorgeous colored silks and velvets and plumes; her favorite hat was purple.

As the tide of the War Between the States swept Nashville, kinsmen urged her to flee South. Her answer was, "No, if the Yankees seized her home or destroyed it, she would pitch a tent beside her husband's tomb. She would not leave."

She remained neutral and was treated with "consideral" respect; even given military protection to visit her sick mother, Mrs. Joel Childress, in Murfreesboro.

Valuables of the Tennessee Historical Society were stored in her home for safe keeping. Impoverished, she would not sell Polk Place. She received a pension of $5,000 a year from Congress when she was seventy-nine.

ASLEEP IN JESUS
Mrs. Sarah Childress Polk
Wife of
James Knox Polk
Born in Rutherford County
September 4, 1803
Died at Polk Place
Nashville, Tennessee
August 4, 1891
"A noble woman, and devoted wife,
A true friend and sincere Christian."
"Blessed are the dead which died in the Lord."

(The letters published below were found among the 150 volumes of the James K. Polk papers in the Library of Congress. As will appear, the wife's letters are only a cover for her campaigning husband's mail.)

Columbia, June 15, 1839

Dear Husband,
You did not leave me any directions where to write or direct anything - These letters contained information I thought might be useful to you, and I have thought proper to enclose them to Major Bills with a request that he would send them to you—There is nothing occurred since you left of importance. I have only heard from you by Genl. Pillow

since you left. Why don't Knox write to somebody? I am anxious to hear from you, not political prospects only, but your health.

Your affectionate Wife
Sarah Polk

Nashville
Dec 31, 1840

Dear Husband

There has nothing happened that is of much importance since you left here—appointment of senators as far as I have learned has been well received. Letters from Brown, John and Turney have come to you from Washington, written before Mr. Grandy's death but anticipating the event, proposing or making suggestions to you that it may be necessary and proper to call the legislature together for the purpose of electing senators, for it is almost reduced to a certanty **that here will be** a call session of Congress in the spring—In which event Brown and Turney both write that you should be the person to be elected. I have given you their views written to you privately in as few words as I could express the intention. I do not understand matters sufficiently well to form an opinion yet it does not strike me that it is the right thing for you to do. They all seem to think there will be a call session of the Congress early in the spring. Johnson wrote that he could not run again and that it was necessary to have his successor settled and ready to take the field— This is the Washington news. As to home there have come some letters from Memphis which seem to be of some interest about the Rail R Directors & one from McLemore and one from Gaines. There appears to be much feeling and excitement on the subject, but I suppose at Memphis you learn all about it. Here are some sheriff returns, which is all that have come to hand. I saw Mr. Jerry George last evening but he does not seem to know much about anything—I have just given Maj. G. such letters as you directed me, all he seemed to know was the speculation about the new Clinick, all of which is to be seen in the papers now and before you left. Now as to **myself,** I have been waiting to receive the meat before I would leave from Murfreesboro. This is Monday and it has not yet come. I sent Elias to the man on Monday, he was not at home so you may see that I am in a state of uncertainty yet. I will go on Saturday, I think, **meat** or no **meat**—though I do not know that it will make a man think any more of his **wife** for her to neglect the domestic duties of the household. I will risk it at all events. As directed I will write again at Murfreesboro and hope to hear from you soon.

Your affectionate Wife
Sarah Polk

His Excellency   Nashville
James K Polk   April 8, 1841
Somerville, Tenn.

Dear Husband

There is not as yet any business to call your attention, no letter from Jackson by last night's mail. But a letter from the President and directors of the Lagrange and Memphis railroad company, asking for bonds to the amount of $7000, and asking immediate attention to it, and also stating that James Renbert was dead, and that the board had that day unanimously recommended Gilb Thomas G. Polk to fill the vacancy.

I will enclose a letter from Knoxville on the same subject or road commissioners—something which you could attend to where you are. A letter of invitation to a dinner given to A. V. Brown at Savannah on the 22nd—This is about all that has come since I wrote last to you. If you wish me to send letters or newspapers to you write—

The Banner was out on you a few days ago, on your reasons for not calling the legislature together. The article, said to be written by **Allan Hall an Office Holder.** The Union of this morning charged it upon him, and also had some good articles relative to your prospects. The Banner of today has two letters from **Big Spring** and **Sparta** telling what an extraordinary Lean Jones proves himself to be and that he uses you up so that they (I suppose his traveling companions or puffers) think that you will leave them by the 15th with an excuse to attend to executive business. There is rather a slam here on politics and everything else, there is not much said only what appears in the papers. I do not think it likely that the Democrats will get out any candidate in this county, there seems to be no prospects of doing so. I have not gotten much news as I see but few persons to talk to. I have written all I know at present—You must write where to direct my letters to. I am not at all discouraged at anything I see in the papers or hear from any quarter, but when I think of the labor and fatigue you have to undergo I feel **sad** and melancholy, and conclude that **success** is not worth the

103

labour. Dr. Young is not in his room but attends to his business that I send him faithfully. If Jones does frighten you home by the 15th you may tell him your wife will be glad to see you.

Your affectionate
Wife
Sarah Polk

Gov
    James K Polk
        Athens
            Tennessee

Since writing I have received the Columbia **Observer** which has changed editors from Zolly to two Roseboroughs and had Barkely Martin candidate for the Senate, William Dean for the House of Representatives.

(No heading or date. Post Marked 4/9)

Dear Husband
    Enclosed is a letter from Edwin Polk which contains a statement from George Alexander. I thought you might need it in the region where you are. As it was only a copy, it could be risked by mail—

Yours &c
Sarah

Nashville
April 10th, 1841

Dear Husband
    The application for a special judge at Jackson did not come until last night. Gen'l Armstrong attended to securing some person to go with it according to your directions.—I suppose the appointment will reach there in times as I understand that it is likely that the Court will hold four weeks. I had written to you by the mail yesterday morning, and sent some papers which I could have sent by the messenger if I had known that one would be sent.—The Banner & Whig of yesterday give you a touch. Their attacks amount to but little and only proves to me they are uneasy. Allen Hall is here writing for the Banner, and the Whig is not severe. The article yesterday was a rally to the Whig candidates for the legislature, saying that to you defeat would be nothing if the legislature was Democratic, your ambition now was the Senate of W. In my last I wrote you that Jones letter writer had appeared in the Banner representing you as used up by

Jones &c, &c, &c. I do not believe that anything they have put in the papers will have any effect on you, so you must not be uneasy. I am not troubled by anything that has yet appeared. **Old Tip** is dangerously ill, so it is understood from the mails of last night. I believe I wrote you all the business in my last letter—directed to Athens.

Yours affectionately
Sarah Polk

Gen'l Armstrong found great difficulty in getting a competent person to go which delayed the starting of a messenger.

Nashville
April 14th, 1841

Dear Husband

I enclose you a communication given me this morning by Mr. Walker from David Dobbins. Mr. Walker said he retained a copy and requested me to send you this. There is nothing since I last wrote you that is worth writing. The Whigs I am told are in a good deal of concern since the death of their President, now knowing what **Tyler** will do &c &c According to my judgment the same powers will control, Clay &c. The Banner is still harping on your two addresses—In their articles now, they award to you what they never did before—that you are able talented and a great leader and that the Whigs are in danger of another defeat. I am told that they have become here very uneasy fearing that there will be a Democratic legislature. They says in their articles that you are a **wily and dangerous foe,** so I think that they will level all their articles against you. They are more respectful towards you than they were in former times. They make no new charges, and all they have said does not amount to much in **my** judgment.

I have felt some uneasiness since you wrote me that you were not at all well, and seeing in the papers that you declined speaking on one occasion because you were unwell. I hope to hear from you tomorrow and hear that you are well again. Success is not worth the trouble, much less ruining one's health by it, and do take care of yourself.

Thursday, April 15th, I was much disappointed that I did not hear you today. If I do not hear in a day or two I shall be uneasy as the last I heard that you were sick. I have a letter from the overseer in Miss. dated the first of April. All was well, he had planted corn and commenced planting cotton on that day. Nothing more at present.

Your affectionate
Wife
Sarah Polk

Nashville
April 25, 1841

My dear Husband

I have just returned from Columbia where I have been during the last week. Sister Walker I left some better and her family in fine spirits with the hope that she will now recover though not sure. I was sent for a week ago. She was not expected to live. I think that she may get well, but it will be a great while before she is entirely restored, so thinks her Physician. S. P. Walker promised me to write you all concerning the politics of the county. As far as I could learn all would go on well. Cabal is a candidate but no one thinks of him being elected. Watterson was there. As to the vote, they think you will get as good a vote as you ever did. There is no enthuasiasm for Jones here or anywhere else that I hear from but rather an indiference (sic). Here I am told nobody seems to care or to be uneasy except E. H. Foster. He is might troubled about your address and the legislature. The articles are weak and feeble in the Banner once a week, headed Gov. Polk's Address. They cannot hurt you anywhere. I have not seen Harris since I returned from Columbia, indeed I have seen but few persons not even Young, because he is sick again. I suppose he has **over-eat** himself. He attends to the business faithfully as far as I know—I hear no complaints on your absence—Only such **as your wife makes** and I confess that I feel much anxiety for your health and I do not know how you are to stand the fatigue of the campaign. It makes me unhappy to think of what you must suffer, and for what? You cannot be honored by success, nor dishonored by defeat, so I have not much to stimulate me. I received since I got home Thomas letter from Madisonville. Tell him I am much obliged to him for his kindness in writing me. I wrote to you at Knoxville and enclosed a paper from David Dobbins which I suppose you received. I learned when at Columbia that William's nomination was well received and he would probably get a better vote than anyone of them so you need not be uneasy about him.—I have nothing more. Nashville is dull and quiet in everything.

Your affectionate Wife
Sarah Polk

Tell Thomas all are well at his Father's.

Nashville
Sunday, May 2, 1841

Dear Husband,

I write because you requested me to do so, not that I have anything to say of consequence. As far as you are concerned everything is quiet, nothing in the Whig papers for the last week or two. No business came into the office requiring your attention, and nothing, said about your absence. Mr. Harris promised me to attend to your appointments. They will appear in the Union tomorrow morning. I suppose that you have seen that John of Wilson is a candidate for Congress. He spoke here on Thursday, Robert Caruthers will speak tomorrow. I see so few gentlemen that I do not get much chance to pick up news. Cox I am told is running for Congress in the District. If I can pick up anything tomorrow or next day, I will write to you again. But tonight I know nothing to write about. So you must excuse me, for I know it will be a tax on your time to read a long letter about **nothing.** I hope soon to see you.

Your affectionate Wife
Sarah Polk

Nashville
June 18, 1841

Dear Husband

Your letters from Lawrenceburg I have received and will try to impress on your friends that necessity of attending to your requests contained in them. Any business you wish attended to through Genl Armstrong I know will be faithfully and immediately done, for he seems willing and alive to the canvass, but **Harris** is **wild** and crazed about the widow or her fortune. I saw Genl A. today and he says that Harris is a common subject of remark and can do nothing with him and cannot even get to see him to converse with. I do not wish to give you uneasiness of mind, but he is no

107

account. Him and the paper has been so much abused that I do not think he can do any good, so in my opinion you do not loose (sic) much from the inefficiency of his paper. Hollingsworth will be a candidate in opposition to Jennings, and it is understood that he is out but not yet announced in the papers. I understand there has been some money made up for him and he takes the field. They cannot get anyone for the **House** to run. The Whigs are not in good spirits here. They I am told think or fear that they will loose (sic) the legislature. Foster is dispirited and is sick again with the wound, had three doctors to go out to probe it for the **knife blade.** I expect it is half pretence.

Judge Catron told me he had, in a few instances, in his tour in the District intimated to some of the Whigs that Judge Green would be a more reliable candidate for the Senate than Foster, a broken down hackneyed politician, and it took well. I suppose you get the Washington news through the papers. If you desire me to send you the Globe and other papers that are on file here write me. I do not send them more frequently because I thought you wished the files kept. I believe I have written all I can think of now. I have kept my letter open for the mail this morning. You had no letters to come, and I of course have no information. I send you the last papers. I had scarcely time to look at the Globe or Intelligencer, but supposing they contained the Abolition and repeal of the Sub-Treasury I send them. I saw Harris to day and gave him your letter from Lawrenceburg. He promised to have all attended to and in the Union of Monday. Hollingsworth is a **candidate** and Ken (?) Walker (from whom you know that I got a good deal of news) says it makes some sensation among the Whigs. Dr. McNairy will vote for him and Joe Nowell thinks he will be elected. This of course is women's gossip and not worth much. This is rather a long conclusion to my letter.

Your affectionate
Wife
Sarah Polk

Nashville
June 25, 1841

Dear Husband

I have been absent for a few days in Murfreesboro, returned last night when I received your letter from Savannah.

I found Dr. Young anxious to hear something about the Bonds sent to you. Graham left I suppose without giving Young any information concerning them. Graham I presume did send them and papers to you, and they have not had time to be returned of course, and I have so informed him. You can see by the Union (which I send you by the mail) that Hollingsworth is a candidate and I have just seen Donelson and Dr. Esselman who says his chances for success is pretty good. They cannot get anyone out for the House and think it will be an advantage to have none. Ewing and Campbell will not take the field to discuss; they have no opposition and Jennings is unpopular, so you may see that they have no hope of electing their man Hollingsworth. You may discover that the last **Union** is better filled than usual. I am in hopes that Harris will do better in future—I learn no news since I came home but that Genl Jackson has been dangerously ill and now much better, the **knife blade** has been cut from E. H. Fosters side and he is well. Genl Anderson is here from Knoxville, gives a flattering account of the prospects in E. Tennessee, says that you will increase your vote of '39, told me of many counties he had been in and traveled through. His account is flattering. In Rutherford the Democrats seem to be sure of success. The removal of the Post Master at this place will do good, Henderson being a poor Methodist preacher, the Whigs will loose (sic) some vote wherever the towns have no influence. There is a good deal of excitement in the latter place about the removal. There comes to you now but few letters &c &c. Young says there is no business in the office. Sister Walker is here and much improved in health and intends going the Spings. I hope that you will take care of yourself. I think sometimes that it is impossible for you to stand the fatigue until August but I pray that you may have health which is more than success.

The mail of this evening brought you a letter from A. V. Brown which I send you. Nothing else came.

Your affectionate
Wife,
Sarah Polk

Nashville
June 30, 1841 (?)

Dear Husband

I do not write because I have anything to communicate, on the contrary I have nothing and have heard nothing since

109

I wrote you last. Everything as far as I can learn is quiet, remarkable so at this place. The Whig papers have not noticed nor denied the charges against Jones as published in the Union. All the Democratic papers has the Certificate and comments in them, yet I have not seen or heard a single denial in the papers. Harris's two or three last papers are more spirited, and I think probably his senses are returning for he appeared more rational when I last saw him. I am a little surprised not to have heard from you before this. E. P. McNeal was kind enough to write me how you were at Bolivar, which is all I have heard from you in ten days. But I hope to hear from you this evening.

Your affectionate Wife
Sarah Polk

Nashville
July 5, 1841

My dear Husband

I am afraid that you will think me troublesome in imposing on you the necessity of reading my letters which in truth contain nothing. For I assure I know nothing to write and have a poor opportunity of learning anything. Sister Walker being here has confined me at home for the last two weeks and I know but little that is going on only from newspapers, which you see. There is as far as I can learn no excitement and very little interest in Politics—I send you the Union of today. I think of late that Harris seems to give more attention to the paper and it is more spirited. The Whig papers say but little about the election, do not abuse you, nor do they praise Jones, nor defend him, if anything, I think the Democrats are more active and spirited here than the Whigs. But I hear so much less of politics here than I ever did before that I am at a loss what to think of their prospects—Let the result be what it may, so you do not destroy your health or kill yourself with fatigue, I should not grieve but he thankful. You have scarcely any letters of any sort, and there is no business in the office. **Young** is going about, I have heard nothing of the Bonds. Indeed everything as far as I know is quiet.

I will not close my letter until the mails of this evening comes in. I received no letter from you nor anything else. You need not be alarmed when I tell you that there is an addition of **ten** to our family this evening. Mr. and Mrs.

Walker Maj Bills Mr. McDowell Jane Sally Andrew &c &c &c.
Do you think I am lonesome?

Your affectionate
Wife
Sarah Polk

Nashville
July 25, (1841)

My dear Husband

I am distressed that I know nothing, nor have learned nothing since you left to write you. As far as I know there is as yet a calm and quietness in politics. Though I confess to you the truth that I have had no opportunity of learning much. The house full of **kin** that I have had ever since you left, and indeed all the **summer,** has made me nothing more than a servant—and a senseless round in my house keeps me at home and keeps away such company as I might gather information from. So you can perceive that I have no means to learn anything to write you which I offer as an excuse. I sent you the Banner containing Jones letter to the people in the Clarkesville District. I directed it to Blountsville. As far as I can learn it made no impression here for nothing is said about it, and there has been nothing said in the papers. I regret that I have nothing to write you. The truth is I learn nothing, I hear nothing, and of course to read a long letter from me would be a loss of time, so I will leave off.

Your affectionate
Wife
Sarah Polk

Nashville
July 29, 1841

Dear Husband,

I have not heard from you since you left Nashville, but hope to hear today. I am told that there is more interest, and I may say excitement, within the last few days on the subject of the Election. The Whigs it is said are uneasy, the Democrats in good spirits. I hear from W. Curria that there has been many changes in Williamson since you were there, among them old **Beaufort** who interrogated you at the speaking—But whether there can be changes enough to elect you next Thursday is another question, but I shall have philosophy to stand it and think that I can be as happy with my husband **at home** defeated candidate, as to have a suc-

111

cessful one always from me, and you have now character enough in the country to stand a defeat temporary as it must be without injury to your future prospects.

The Banner of this day has two articles rallying the Whigs and urging them not to let personal considerations induce them to vote against their principles at this important time. If you can get through the canvass, **health unimpaired**, and at home safely once more, I will be content, let the result be what it may, but I hope for the best in all things.

Your affectionate
Wife
Sarah Polk

Wednesday night (1841, August 4, in
pencil)

Dear Husband

You told me I must write to you by Thursday's mail. In order to prove to you that I am an obedient wife, I send you this form of a letter, for I have nothing to write. Since you left I have heard nothing and know nothing. I was sorry that you had to travel alone to E. Tennessee, but hope that you will pick up some one on the way. I hope that you will write me according to promise. If I can gather anything worthy of your attention I will write you to Knoxville. But I do not think my letters worth the postage.

Your affectionate Wife
Sarah Polk

Honl James K. Polk

The **Observer** this morning says you are **peevish** and **fretful** of late indicating that you expect to meet with some disappointments. As to the V.P. I though t you were **right good natured** when at home. So take care how you show your **bad temper.**

Murfreesboro

Dear Aunt

We received your letter a few days since and were amused to think you thought it a quiz that I should write that I was to be married, but I am sure you will believe it now. Aunt, my motive for writing at present is to..... ask you to purchase me a suitable bonnet for 10 dollars, and Pa will settle with you. Our merchants have not received their

112

goods. You and Uncle must be certain to come. William
Childress and his family are invited.

Your neice
Elizabeth R.

ANCESTRAL HOME OF JAMES K. POLK
AND SARA CHILDRESS POLK

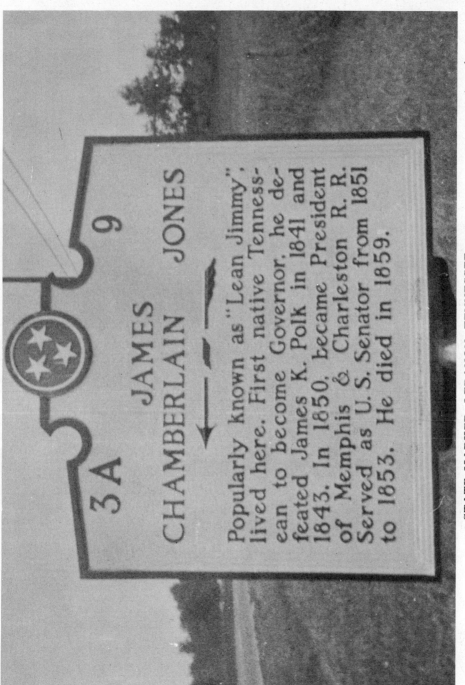

STATE MARKER, LEBANON, TENNESSEE.

The marker text reads:

3 A

9

JAMES
CHAMBERLAIN JONES

Popularly known as "Lean Jimmy", lived here. First native Tennessean to become Governor, he defeated James K. Polk in 1841 and 1843. In 1850, became President of Memphis & Charleston R. R. Served as U. S. Senator from 1851 to 1853. He died in 1859.

JAMES CHAMBERLAIN JONES' HOME, LEBANON

Sarah Watkins Munford Jones

B. 1812 — M. 1829 — D.

Wife of Governor James Chamberlain Jones

Sarah Munford Jones, a Tennessee First Lady in 1841-45, like her sister, Matilda Hudson Mooney, was a beautiful Kentucky girl. Her sister was gifted with both pen and tongue, with a magnetism that drew people around her. Sarah had a charming manner of relating her family history.

"The Munford family sprang from English-Welch blood. Grandfather, Thomas Bowling Munford, was a member of the Virginia House of Burgess from Amelia county. He left four sons: William, Richard, Thomas and James, who settled in Hart and Green Counties, Kentucky. Richard built the town of Munfordville, was a farmer, a merchant and several times a member of the Kentucky Legislature." William Munford, father of Sarah, was born in Amelia County, Virginia. He went to Kentucky when a young man, was one of the early settlers and died at Lebanon, Tennessee, in 1844, age sixty-six.

"William married Lettice Ball, born in Lincoln County, daughter of Thomas Ball originally from Virginia, but who early started out as a carpenter at Lexington, Kentucky; he became a prominent farmer and owner of a large canning factory. He married a Miss Reid, of a very distinguished legal profession family of the early history of Kentucky;" thus through her maternal grandmother, Sarah Munford Jones, was related to the Marshalls, Reids, and Greens of Kentucky.

Sarah Munford Jones was the fifth of nine children of Letitia Ball and William Munford. She was born June 18, 1812. At the age of seventeen she married James Chamberlain Jones on August 27, 1829. They started life on a farm near Lebanon, Tennessee not too far from the Andrew Jackson Hermitage.

James C. Jones was the son of Catherine Chapell and Peter Jones. He was born near the Davidson and Wilson County line on June 7, 1809.

He attended the Old Field Schools; his father died when he was a small boy of ten years of age. With an uncle as guardian, his education was little.

He grew into a long, lean fellow, about six feet tall, weighing one hundred and twenty-five pounds, with a prominent nose, small deep set blue eyes overhung by massive eyebrows. He had a melodious voice, unmatched burlesque and prompt wit. His friends nicknamed him "Lean Jimmy Jones" and during his campaign for Governor of Tennessee, he was referred to as "Blue Jeans Jones."

It was said, that his guardian disapproved of his marriage to Sarah when he was twenty-one and withheld his father's estate, causing Jones to do hard farm labor.

The Jones, when he first entered politics, had become the parents of four children. He was elected to Tennessee State Legislature in 1837, and again in 1839, and by 1841 he was Governor of Tennessee.

The children of the Jones were Mary Letitia Catherine, born September 27, 1830; Amelia Matilda, born February 23, 1832; Peter Munford, born September 18, 1834; Ann Frances, born February 23, 1837; and Sarah Elizabeth, born December 7, 1839. The sixth child, Hugh Lawson White was born while his father was Governor, September 2, 1842.

The Whigs put up James Chamberlain Jones against James Knox Polk for Governor in 1841. It was a round of "stump speaking;" Polk a more educated man than Jones, but Jones a more natural mimick and actor, ridiculing James Knox Polk and telling jokes that caused the people to howl with laughter. Polk was disgusted and mortified. In the final vote Jones won the nomination for Governor in 1841 and again in 1843.

In 1843, the Legislature made Nashville the permanent Capital of the State and the corner stone of the capitol was laid in 1845.

Jones accomplished little from 1841-1842, but in his second term the Legislature appropriated funds for the Blind School in Nashville and the Deaf and Dumb School in Knoxville, these two schools being the first institutions for handicapped children in Tennessee. The first train in Tennessee made its exhibition run over Lagrange and Memphis Railroad and James K. Polk became the first Dark Horse in American politics to become President of the United States. The Methodist Episcopal Church was established and also the Southern Baptist Convention. It turned out that James Chamberlain Jones was not the Country Clown some people believed him to be.

Even with so little education as he had acquired, he said,

"Colleges and Academies are more to be relied on than all the armies and Navies the government can command."

He also said, that the Tennessee Legislature should become more local and less National in their proceedings.

In 1850 ex-Governor and Sarah Jones moved to Memphis, Tennessee to live. James Chamberlain had been born June 3, 1847 and Felix Morgan arrived on November 14, 1848. The last and ninth child, Robert Brinkley, was born in Memphis on October 14, 1851.

The ex-Governor Jones became President of the First Memphis-Charleston Rail Road. He was chosen as one of the first West Tennessee Senators of the United States Senate for six years. He was seriously considered for the Vice Presidential nomination in 1852. Retiring from public life, he died in Memphis on October 29, 1859, age fifty years.

Sarah, age forty-seven, a widow with nine children, the youngest just eight years old, was a devout Christian woman, as all her family before her. Her family were intellectuals— lawyers, Representatives in Legislature and well-to-do farmers.

Sarah's mother, Letitia Ball Munford, was a most lovable woman and devout. As a daily habit she would take each of her nine children, Matilda, Mary Jane, Thomas J., William B., Sarah, Robert, Kitty Ann, Richard, and Edward into a room and pray for them. On her death bed in 1815, with her children and husband gathered around her, pointing to heaven, said to William, "Meet me with the children there."

More of Sarah's family history: "Matilda was twice married, first to Joseph N. Hudson, second to Major Mooney, a United States Officer in the Mexican War; she was not only beautiful, but a heroine for her day. Her son Samuel was ill in Mexico during the war; she made the hazardous trip, nursed him to health, and brought him home."

"Mary Jane Munford married Albert Ward of Davidson County and lived near the Hermitage."

"Brother Thomas was the marrying type; he had three wives; also he was called the super human athlete; he weighed only one hundred and forty pounds but was remarkable in his activity, and strength; he was a fine classical scholar, a member of Tennessee Senate from Wilson county and was for many years Clerk and Master of Chancery Court of Clarksville, Tennessee."

Thomas died on his plantation in Kentucky.

"My father William was an excellent farmer, very affectionate to mother and all the nine children. If any disputes came up in the neighborhood, my father was the peace-maker."

"Brother William represented Montgomery County in the Tennessee Legislature—a good man like a pure diamond, without a fleck or flaw, a praying elder in the Presbyterian Church, a devout Christian with implicit faith in the Bible. He literally walked with his God, and when he died, ones who knew him said, "We shall never again see a man so grand!"

"Richard, the eighth child, died early in life, also Robert, the sixth of the Munford children."

"Edward was the youngest Munford, born October 16, 1820. Father entered him in Primary Department of Center College, Danville, Kentucky, when he was eight years old. Among his classmates was John Breckenridge. Edward was a brilliant student, a Colonel in the War Between the States. But with all his college learning, he had never been taught his multiplication table, English or geography. When he was fifteen years old, father came to Lebanon to visit Kitty Ann who had married Dr. Miles McCorkle, a prominent man, one of the directors of Lebanon Law School at one time and represented Wilson County in the Legislature.

"At this time he entered Edward under Reverend Thomas Anderson. He later studied law with Robert L. Caruthers. When the Jones moved to Memphis, Edward went along."

Sarah Munford was famous for her fine humor, the many anecdotes; she was known as a superb business woman, also her tact of entertaining their guests as Governor's First Lady by her brilliant conversational powers and her lovely charming manners.

Cynthia Pillow Saunders Brown
Sarah Woodford Burrus Brown

Wives of Governor Aaron V. Brown

The two wives of Aaron V. Brown, the eleventh governor of Tennessee, were Sarah Burrus, born a Virginian and became a Tennessee Plantation lady of great charm and beauty, possessing qualities that made her a favorite social attraction, and Cynthia Pillow Saunders, Belle of Columbia and a socialite of Nashville, Tennessee, a lady of the world of fashion, the wealthy widow of J. W. Saunders who left three children and the beautiful Melrose Mansion to Cynthia at his death.

Aaron V. Brown was born August 15, 1795, the son of a patriot soldier Reverend Aaron V. Brown Sr. born February 18, 1767 in Brunswick County, Virginia, who died in Giles County, Tennessee.

Aaron V. Brown Sr. had three children by his first wife Nancy Howell; Elizabeth, Thomas and Nancy.

The second wife Elizabeth Melton born May 13, 1757 in North Hampton County, North Carolina was the mother of Mary Brown Trotter, Lewis born in 1791, died 1811. John Frazier, William, Penelope who married David McEwen, Rebecca who married Christopher McEwen, Sarah Born 1797 and Rebecca born 1799. Aaron the future governor of Tennessee was the ninth child of the eleven.

The Brown family moved to Giles county in 1813. They sent Aaron to the University of North Carolina to study law. He graduated in 1814, studied law in Nashville and became a law partner of James Knox Polk in Pulaski, Tennessee.

He was a State Senator from 1821 until 1827. A Representative from Giles county in 1831 and a member of Congress in 1839.

Aaron V. Brown first married Sarah Woodford Burrus. Spears in "Prominent Tennesseans" says she was the daughter of Judge Joseph Burrus of Scotch-Irish descent.

Judge Burrus was born in Amherst County, Virginia in 1765. At the age of fifteen he enlisted as a volunteer in the Revolutionary war and as a private soldier participated at the surrender of Cornwallis at Yorktown.

He was several times a member of the House of Burgesses of the state of Virginia.

He moved to Rutherford county, Tennessee in 1805 and upon the advice of General Andrew Jackson purchased lands on Stone River and remained upon his plantation until his death in 1821.

Mrs. Elizabeth Ridley of Murfreesboro, Tennessee, a great grand niece of Sarah Brown, says, "Judge Joseph Burrus left a large family of fourteen sons and daughters who were prominent in the political history of Tennessee."

Layfayette Burrus and Captain W.C. J. Burrus were very prominent men, the latter serving several times in the Tennessee Legislature.

Sarah, like the other Burruses was a beautiful and intelligent girl. Her parents, cultivated people, spared no means in educating their children.

They were an entire family of fine looking people, with not a member having an ungainly feature.

The girls were: Martha who died young, Ophelia Palmer, Elizabeth Howse, Lucy McCullock, Sanny Alexander and Sarah. They were referred to as, "The Beautiful Burruses."

The Burruses were modest, retiring in disposition, they were democrats in politics, and Methodist in religion.

Sarah married Aaron V. Brown when she was quite young. She was interested in her home, entertaining kin, friends, and neighbors with warmth and kindness or sitting gently by her child's cradle, reading, sewing or knitting. It was as a wife and mother that she found her vocation.

She was the mother of six children: Charles Joseph, William Erskine who died at the age of three, Charles Walter, Aaron V. Jr., Laura who married at Melrose, Dr. Flavis Joseph Robertson, a son of Dr. Peyton Robertson who was a grandson of James Robertson.

Mrs. A.B. Herron of Brentwood has an oil painting of her great grandfather Governor A. V. Brown and Sarah Brown hanging on her wall that shows the great grandmother as a beautiful dark haired young lady.

Sarah died at the age of thirty five. The girls Laura, and Medora grew up at Melrose where Medora Brown married Wylie Blount Dortch, the grandson of Lucinda Baker and Wylie Blount, third governor of Tennessee. Medora's daughter Laura Dortch became the wife of William King McAlister of Nashville and were the parents of Hill McAlister who became Tennessee Governor in 1933.

The two McAlister girls; Louise Love and Laura Bathrick live in Fort Lauderdale, Florida.

The gubernatorial contest in 1845 was between Aaron V. Brown a Democrat and the Whig Ephrain Foster.

Brown was a member of Congress since 1839 and had won more than local distinction.

Ephrain Foster was eloquent, fiery and impulsive. Judge Joe Conn Guild at one time remarked that he was on his way to study law in the office of William Brown, but sauntering along into the court room he witnessed Foster's splendid outbursts of passion when he threw a book at the presiding Judge with such gallant and noble bearing, Judge Guild determined then and there to read law under Foster.

Part of Brown's Mount Pisgah Speech that was said to have elected him to office: "Moses when standing on top of Mount Pisgah, looking over on the promised land, gazed not on a scene half so lovely. Oh let us this day vow that whatever else we do, by whatever name we may be called, we will never surrender one square acre of this Godly heritage to the dictation of any King or potentate on earth. Swear it! Swear it! Swear it! my countrymen and let heaven record the vow forever."

The allusion was to Texas in South, Oregon in the West, "Fifty-four --forty or Fight."

Senator Brown was on his way home from Washington when he received the news that he had been elected Governor in 1845.

One month after he became Governor he married Mrs. Cynthia Pillow Saunders in November 1845, the widow of John W. Saunders and a daughter of General Gideon Pillow.

Gideon Pillow was born in 1806, educated at the University of Nashville. He practiced law at Nashville; he was a Major General in the War Between the States and had been a Brigadier General in the War with Mexico.

He had moved to Maury County as a young man and a surveyor; he purchased 5000 acres of land from General Nathaniel Green and selected the spot where Pillow Place now stands at Columbia, Tennessee.

Cynthia grew up with her three brothers: General Gideon Pillow Jr., Granville and James Pillow; her two sisters were Mrs. George Martin and Mrs. (Judge) West Humphries.

She often listened to her grandmother Pillow who was a sister to Dolly Payne Madison tell how the Indians stole her father Gideon out of his cradle and how she went after the

SARAH W. BURRIS BROWN

BEAUTIFUL MELROSE

Indians and rescued her baby from the Indians.

The stones of their antebellum Clifton Place were quarried by the slaves, and the interior woodwork of wild cherry was cut from their forest and dressed by cabinet makers, who came from Nashville for the purpose. The house at Columbia contains the furniture, mirrors, portraits, and silver that was used when Cynthia grew to young womanhood.

Melrose in Nashville, the home of the Browns, was a gift to Cynthia when she became the bride of John W. Saunders. There was no Governor's Mansion in 1845. It was here that the Gubernatorial Melrose began a career of unsurpassed distinction. Entertaining was frequent and lavish. Notables from every section were guests.

The picturesque site of the winding driveway from the entrance gate was over a stream spanned by rustic bridges, through a rolling lawn of bluegrass, then a formal heart shaped, box bordered garden with a marble fountain in the center.

Melrose was filled with many lovely furnishings and the finest collection of paintings in the United States.

This period in history was one of such struggles and war excitement that papers of that day carried very little of the peaceful pursuits of the inhabitants of Tennessee.

Melrose was one of the national ideal mansions of the old South, to Tennessee a proud possession. It was here that an only son Granville Brown was born to Cynthia and Governor Brown.

Mrs. Brown's great beauty and hospitality and entertainment made her a leader in Washington society while her husband was Post Master General under President James Buchanan.

The bachelor President frequently called upon Mrs. Aaron V. Brown to preside at the White House and her many graces won her general applause.

Her daughter Narcissus Saunders was one of the Belles of Washington. She and her mother Cynthia were frequently mentioned of their notable entertaining in Washington, D.C.

Aaron V. Brown died of pneumonia March 8, 1859 in Washington. He was brought to Nashville and Buried in Mt. Olive Cemetery under the auspices of the Masonic Fraternity.

Cynthia and the children returned to Melrose.

126

IDLEWILD

MARY ANN TRIMBLE BROWN

Mary Ann Alexander Trumble Brown

B. 1816 — M. 1839 — D. 1895

A Distinguished First Lady

Mary Ann Trimble Brown had been a Tennessee First Lady in 1847-1849. Residing at the Mansion "Idlewild" at Nashville, Tennessee; its grounds redolent of antique hospitality, with its large airy rooms, the imposing staircases, the great hall, where hung on the oaken Wainscots portraits of deceased grand dames: Cousin Dolly Paine Madison, Grandfather Thomas Clark, statesman of the far distant past, tables of mahogany and curios from foreign lands innumerable, fragrant with an undeniable charm in the quiet of its repose.

It was summer of 1851, the landscape was at its fairest on fair mornings: the foliage of the wide branching elms stirred and rustled in the soft westerly breeze. The air breathed through the trees; the sun lay softly on the blue grass. Mary Ann's flowers dispensed their sweet fragrance with a lavishness that knew no stint.

There were no Negro settlements in Edgefield, only family servants and the new baby's black mammy.

It was she who kept the Brown brood in hand by professing to know a red bird in the Edgefield bush, that could fly through its shady lanes and avenues while the children played the fascinating game of "cat" and lined up the gang for a battle of rocks.

The red bird could perch on a window still at the Governor Brown Mansion and report on the conduct of each little Brown's misdoings. James, Tully, Neil S., and Duncan came to know the bird quite well.

July, 1851, the apples hung red in tree tops of Idlewild's orchard, the pink faced peaches ready to be picked and dried. Mary Ann's trunk and carpet bags were packed, the baby's satchel held lobelia, paregoric, assafetida, castor oil, and other remedies for the baby girl and the four boys—ages nine, seven, five, and three. They started on their journey to Russia to visit the ex-governor Neil S. Brown, now U. S. Minister to Russia. Their journey began by stage coach, then by steamboat to New York.

After a five-week voyage from New York, the Brown family was met in London by Neil S. Brown. August 6, 1851, they registered at the Hotel Bristol in Paris, France. Their friend, Randal McGovock, of Nashville, was touring Europe— he and Neil had roomed together in London, while awaiting Mary Ann's arrival—called on them at the Hotel Bristol to find they were out searching for the nurse, Sue Lou, and a carpet bag that had been missing for four hours. They were located by the help of Paris Police.

They had breakfast the next morning at 7 a.m., at Hotel Maurice, and left soon after for Brussels, Belgium, reaching their destination around five o'clock in company with William Johnson of South Carolina, and Bishop James Otey. Mary visited Axlo Chappelle. They were to meet again on the Rhine.

At the summer's end Mary Ann returned to Idlewild with the children and the Black mammy, Prudelia. Although duty bound Neil S. Brown remained at his post—aggravated by Russia's bitter cold, and endangered by cholera until June, 1853, he urged the New Administration to hasten his recall— he was literally worn out by Russia's climate.

He and his secretary, Edward H. Wright, had sailed into St. Petersburg harbor July, 1850, and had reached Peterhof. They were presented to the Emperor Nicholas and the Imperial family on August 13, 1850. Neil S. Brown was much impressed with the simplicity, cordiality, and apparent frankness of the Emperor. Brown dedicated himself to the promotion of American commerce with the Russia Empire. He thought that the United States should compete for the Russian growing market for cotton, tobacco, and north western furs.

He thought Russia was too remote to become a rival in arms and her outlets to the ocean too limited. He attributed their backwardness to their want of inventions.

"Russia cannot boast of a single invention, that has not been copied—out of the empire, all they have is borrowed, except their miserable climate. No nation has more need of foreigners and none so jealous or ungrateful toward them."

Neil S. Brown was not allowed enough money from the United States Department to pay for postage, stationery, or subscription to the St. Petersburg paper.

"I regard my style of living as a medium one," (he wrote Daniel Webster, Secretary of State, after cutting corners for a year.)

"It would be difficult to reduce it with respectability and difficult to exceed it without bankruptcy.

"With my family here, my expenses would absorb my whole salary and not be considered extravagant."

After his first winter in St. Petersburg, he asked for a leave of absence, met Mary Ann and the children in London in August, 1851.

Neil S. Brown had married the auburn haired, large brown eyed Mary Ann on December 26, 1839, at her Nashville home. She was the daughter of Judge James Trimble and Letitia Breckenridge Clark. Her grandmother, Susan Paine Clark, was a cousin to Dolly Paine Madison. Her grandfather was the first merchant of Kingston, Tennessee.

Mary Ann's sisters were: Louisa, married to John Reid; Eliza, who married Adrian Van Lindsley; Susan, who married Col. W. B. A. Ramsey of Knoxville, Secretary of the State of Tennessee. Her brothers were: Andrew, Thomas who married Penelope Williams, and Hon. John Trimble, several times a member of the Legislature.

Mary Ann was a lady of intellect, of pleasing, amiable manners. She possessed a strong and rounded character, religious; a member of the Presbyterian Church in which she was very active. She was endowed with tact and native politeness which were beautifully manifested in the practice of a genial and elegant hospitality. Her father, Judge James Trimble, was born in 1781, in Rockbridge, Virginia; his ancestors were of Scotch-Irish descent. The Trimbles and the Alexanders were educated, religious people in the middle class.

Dr. Archibald Alexander and sons were well-known directors at Princeton College. James Trimble was educated at Washington College, East Tennessee. He studied law in Staunton, Virginia and settled in Knoxville—a clerk in the General Assembly.

He moved to Nashville in 1813, three years before Mary Ann was born. He was a Republican, a member and elder in the Presbyterian Church, and a leading member of the Nashville Bar, director of a Branch Bank of U. S. Nashville, trustee of Cumberland College, afterward University of Nashville.

Among the young lawyers who read law in his office was Neil S. Brown, who found something more interesting than the law books. He wooed and won the lovely daughter, Mary Ann.

Their first home was in Pulaski, where Neil practiced law. He was the son of Duncan and Margaret Smith Brown who had emigrated from Robeson County, North Carolina to Giles County with his brother-in-law, Daniel McCallum and his wife Sarah Smith. His grandfather, Neil Smith and his wife Mary Little, were born in Scotland in 1756. Mrs. Smith died in 1852 in Giles County.

His grandfather Angus Brown, brown in 1745, the son of Rebecca and John Brown, who was born in Scotland and came to America in 1750. He married Mary McFarland, born in 1745, in 1762 and died in 1824.

Angus Brown served in the Revoluntionary war under General Marion.

The Browns were farmers. This is where Neil grew to manhood height—six feet two inches—with the manners of a perfect gentleman.

In youth he had followed life as a farmer, acquiring the rudiment of an elementary education at night by a pine knot lighted fire after a hard day's work. His education did not begin until he was seventeen years of age. He taught school to acquire means to further his higher education. He was twenty-one when he entered Manual Labor Academy, Maury County, for two years.

In 1834 he studied law in the office of Chancellor Bramlet of Pulaski, and made a trip to Texas—law practice was not encouraging there—he returned to Tennessee.

He entered as Private in Armstrong's Brigade for the Seminole fort. He fought in the battle of Withla Coachee and was promoted to Sergeant Major.

Soon after his marriage he was nominated as the Whig candidate for Presidential elector on the ticket of Hugh L. White of Knoxville.

Though women did not voice their political views yet, Mary Ann and Neil shared their political interest. Both were Whigs and ardent supporters of Henry Clay, for whom he took the stump in 1844.

After six years in the State Legislature, he became Governor in 1847-49, succeeding Aaron V. Brown.

Neil S. Brown was the second native son to become a Tennessee Governor.

His record as a speaker was that of an earnest young man, persuasible kind, mixed with ancedote, keen wit, and satire, which rendered him popular and effective with juries and people.

During his administration, 1847-49, his record may be considered unique of political life: the New Orleans and Ohio Telegraph chartered the first telegraph company in Tennessee; with the first telegraphic dispatch, announcing the Presidential election returns in Tennessee. In 1848 the first Tennessee Historical Society was formed.

Someone once asked Neil S. Brown how he became Governor. He replied, "I started life on nothing. I was as poor as any man in Tennessee who ever became at all known. So there was no method, beyond taking hold of whatever there was to do and doing with all my might. I had native ambition to rise from obscurity and make myself useful in the world."

The last political position of Governor Brown was a member of the Constitutional Convention of 1870. In 1880 he went on the platform on the state debt question—to put in one more plea for the credit and honor of the State Debt question. He was recognized as the Old Man with eloquent pleading. The great-grandson, Attorney, Neil S. Brown of Nashville, Tennessee, and Mary Ann says I have often heard my father Lytle Brown, say of Mary Ann Trimble Brown, "a woman of the strongest character and greatest courage, particularly as he saw her in times of family trouble and tragedies, a woman possessed of an intellect of much force."

She suffered the untimely death of four sons: Henry at the age of thirty was killed on March 11, 1881, at Albuquerque, New Mexico by a bandit, who apparantly was one that he had driven from robbery at the Railway Express, as agent on the Atcheson, Topeka and Santa Fe Railroad.

Neil S. was killed in a railroad accident. Duncan, age thirty, died of a cerebral hemorrhage. At the time he was circuit court clerk of Davidson County. James Trimble died at age of thirty-six of pneumonia on May 31, 1878.

During the War Between the States, Neil S. Brown was arrested as Confederate sympathizer.

Idlewild, consisting of some fifty acres in Edgefield community, so named by Reverend John B. McFerrin, a neighbor, and Neil S. Brown, was surrounded by rail fences and burned by the Yankees. Mary Ann did her best to defend her chickens and country hams during the siege of the thieving Yankees, who talked to themselves rather strongly during the burning and looting at Idlewild.

In the long summer afternoons after his retirement from public office, lawyers, friends of the Governor, wearing their long black broadcloth coats, shining top hats, slinging their gold handled canes, came to Idlewild for a game of croquet, archery, a cigar, or just a peaceful talk with Mary Ann and Sue Lou, presiding with grace and dignity in their social life.

Mary Ann was a typical Southern lady. She was generous and true to all that was noble and good. Her life was one of long exemplification of Christian virtues, a pattern of order, system and neatness.

She died at Idlewild on October 24, 1895, at the age of seventy-nine.

Her life since the death of her husband in 1886 had been spent in the retirement of her own home and in the companionthip of the four of her eight children who surrounded her: Attorney General Tully Brown, John Calvin of Railway Mail Service, Mrs. Vincent Donelson and the lost baby girl in Paris, Miss Susan Brown.

Mary Ann Trimble Brown will be remembered for her grace and charm and dignity, as well as hospitality and attentiveness to their many guests and political gatherings as Tennessee's First Lady.

Mary Ann and Gov. Trousdale home at Gallatin, Tenn.

Trousdale Place, Clark Chapter U.D.C., Gallatin, Tennessee.

Mary Ann Bugg Trousdale

B. 1807 — M.   — D. 1887

Wife of Governor William Trousdale

Mary Ann Bugg married the "War Horse of Sumner County", William Trousdale, who became Governor in 1849. She bore the honors of First Lady of Tennessee from 1849-1851, as described by her great, great grandson, Attorney Allen Guild.

"She was the daughter of Frances Lewis and Samuel Bugg who lived in Mecklenburg County, Virginia, born February 1, 1807. The Buggs moved to Sumner County, Tenn., in the eighteen hundreds. The Buggs Island Dam in Virginia near Chase City was named for her father Samuel Bugg. Later the name was changed to "John H. Kerr", a North Carolina Congressman who sponsored it. The reservoir covers land in both Va., and North Carolina.

Mary Ann Bugg was of slight build, fair with brown hair and blue eyes, very quiet and retiring, fine and delicate in mind, her heart went out to her husband and children, carrying on her Presbyterian religious heritage within her family tradition, teaching her children the Christian faith through daily acts, living out the understanding relationship to family, church and God.

There were seven Trousdale children: Mary Louise who became the wife of B. T. Allen, a brother to Eliza Allen who became the first wife of Governor Sam Houston, when he was a small lad of four years attending the wedding in his ancestral home in Gallatin, Tennessee. Caroline Valeria Trousdale became Mrs. Frank Lafferty, Frances Elizabeth married Senator John Bell Peyton, a prominent man of Middle Tennessee, two children died in infancy; the two sons were Charles William and Julius Augustus Trousdale.

William Trousdale was born 1790 in Orange County, North Carolina; his father, James Trousdale was a Captain in the Revolutionary Army. He was of Scotch-Irish descent. The Trousdales migrated from North Carolina and settled on the present site of Gallatin. He received a land grant in 1784, for his Revolutionary services from North Carolina, which embraced a large portion of the site of Gallatin, Tennessee.

The Trousdale Mansion on West Main Street in Gallatin was closely related to every war in which this country has been engaged down to the War in Spain.

The house was built on part of the land grant of December 4, 1784 to Captain Trousdale. He rebuilt and settled the year Tennessee became a state.

In 1801, The Legislature of Tennessee appointed commissioners to locate and purchase a site for the county seat of Sumner County.

They selected Captain Trousdale's farm, a town was laid off, and one of the lots was bought by John H. Bowen, a distinguished lawyer, who built a large brick house, which was not completely finished until 1820.

Governor William Trousdale bought the house soon after the death of John H. Bowen. Here, he and Mary Ann Bugg lived while he was Governor from 1849 until 1851. He was appointed to Brazil, as Minister, under President Franklin Pierce in 1852.

Brazil was a far cry from the day Governor Trousdale, a small lad of six years, came with the family in covered wagons and made the hazardous trek over the rough mountain roads to the Tennessee country.

He was a student, as a boy, of Reverend Gideon Blackburn. William left school to take part in the Creek War and was at Tallahatchie and Talladega. He won great fame in the War with Mexico. He added to the purity of his character, and the manly, homely virtues by which it was adorned, an exalted courage, capable of the most daring feats of valor. Captain Trousdale was twice wounded at the Battle of Chapultepec and was promoted to Brigadier General in the United States Army. During one of his campaigns, he performed the daring feat of swimming the Tennessee River on horseback, though he could not swim himself. So many and so brave had been his services in camp and battle that he was called, "The War Horse of Sumner County."

He held office one term. One of the outstanding events during his administration was the meeting of the "Southern Convention" at Nashville in 1850, to consider the compromise measures before Congress asked what the Southern States thought about slavery.

He retired to his home in Gallatin, where he died in 1872. His widow, Mary Ann Bugg Trousdale continued to live there until her death in 1887, then Julius Augusta Trousdale came into possession of the Trousdale Home. He was the fourth

LANGLEY HALL, GALLATIN, TENN.

Home of Atty. Allen and Mrs. Guild, great grandson of Gov. Wm. Trousdale

child. He married Ann Berry of Nashville in 1880.

Four of their five children died in infancy. Mary completed her education in New York, returning home in 1889. She died in August 1889. Her father, much attached to her, followed her in September.

By his will, his property went to his wife, Ann Berry Trousdale. A short time after his death she gave the house and grounds to a corporation, charted for the purpose of perpetuating the history of the Confederate States and the Confederate Soldiers, under the control of Clark Chapter, United Daughters of the Confederacy.

The house and grounds were in the possession of the Trousdale family from 1784 until 1900 (except a short ownership by Mr. Bowen).

In this home Mary Ann Bugg, who was more interested in home than social life, entertained with apparent ease, grace, charm and regularity in the "Trousdale Mansion," over which she presided. She was ever cheerful and happy for her whole mind and heart was to promote the happiness of her family.

Langley Hall, takes its name from Mrs. Trousdale's brother, Langley Bugg, who formerly owned the land on which the gorgeous home is built. They did not want to call it "Bugg Hall" hence its name Langley Hall.

It has recently been recopied on the site of old Langley Hall. The house was first built by Katie Trousdale Allen. It is located at 416 Coles Ferry Road and now the residence of Governor and Mrs. Trousdale's Great Grandson, Attorney Allen Guild, and his wife Edna, who is Regent of Daughters of the American Revolution, in Gallatin, Tennessee.

MRS. FRANCES OWEN CAMPBELL
And Infant Son, William B.
She Was Born in 1818; Died in 1864.

CAMP BELL AND FRANCES O. CAMPBELL

Frances Isabella Owen Campbell

B. 1818 — M. 1835 — D. 1864

Gave Grace and Charm to All Living Things

Frances Isabella Owen, who became a First lady in Tennessee in 1851 until 1853 was the charming blue eyed lady with auburn hair who had become the bride of Governor William B. Campbell at the age of seventeen, in 1835.

She was born at the "Bower" in Smith county, Tennessee near the town of Gordonsville to Mary Goodwin and Dr. John Owen who had moved to Smith County shortly after the county was organized. They had married during the war of 1812.

Frances' maternal grandparents were Frances Amis and Lemuel Goodwin of Halifax County, North Carolina; her paternal grandparents, Amelia Grant and John Owen, were from Granville County, North Carolina.

Doctor John Owen and his wife, Mary Amis, were both educated in the best schools afforded by North Carolina in the nineteenth century. Dr. Owen and his oldest son were both educated at Philadelphia Medical school, under the famous Doctor Benjamin Rush for whom he named his oldest son, Dr. Benjamin Rush Owen of Lebanon, Tennessee.

Frances and her other brother Dr. John Owen, Junior were educated at the best institutes of learning of their day.

Governor William B. Campbell was born on Manker's Creek in Sumner County near Nashville, February 1, 1807. He was the oldest of six children of Catherine Bowen and David Campbell; his paternal grandparents migrated from Scotland to Ireland and then to America in 1726. They first settled in the state of Pennsylvania and then moved to Virginia in 1730.

William studied law with his Uncle David Campbell in Arlington, Va., he was a cousin to Ann Campbell Roane who married Archibald Roane, the third Governor of Tennessee.

William located at Carthage, Tennessee in 1829; he was elected Attorney General and district judge, member of the state legislature and of the United States Congress. He fought as a Captain in William Trousdale's regiment of Tennessee Volunteers and through the Seminole War.

A delightful anecdote has been handed down among Mrs. Campbell's descendants as told by a granddaughter Miss

Margaret Campbell of Lebanon, Tennessee, "While Grandfather William Bowen Campbell was in Mexico in 1846, Grandmother sent a very good picture of herself and infant son, William Junior. When the picture arrived at Military Camp the story spread that Colonel Campbell's wife and baby had arrived. The soldiers flocked to his quarters to see the wife and baby from home. Colonel Campbell was happy to pass the picture among the boys."

Colonel Campbell took part in the battles of Vera Cruz, Cerro Grodo and Monterey. It was at Monterey that he gave the command, "Boys, follow me" which became a celebrated phrase in Tennessee History; his regiment was nicknamed the "Bloody First".

In 1851, William Bowen Campbell, the third native Tennessean and the last Whig Governor of the State, was in office one term.

Frances Owen Campbell spent many winters in Washington, D.C. when her husband was Congressman for years; here she enjoyed the challenge of Washington political and social life. Perhaps during these years her very definite national views, rather than sectional ones, were enhanced. In her diary of 1860 and 1861 this viewpoint is clearly expressed.

Every account of Frances Campbell as revealed by her children stress her as an insatiable reader of books from which her remarkable, retentive mind gleaned passages that she sprinkled deliciously through her conversations.

The children often listened to Frances and their grandmother Mary Amis Goodwin when they were conversing in French; this they later thought was also a clever design used when the youngsters were present. "Little pitchers have big ears", and there were nine little pitchers growing up in Governor William and Frances Campbell home.

Mary Campbell became Mrs. D. C. Delley. Margaret, who married James Pitcher, was interested in history and genealogy, and wrote the history of the Campbell family who originally were from Scotland. The other children were William Bowen, Frances Amelia, who became Mrs. Willis Bonner, Dr. John Owen Campbell and Lemuel Russell Campbell. Two children died in childhood: David and Catherine.

A contemporary friend wrote of Frances Campbell, "Vigorous in mind, perservering and endowed with extra ordinary energy, she matured into an accomplished woman of highly cultivated understanding."

Every account of Mrs. Campbell in her home and church

shows her as having a very deep faith and being a consecrated Christian. In her diary repeatedly she refers to her church work and to her charity visits and gifts. Even with her large family she found time to do much for the unfortunate, then make visits to take the garments where needed.

In Mrs. Campbell's letters written during the War years (1861-1863) she was constantly asking for publications — Harpers and Lady Godey's Book in particular. She was asking for publications from both sides of the political questions; several times she reminded her absent family in Lebanon, Tennessee to see that the subscription to the National Intelligencer, the leading Whig publication, be renewed. She was a woman with a thirst for knowledge and a keen sense of the condition of her times.

Frances Owen Campbell had time to use her gardening spirit, that possessed her at her home Camp-Bell in Lebanon. She planned the garden, filled with old fashioned flowers, shrubs, arbors, and cherry blossoms with the bees, birds, and butterflies flashing their gorgeous colors among them.

In 1862, President Lincoln gave ex-Governor Campbell a commission as Brigadier General in the Union Army but he resigned without having seen active duty.

On March 22, 1864, the beloved Frances Campbell died at her Camp-Bell home.

In 1865 William Bowen Campbell was elected to Congress. He spent his last days at the beautiful old White Colonial home where he and his family had lived for so many years. Here he died in 1867.

They had spent thirty full and fruitful years together amid the struggles of Civil War. A man of courage, unquestionable integrity, all who knew him respected him highly; his private life was without reproach.

Mrs. Robert Sewell Brandau says of Mrs. Campbell and her Garden- "The guiding spirit of this garden was the devoted wife, and lovely auburn haired lady with the soft blue eyes whose loving care gave charm and grace to all living things."

Some Governors' wives are remembered for this or that. The First Lady Campbell will be remembered for a woman with the urge to push forward into something seen dimly ahead, who went to the root of things with delight in her homemaking and learning, showing the lasting grains of character of a woman who "gave grace and charm to all living things."

Eliza McCardle Johnson

B. 1810 — M. 1827 — D. 1876

Wife of Governor Andrew Johnson

The year was 1826. Eliza McCardle was standing in her yard with some girls in the town of Greenville, Tennessee. They were aware of a wind blowing a cloud of dust in the road near by.

It was a late Saturday afternoon in September. Two men, one middle aged and the other a young man of perhaps eighteen years, were walking, while a woman rode in a cart drawn by a blind pony. Dust laden, arriving in the country village, it was an unpretentious procession but it did not go unnoticed by Eliza McCardle, who watched the red haired youth and his worn mother, moving down the road in the creaking cart.

The attractive mountain girl remarked to her friends, "I like what I see."

Young, aspiring, and ambitious, Andrew Johnson was not long in making friends, and among them the beautiful Scotch-Irish daughter of Sarah and John McCardle, a shoemaker. Eliza's mother was one of the beautiful women of her day in that section of the country and legend says Eliza resembled her mother.

Eliza had a good common school education for the period. Although her life was not one of wealth, it would have seemed a luxurious life, compared to the life of Andrew Johnson, who knew only searing, grinding poverty from his earliest childhood. He was four years old when his father's death resulted from his rescuing two drowning men.

When Andrew was ten years of age he became the bound boy of Mr. Shelly, a tailor in Raleigh, North Carolina. When he was sixteen he left Mr. Shelly and worked as a journeyman in Laurens Court House, South Carolina.

He returned to Raleigh, only to find a ten dollar reward out for him, as a run away. He offered to work the balance of his time, but he would have to give bond and this Andrew would not do.

He had toiled the long hours away applying the needle and thread while other boys romped, hunted and enjoyed a youth which Andrew Johnson never knew. Poverty is a grim

145

and cruel master; he teaches his lessons with long hours, sour looks and hard knocks. Andy had a thorough knowledge of his tutor.

Many years later he told Congress, "If being poor was a crime. . . . .I would have to plead that I was guilty; that I was a great criminal. . . . .Yes, I have wrestled with proverty, that gaunt and hazard monster. I have met him in the day and in the night. I have felt his withering approach and his blighting influence."

Andrew worked for the only tailor in Greenville, Mr. George Boyle. He then went to Grainger County for six months. Learning that Mr. Boyle had left Greenville, he returned and made that his home.

On May 17, 1827, Eliza McCardle and Andrew Johnson were married by the magistrate of Greenville, Mordecai Lincoln; she was just seventeen and he was not yet twenty-one.

Education in those days did not embrace the scientific accomplishments it does today. It is a mistaken idea that Eliza taught her husband to read. Mrs. Martha Johnson Patterson's granddaughter, Mrs. Margaret Bartlett says, "My father said that Andrew Johnson had mastered words and sentences after shop hours, until he was advanced as far as the third grade when he was married."

While other people slept in the silent watches of the night, Eliza and Andrew studied together, she often reading to him as he stitched a garment, more often she was guiding his hand in writing.

She took Andrew in hand mentally and taught him from well thumbed text books as he worked in the little shop, the front room of their two-room home on Main Street. The back room was their kitchen, dining room, bedroom and parlor; here Eliza was wife, housekeeper, and teacher. She read books on the British Statesmen and other classical and political works. He had to work hard to make a living. Eliza taught in the mountain school when she could.

She was the mother of Martha and Charles before Andrew bought a house on Water Street in February, 1831. Mary was born in 1832, Robert in 1834, and the youngest, Andy, was born while his father was serving as Governor of Tennessee.

In those first years when Eliza was a First Lady of Tennessee from 1853 until 1857, they lived in the George Campbell home in Nashville. Mr. Campbell had purchased the property for a pony and a rifle.

Mrs. Johnson once remarked to a friend who had asked about her private life as the wife of the man who was first Alderman of Greenville, then the Mayor, legislator Congressman, Senator, Vice President of the U. S., a Governor of Tennessee twice, and President of the United States that she was opposed to any publicity about herself. Her life had been spent at home, caring for her children, and practicing the economy rendered necessary by her husband's small fortune.

Previous to the War Between the States, the Johnsons became land owners, and slave holders in Greenville. Eliza, a gentle, devoted mother, looked after his personal affairs when Andrew Johnson was away from home for long periods at a time, collecting rents, managing his real estate and other things.

She had a mild, affectionate nature; she could soothe her husband's stormy rages by placing a hand on his shoulder and saying softly, "Andrew, Andrew."

When tragedy began to strike the Johnsons in June, 1861, in his home at Greenville on a brief visit from Washington, Mr. Johnson was ordered to get out of the State if he wanted to live. He had to leave Eliza sick and the younger children in Greenville while he hurried back to Washington. Eliza had spent two months in Washington but had to return to Tennessee because of her health.

Long and stormy were the times before she again saw her husband. At home quietly attending to her own affairs, one moring she received a message:

Headquarters Department of East Tennessee
Office Provost Marshal, April 24, 1862
Mrs. Andrew Johnson, Greenville,

Dear Madam:- By Major-General E. Kirby Smith I am directed to respectfully require that you and your family pass beyond the Confederate States' line (through Nashville, if you please) in thirty-six hours from this date.

Passports will be granted you at this office.
Very respectfully,
W. M. Churchwell,
Colonel and Provost Marshal.

Eliza was ill and her affairs were unsettled; she did not know where to go. Rumors she had heard were that her husband had been murdered in Kentucky or Nashville, and other upsetting false rumors did not help her health, and it was not until September that she left Greenville.

She did not know her husband was Military Governor of Nashville. In February, Lincoln had asked him to give up his Senate Post and return to Nashville, giving him absolute power over the State of Tennessee.

Johnson shouted vengeance at Confederate sympathizers and imprisoned men who would not swear allegiance to the Union. At the same time he levied taxes on the State, took control of the R. R. and ordered elections. He was shocked to learn that Eliza and the children had been ordered out of their Greenville home.

After a long journey from East Tennessee, Eliza and her children reached Nashville, where Andrew shed unashamed tears at the reunion.

Confederate General Bedford Forrest made it possible for a two-horse wagon to bring their baggage through the Confederate lines under a flag of truce as an exchange of Federal prisoners and refugees, but there was no transportation for Eliza. When they reached Murfreesboro, exhausted and weary, they could not go through the line and no night accommodations could be found, no food except a little for the children. They spend the night in a vacant eating house across the road from the depot, where they slept on the floor.

With all the trials, exposure to weather, insults to her sons, Eliza never gave a hasty word or look to show her feelings, and was remembered by friend and foe as a lady of sweet winning manners.

The two years Eliza and children spent in Nashville were full of personal sorrow. They arrived in October, 1862, and spent almost two years there. During that time the older son, Dr. Charles Johnson, was thrown from a horse and killed; the youngest, Andy, like his mother, was suffering from tuberculosis.

While the Union army occupied Nashville, Andrew Johnson saw little of his family. The Capitol was fortified and known as "Johnson's Fort." His Union stand had so endeared him to Lincoln, that he became one of the select committee who often met with the President to plan the conduct of the war.

When selected by Lincoln in 1864 as his running mate, Johnson observed wryly, "What will the aristrocrats do with a railsplitter for a President and a tailor for Vice President?"

By the time Lincoln's death had placed Andrew Johnson in the White House, Eliza was almost an unknown figure, confined to her room by poor health. However, the White House became a livelier place under Johnson's administration than

GOVERNOR ANDREW AND ELIZA McCARDLE
JOHNSON HOME, GREENEVILLE, TENNESSEE

during the gloomy war years, with the two sons, Robert, who was Secretary to his father, Andy, and the two daughters, Martha Patterson, Mary Stover, Judge Patterson and five grandchildren. Eliza, in her northwest bedroom, sewed, knitted; she was the center link of the family.

Martha Patterson acted as hostess at the White House. As a girl she had often visited President and Mrs. Polk. She was a friend of the Blairs, Lees, and other old families of Washington. With her charm and grace she filled her position with dignity and clear judgment.

Martha was a woman of rare tact, "We are plain people from Tennessee," she announced, "called here for a short time by a National calamity; I trust too much will not be expected of us."

It was Martha who donned a calico apron in the early hours at dawn to go to the kitchen and dairy to skim the milk before breakfast.

At Johnson's last reception the blond Martha wore black velvet, trimmed with bands of satin and lace with a white lace shawl over her shoulders. She stood by her father, smiling as she received the guests.

Eliza McCardle Johnson's features in her later years of ill health show the physical and mental suffering she had endured. Heavy lines plowed her once beautiful face and mouth set in pain with sad eyes. The years had taken much, including the loss of her children; Robert had died in 1868. Only the daughters Mary and Martha remained, a bright glow; they were successful wives and happy homemakers, that were a joy to Andrew and Eliza.

The ex-governor of Tennessee and President of the United States, called a "Pillar of Cloud and Fire," died on a visit to Mary Stover in Carter County in 1875; Eliza died in 1876, at the home of Martha Patterson.

Mrs. Margaret Patterson Bartlett, who occupies the Andrew Johnson Home in Greenville, Tennessee says, "My great-grandmother, Eliza McCardle Johnson, was born at Leesburg, Tennessee, Washington County, 1810. Having a good common school education, I suppose she was a Democrat, since that was the political faith of Andrew Johnson. Andrew Johnson was a member of no church, but he definitely had a belief and I presume she did, too. There was not too much stress put on church membership in those days, and neither was Lincoln a member of any church. Eliza was ever her husband's inspiration and although she was in the

White House, my grandmother, Martha Patterson, served as First Lady. Eliza Johnson was only able to attend two parties there; one was a Children's party."

"She was ever Andrew Johnson's inspiration. Each evening he went to her room and there they had coffee. They discussed the affairs of the day. Andrew Johnson did not tell jokes. He loved children, and he was always happy with theirs and other children, too, but as you know he had serious business. Mrs. Johnson was gentle and helped him as much as her physical health allowed. She had this terrible disease for a long time. I do not know when it developed; I can not say whether when Johnson was Civil Governor or Military. Three sons died, leaving Johnson no heirs to the name."

"There does not seem to be much found relative to her life, though I wish there was, for she must have been a wonderful person."

MARTHA TRAVIS HARRIS

Martha Maria Travis Harris

B.　　— M. 1843 — D.

Wife of Governor Isham Green Harris

After a thrilling and aventurous exile in Mexico, Martha Travis and Governor Isham Green Harris lived in a quaint, weatherboarded house on West Main Street in Paris, Tennessee.

The house was surrounded with evergreens, magnolia and holly trees from the Botannical Gardens in Washington and boxwoods they brought on their return from Mexico.

Governor Harris went to Mexico in 1866, where he was in exile for a while. In 1868 an article appeared in a Nashville paper:

"The State School Fund"

"Within the last two years our people have heard a great deal about the Rebels stealing the Tennessee school funds."

General Robert E. Lee had surrendered in 1865 ... During a greater part of the War Between the States Ex-Governor Harris served as a volunteer aid to General Albert Sidney Johnston. When Johnston attacked General Grant's forces at Pittsburg Landing, Johnston was killed in the afternoon, Harris lifted him from his horse and placed him on the ground. This was April, 1862. Harris in early 1862, had left Nashville by special train for Memphis with other State officials and the state records for safety.

Under the Reconstruction Governor William G. Brownlow disfranchised all Confederates who aided the Confederacy in any way, and offered a $5000 reward for the capture of Tennessee's Wartime Governor Harris. He had expected this and was safe in Mexico.

Martha Travis Harris and the children were also in Mexico. She had packed her china and other valuables between the straw in large barrels and among her possessions she placed the $60,000 in gold of the school funds and took it to Mexico so the Federals could not get their hands on it.

She stayed on in Mexico while the Governor went on to Liverpool, England where he engaged in the Cotton business.

When it was safe to return to Tennessee, he went to Mexico for Martha and the children, and returned to Nashville. All this time the gold stayed in the barrels in Mexico. When Governor Harris with gold in hand approached the Capitol, Governor Brownlow was standing in the doorway. Seeing Gov. Harris he said, "While the lamp holds out to burn ... " Governor Harris quickly replied, "the vilest sinner may return."

Mrs. Georgia Harris Cox states she heard Mrs. Harris tell of her exile, and the school funds being kept intact.

Martha Maria Travis was the daughter of Major Edward and Martha Blanton Travis of Henry County, Tennessee. Her paternal grandparents were Colonel Edward Champion and Booth Travis of Virginia.

Martha, nicknamed "Crockett", married Isham Harris in 1843. He became Governor in 1857 and held this office until President Abraham Lincoln appointed Andrew Johnson Military Governor of Tennessee March 5, 1862.

Martha was a large, beautiful girl with an intellectual interest in the world around her. She grew up with her brothers James L., William Edward, Leedson, and her two sisters Sarah and Mary Travis. She also had six half-brothers and sisters, making a round dozen to enjoy farm life and the race horses that Major Travis had on his farm. Martha retained the grace of an experienced horsewoman.

She was educated in the schools of Paris, Tennessee. The early settlers of Paris were men and women who understood and appreciated the meaning of schools to their community. Schools were organized for the girls as well as for the boys as early as 1823.

Martha could dance, embroider, sew, make apple butter, and feed guests, though she much preferred her riding habit and the spirited horses to telling servants what to do.

Martha's many advantages fitted her for the role as Governor's wife. She had a mind equipped with wit, courage and forethought of what to do in crisis. Plenty of crises were her share during the War Between the States.

Governor Harris was the fourth man born and raised in Tennessee up to 1859 to become Governor.

He was the son of Lucy Davidson and Isham Harris. He was born in Tullahoma, Franklin County on February 10, 1818. His parents were from North Carolina of Revolutionary stock. They migrated to Tennessee, settled on a farm and reared nine children in a log house.

Isham Harris Sr. owned a thousand acres of land but at the age of fourteen Isham Jr. left the paternal roof, going to Paris, Tennessee, where he hired out as a clerk in a mercantile establishment, studying law at night. He entered the office of Judge Andrew Campbell for supplementary study and was licensed to practice law in 1841.

He and Martha Maria Travis married in 1843. Five years later he became a member of the Tennessee Legislature in 1847. Candidate for Presidential elector in 1848, he was a member of Congress from 1849 until 1853.

Martha and Isham moved to Memphis in 1853, where he opened a law office, and was chosen Presidential elector in 1856. He was elected Governor in 1857 and again in 1859.

After the evacuation of the state, civil Government was paralyzed, and subsequent elections were held irregularly, and for the most part by the soldiers in the Confederate camps.

In 1863, Robert L. Caruthers was elected governor, but failed to qualify as such, and Isham G. Harris continued nominally in office.

Slavery was the cause of secession; secession was the direct cause of Civil War.

The North had freed and sold slaves to the South, and after Eli Whitney invented the cotton gin they established factories to spin and weave cotton. The South needed her slaves to raise more cotton for the Northern factories. That is the reason they kept slaves in the South.

Lincoln was elected President and the Confederate States' Government was formed in Montgomery, Alabama in 1861 in February. He declared that he had no right to interfere with slavery in the States and had no desire to do so.

But after Fort Sumter was attached, Lincoln called for seventy-five thousand soldiers to force the seceded states back into the Union. With anger and sorrow the people of Tennessee were forced to take part in the War.

President Lincoln called for soldiers from Tennessee. Governor Harris refused to send them, and said, that if Tennessee must fight she would fight with the South. He said he would not send five thousand, but fifty thousand for the Southern cause. At the close of the War, Governor Harris practiced law at Memphis, Tennessee until 1877 when he was elected to the United States Senate. He served in the senate until his death in Washington July 8, 1897, and was buried in Memphis.

He served as Governor 1857-1862, at a time in Tennessee of great excitement and change. The Whig party was dying, the Abolition party growing in the North, and in the South the Democrats were sweeping everything before them.

Martha Maria Travis was the mother of eight children, the four sons were Dawson, James E., Isham and Eugene Harris. There are three great grand children: Lula Harris of Memphis, Glen Harris of Capleville also Dawson Harris.

GOVERNOR ISHAM G. HARRIS HOME

R. L. CARUTHERS HOME

Sarah Vaughn Lawrence Caruthers

A Would-Be First Lady, 1863

Sarah Vaughn Lawrence Caruthers never had the pleasure of acting as a First Lady of Tennessee. She endured the cruel misrepresentation of political strife and the war, with crushed heart over her husband's not being allowed to serve in 1863 after he was elected Governor, but was not inaugurated.

Sarah was the daughter of Miss Thomas and David Vaughn, who came from North Carolina when young and settled on a farm in Davidson County. Her father was a man of energy and perseverance—bought farm land and negroes and left an estate of 2000 acres, dying, leaving a wife and six children in 1864.

Three of the children were Hiram Vaughn and Judge Mitchell Vaughn and Sarah, who first married a Mr. Lawrence. They had one son, Vaughn Lawrence, who served under General Nathan Bedford Forrest during the War Between the States. The Federal authorities put a "price upon his head." Finally—when sick in bed—they arrested him and took him to prison. Here he became so critically ill that his release was secured and he was allowed to return home, but his house was burned to the ground soon afterwards.

Sarah married second Robert Caruthers, the elected Governor in 1863. As the whole state was in possession of contending armies, he did not take the oath or exercise the duties of the office, the governorship having been turned over to Andrew Johnson as Military Governor by President Lincoln.

Robert Caruthers was intensely Southern in his sentiments. Although frail in health, he volunteered twice; but each time was refused because of his health. Later he entered the secret service of the Confederacy, and experienced many thrilling adventures.

He was a member of one of the oldest and most prominent families in Tennessee. His people came from Scotland to America, first settling in Virginia and North Carolina. Soon after the state of Tennessee was formed, the Caruthers located in Maury County near Columbia. Here Robert L. was

159

born on December 13, 1827, the youngest child of Elizabeth Porter and Robert Caruthers. Both his father and grandfather, Robert Caruthers, were Revolutionary soldiers.

His four sisters were Mesdames Richard Looney, Mitchell Davidson, William J. Sykes, and Leonard D. Myers. His brothers were James and Abram.

Abram and Robert Caruthers were co-founders of the Law School at Lebanon. Robert and Mrs. Caruthers moved from Smith County and built their Mansion in Lebanon on West Main Street—designed by William Strickland.

Judge Caruthers maintained his law office in the right wing of his residence and the Law School was first conducted in one of the substantial brick servant quarters opening on the garden in the rear.

Their home was typical of the old South, with its stately columns and well-balanced facades. The interior and decorations were impressive of Sarah Caruthers' elegance and hospitality. Nothing escaped her watchful yet kindly eye, either within or without the mansion. She loved all pure and beautiful things, whether in nature or in art. Here were the portraits, silver, and rare books that added to her home elegance.

The formal gardens, under her immediate inspection were unusual; the residence was included in the design. Walkways of both brick and white shell were used to give variety and many boxwood and crepe myrtle gave formal dignity to the planting.

Sarah Caruthers was the mother of Robert Caruthers, an only son who died without an heir to carry on the name of Robert. The daughters were Mrs. W. H. Simonton of Fort Scott, Kansas, and Mrs. Newson of Huntsville, Alabama, where ex-governor elect Caruthers lived and died after the death of Mrs. Caruthers. He died January 3, 1907. He was a devout Christian of stainless honor, a cultured, chivalrous Southern gentlemen of the old school.

No American lady was ever more skilled and accomplished in domestic culture and economy than was Mrs. Caruthers, and was never so happy as when in the enjoyment of her own home; which was a pattern of order, system, as well as of hospitality, charity, benevolence and attention to the management of her husband's interests and public affairs.

GOVERNOR WILLIAM G. BROWNLOW

old print
Eliza O'Brien Brownlow, age 91.

Eliza Ann O'Brien Brownlow

B. 1819 — M. 1836 — D. 1914

Wife of Governor William Gannaway Brownlow

Governor William Gannaway Brownlow once remarked, "I never courted but one woman and her I married."

The woman was Eliza Ann O'Brien, born in Kingsport, Tennessee, September 25, 1819. She was the daughter of Susan Dabney Everett and James O'Brien.

Her father was a Methodist who emigrated from Pennsylvania to Sullivan County about 1814 and married Susan Everett in 1816. For over twenty years he was a merchant in Kingsport, but later he entered the manufacturing of iron.

Eliza had three brothers who died unmarried before the War Between the States. Her younger brother, Alfred Gaines O'Brien, was in the thirteenth Mississippi Regiment, Confederate States Army. She grew up with her two sisters Sara and Mary O'Brien.

It has been said, "William G. Brownlow had a double history: that of a Methodist minister and that of a politician. He was a man in whom there was much to admire and something to condemn.

His true inwardness and evident outwardness did not harmonize. His character as a blatant politician and violent controversealist stood in marked contrast with the purity of his private life, his gentleness as a husband and parent, and his kindness and liberality to his neighbors, especially the poor and afflicted.

Much history of the state gathers around the name Brownlow. He was associated with many men of great importance and events.

Reverend Brownlow was admitted to the Holston Conference at Abingdon, Virginia in 1826. He was in the Athens Circuit in 1829. After ten years he was in the Scott Circuit and was on a visit to Tennessee. When he returned to Gate City, William and Eliza had seen each other but one time. He remarked to his sister, Nancy Martin, "I have just met a girl in Elizabethton who is the only woman I will ever love." "But, William," Mrs. Martin replied, "it may be the girl won't marry you." "But," said William, "she shall marry me."

It was nearly a year before he saw Eliza again. That he

might marry her, he himself made a special effort to have himself sent to the Elizabethton Circuit. It was the first time in his ministry of ten years that he had sought to influence the selection of his own appointment.

Eliza became his bride at Turkey Town Camp meeting, in Carter County, the Reverend L. S. Marshall performing the ceremony on September 11, 1836, just before her seventeenth birthday. This was for him a happy marriage, for Mrs. Brownlow made him a thoughtful devoted wife.

Judge Temple said of William G. Brownlow, "He was an unique and remarkable character. His early education had been incomplete but he possessed natural ability which enable him to overcome this loss by reading and associations he gained the graces and diction of an educated man.

He was always a friend of the poor and helpless. He abounded in wit and humor. One Sunday afternoon as a teenager he was fishing on the banks of a creek near his home. A Methodist minister came along, asked him what he was using for bait. He replied, "A Methodist preacher". Another incident: Old Brother Aiken, an eccentric Methodist preacher, was a democrat while W. G. Brownlow, the fighting parson, was a Whig. At a camp meeting Brownlow was to preach the sermon and Aiken, who was conducting the opening exercise in his prayer, asked to be delivered from the Whiggery; whereat Brownlow shouted aloud, "GOD FORBID." Turning to him, old Aiken exclaimed: "Billy, keep quiet when I am praying."

Everyone enjoyed his company and his kindness. He was kept in the depth of pverty by appeals for help. His home was open to all who chose to enter, a regular home for all the Methodist preachers and their families and all the people who happened to pass his house.

Eliza, his faithful little wife, contributed her helpfulness and hospitality to all who came to her home.

"There were exciting times at the Brownlow's home. They had been married about four years. One dark, cloudy night while circuit court was in session at Elizabethton, March 2, 1840, between the hours of eight and nine o'clock while the family were around the fireside, Mr. Brownlow was writing. A gun with two rifle balls was fired through the window, breaking one pane and one bar of the sash. Both balls passed near his chest. He instantly sprang to his feet and pursued the enemy and fired at him as he was crossing the fence. Mr. Brownlow had been admonished of his danger and hence was armed. A friend, James Nelson, having heard of threats against his life, had come to spend the night at Brownlows."

Mrs. James O'Brien stoutly objected to giving Eliza to a Methodist Circuit Preacher, because of the hard life to which such a union would subject her. Mr. O'Brien offered no objections to the match. Mrs. O'Brien became reconciled to the son-in-law and after the death of her husband made the Brownlow's house her home.

Colonel John Bell Brownlow one day jokingly asked his mother what attraction his father had for her to cause her to marry him saying, "You knew he was homely, and then he was only a Circuit Rider as poor as Lazarus."

She replied, "I thought he was smart; everybody said he was talented. He was talked about more than any young Preacher in the Conference and when he preached at Elizabethton, he had more people to hear him than any other preacher. I was influenced by my respect for his talent; and besides he was so earnest, persistent and eloquent in his wooing, there was no resisting him."

Col. John Bell, named after the noble statesman, Senator John Bell, was Colonel of the Ninth Regiment of Tennessee Calvary from June, 1863, to the close of the War Between the States. He was also later in the Treasury Department and Post Office Department in Washington, D. C.

He was one of the eight Brownlow children: Susan, first married Dr. J. H. Sawyers and second Dr. T. D. Boynton, James Patton was an officer in the Federal Army. He was shot in both legs and had four hourses shot from under him. He died in 1878. Fannie Brownlow married a Confederate, Captain George C. Latta. Annie and Caldonia were twins; Annie became Mrs. W. F. Patrick, and Callie married Mr. John C. Hale of Arkansas.

The Brownlows lived in Knoxville until the beginning of the War Between the States. He was a Southern Union man and regarded the secession as both foolish and wicked. In no uncertain terms he used abusive and sarcastic language on slavery in his paper and the sermons he preached.

About this time he published a book entitled, "Sketches of the Rise and Progress and Decline of Secession." This book was very popular in the Northern States and brought to the writer a considerable income.

He went North, leaving Eliza and the younger children behind. When the accounts of his reception in the North and the sensation his bitter speeches were creating in the North were read in Tennessee, the following order was issued:

Headquarters Dept of East Tennessee
Office of Provost Marshall
April 2, 1862

Mrs. W. G. Brownlow, Knoxville, Tennessee
Madam; By Major General E. Kirby Smith,

I am directed most respectfully to inform you that you and your children are not held hostage for the good behavior of your husband, as represented by him in a speech in Cincinatti recently and that yourself and family will be required to pass beyond the Confederate States lines in thirty six hours from this date.

Passports will be granted you from this office.

Very Respectively

Colonel Provest Marshall

Similar notices were served on Mrs. Horace Maynard and family, Mrs. William B. Carter and Mrs. Andrew Johnson. At the request of Mrs. Brownlow the time of preparation for departure was extended three days.

The ladies and families were placed in charge of Lt. Joseph Speed of the Confederate Army of Alabama and sent North by way of Norfolk, Virginia. The Lieutenant proved an honorable gentleman and both families were always in praise of his kindness. He left nothing undone for their comfort.

These families were conducting themselves with utmost propriety. The women were amiable and well behaved at all times and under all circumstances. Mrs. Brownlow's brother Alfred Gaines O'Brien was a Lieutenant Colonel of Thirtieth Mississippi Regiment in the Confederate Army and one son-in-law, George C. Latta was a Captain in the Confederate service, but her husband was a Union sympathizer. In this case, it was an ungallant affair sending them through the Confederate line to their husbands, for it was avowedly, at least in the case of Eliza O'Brien Brownlow, visiting the sins of the husbands on innocent women.

William G. Brownlow was a member of the convention that revised the Constitution of Tennessee. He was elected Governor in 1865 and again in 1867, and in 1869 he was sent to the United States Senate, where he remained until 1875. He died in Knoxville, April, 1877.

The four years 1865 to 1869 have been called the

"Brownlow Period." It was the time of Reconstruction and exhibited in its details almost every phase of the stormiest Revolutionary tendencies and the vilest political and personal animosities.

In April, 1865—in a message to the General Assembly, Governor Brownlow warned the legislature that "the demoralized condition" of both races would cause scores to be sent to the penitentiary. "He advised the body to enact more stringent laws to cope with the increasing number of crimes. In asking the death penalty for horse stealing, house breaking and highway robbery, the Governor stated that such laws might look to others like a bloody act, "but the legislators should feel no concern for law violators, but to punish and reform them."

One act of the legislature during the Brownlow administration was a bill to recognize Tennessee's school system with a State Superintendent of schools to be elected by the people. He would have the power to appoint county superintendents. The legislature repealed this bill in 1870.

On November 11, 1865, at the end of the war, Governor Brownlow issued a Thanksgiving Proclamation: "Thursday, seventh day of December next has been set apart by proclamation by the President of the United States as a day of National Thanksgiving."

Tennessee was the first state to leave the Union and the first to return and be restored to the Union, July 24, 1866.

Mr. Brownlow's editorial career was spent in the formative stage of East Tennessee civilization. The first line from the pen of William G. Brownlow that ever appeared in a newspaper was published over a "nom de plume" in a newspaper edited and published in Jonesboro, Tennessee by Judge Thomas B. Emerson. He wrote a number of articles in advocacy of the Whig doctrines of a protective tariff and internal improvements of Federal Government.

The Judge was so pleased with the force and originality of these articles that he advised the young Divine to make journalism his life work. Upon this advice he started the **Elizabethton Whig** the next year of 1839. He changed his paper's title to **Jonesboro Whig** and later to **Brownlow's Jonesboro Whig.**

About 1850 Brownlow moved his family from Jonesboro to Knoxville where he bought a home on Cumberland Avenue and new splendid newspaper equipment for "The Knoxville Whig."

167

At one time Mr. Brownlow sold the office of the **Knoxville Whig** to Charles O. Rice, while he remained sole editor. A criticism of ex-Judge William G. Swan appeared in the paper. Swan went to the office and caned Rice, who was a very pious man. When Reverand Brownlow returned to the city, he took his six shooter and walker back and forth in front of Judge Swan's office and denounced him in the hearing of persons passing the street. The Judge was satisfied with the revenge taken. When the occurrence became known, some democrats said that Brownlow had acted cowardly. To this he replied in the Whig, "Indeed I did everything the code of honor required and more than the gospel justified."

While the Brownlows lived in Nashville, their home was Cedar Hill, once the home of George W. Campbell; the residence at that time was regarded one of the finest in Tennessee. It extended from Vine Street to High Street (now Sixth St. and 7th). The home was surrounded by a group of trees, mostly oaks. In the rear was an old fashioned flower garden which Eliza enjoyed supervising and beyond that the stables for carriages and her horses.

Mrs. Brownlow was a woman of superior physical and mental endowments. She was to Governor Brownlow the best of First Ladies, faithful to him in all his troubles, well poised, symetrical, prudent, a woman without a fault. No one was ever so foolish to speak an unkind word of her. During her long life she was a steady and constant Christian woman. She lived to be over ninety years of age.

A newspaper reporter called to see her at her noted home on Cumberland Avenue where she was celebrating her eighty-seventh birthday, her good health. Cheerful and cordial, "She was a noble Christian of Methodist faith, and the support on which Brownlow, the statesman, orator, preacher and Governor leaned." "He was the kindest man I ever knew," said Mrs. Brownlow on this occasion, "He read and studied and wrote day and night and never a cross word came from him."

But as Governor some one remarked, "Parson Brownlow was a product of his time but his times produced none other like him. He ruled with an iron hand." Another said, "The wrong man, in the wrong place at the wrong time."

Eliza O'Brien Brownlow's one wish was that she live to see a Brownlow great-grandson. She was blessed with this wish while still living at her home on East Cumberland Avenue, with her two slaves, Curtis and Rhodie. Also at that time Boynton Hale was with his grandmother.

A son of Mr. and Mrs. John Bell Brownlow, John Fouche and Margaret Brownlow, recently of Washington, D. C., were the parents of the long waited grandson in 1913. She lived only a few months, dying February 4, 1914.

Mrs. Margaret Brownlow says of her, "Not a beautiful lady but very charming and gracious." "One of the interesting facts in her life was that from the time Andrew Jackson was President through the term of President Taft, every President including these two called on Mrs. Brownlow at her home to pay his respects and to sign her guest book."

HOME OF GOVERNOR DEWITT C. SENTER, Morristown, Tenn.

courtesy of
Mr. and Mrs. Frank Spoon

Harriet Senter Senter, 1869

Harriet T. Senter Senter

B. 1841 — M. 1859 — D.

Wife of Governor DeWitt C. Senter

The inauguration of the Tennessee Senator, DeWitt C. Senter as Governor of Tennessee placed Harriet T. Senter in the exalted social position as First Lady of Tennessee, sixty-three years after Catherine Sherrill Sevier gracefully dispensed the duties as the first First Lady of the State of Tennessee.

Her husband, who had been elected to the State Senate in 1865, from counties of Grainger, Anderson, Union, Claiborne, and Campbell in 1866-67, was reelected from the same counties and when the body was organized, he was Speaker of the Senate. During this session Governor W. G. Brownlow being elected to the United States Senate, Speaker Senter filled out his unexpired term as Governor of eighteen months.

In 1869 he was elected Governor by the people by an overwhelming majority of seventy thousand votes, defeating General William H. Stokes. The campaign was one of the most notable in the annals of Tennesse politics. His competitor Stokes disagreed with him on the franchise law, on the ground that every man as a taxpayer should be entitled to vote. Over this controversy Senter gained the victory and wrested the State Government from the hands of men who heretofore administered its affairs with oppression and bitterness.

However, his wife, Harriet, possessed no ambition to shine in society and enjoyed the farm life, her garden and the prestige of making the greater amount and nicer butter than other women in her neighborhood.

Mrs. Senter was born at Bean Station in 1841, noted as the location of the first frontier log cabin, and as the place where the first white child, Richard Bean, was born in Tennessee.

She grew up on her father's farm with her three sisters: Susan Senter Graves, Columbia Gaines Cozens and Olivia Manley. Harriet was tall, fair, slender with blue eyes and auburn hair. She was educated at the Female College at Rogersville, Tenn., and was an industrious home woman, remarkable for her household economies, not addicted to extravagant living, fine dressing; though we find her in a plaid silk dress with lace bertha and cuffs, wearing the four rings on four fingers as was customary at that period, a gold brooch at the neck and waist-line, her hair parted in the middle pulled back in a bun at the nape of her neck, wearing large earrings as she posed for the photographer while First Lady of Tennessee.

Harriet had led an exceptionally happy life before her marriage on September 1, 1859, at her home in Grainger County. DeWitt was eleven years her senior and a third cousin who frequently visited in their home.

His father, Hon. William Tandy Senter, who was born in Grainger County, married Nancy White, a daughter of Reverend George White, a Virginian and a minister of the Methodist Church.

William Tandy mixed his merchant business, politics and religion. He became a Methodist minister and in 1833 was a member of the State Convention that revised the Constitution of Tennessee. He was district elector on the Harris - Tyler ticket in 1840; a nominee of the Whig party for Congress against Abraham McClellan, but was defeated. He died in 1847 at the age of forty-seven.

Sarah Snodgrass was the maternal grandmother of Governor Senter; his great grandfather, David Snodgrass, of Sullivan County was a Colonel in the Revolutionary War.

Governor Senter was the brother of Susan Sarah Conway, Mary Senter, Ann Eliza Murrell, Rebecca Hodges and Reverend William T. Senter, Jr.

The grandfather, Tandy Senter, a native of Virginia, lived to be one hundred and nine years old and died near Kingsport in 1866. He fought in the War of 1812. A farmer raising fine horses, his wife was Susan Lyon of Virginia. He was twice married and the father of twelve children, six by each marriage.

Harriet's father, Col. P. M. Senter, son of Elizabeth Ore and William Senter, was County and Circuit Court Clerk of Grainger County for almost twenty-five years. He was a soldier in the army that moved the Cherokees from Florida in 1857; a lieutenant in the Mexican War, and a lawyer. Her mother, Adeline McGraw, was a daughter of Gabriel McGraw, whose name is signed to more surveys and locations than that of any man in Tennessee.

During the War Between the States, Harriet, like most of the women in Tennessee while the bitter struggle went on between the North and South, living in the section where the ravages were most dreadful, letting the grass grow undisturbed, kept the home fires burning and hoped daily to hear from her husband. She had been used to loneliness during the meetings of

173

the Senate. When Mr. Senter was repeatedly called, Harriet remained at home; and while he sought honors and support away from home, she found compensation for his prolonged absence in that she best promoted his interest when she lived at home within their means and tried to be a comfort to his mother.

During the War DeWitt Senter was a staunch Union man, and in th e spring of 1862 was arrested by the Confederate authorities and made the Grand Southern tour, as a political prisoner, for over six months. He came home for about a year, went into Kentucky and remained there until quiet was partially restored in East Tennessee by the Federal Occupation.

During the gubernatorial years of 1869-71 there was no Governor's Mansion. Governor Senter boarded in Nashville, while Harriet remained with his mother. She visited him as often as was convenient. It was the days of Reconstruction, and few places were available for rented homes. She was fond of growing things and spent her leisure time among the garden and flowers. She was not a literary woman but was well versed on topics of the day, witty, very graceful and agreeable in her manner.

Prior to the War, Governor Senter was a Whig, born and bred and early instructed in the principles advocated by Henry Clay. He afterward became a Republican.

In 1864 he was district presidential elector on the Lincoln —Johnson ticket and in 1868 was elector for the State at large on the Grant—Colfax ticket. He returned to his farm home at the completion of his term and retired from political life without a remorseful reflection upon himself.

Though raised a strict, pious Methodist by his parents, Governor Senter never attached himself to any church, although a Methodist Church at Panther Springs was built in memory of him. Harriet was a Presbyterian, but became a Methodist after marrying into the family. Governor Senter never had felt the change called conversion; he deemed it would be unwise, if not hypocritical to join a church and assume the responsibilities of a Christian character without first having had an experience of the change that would enable him well and truly to meet his obligations.

He was a Master Mason but belonged to no other secret society.

One of the cardinal points in the governor's character even when a young man was this: "Do nothing that will offend Mother, or cause her to blush for anything I may do."

174

And though wild and fond of gay life, he never did, even in his younger days, anything that was dishonorable. His mother, an old-fashioned, strong minded woman, of the keenest, shrewdest observation, invariably called her children together, read the Bible and prayed with the family or whoever might be present, and to her Governor Senter attributed his success in life, carrying out the right regardless of cost or trouble or time.

The Senters were slave holders, but DeWitt grew up with the idea that slavery was a misfortune and wrong in principle.

He and Harriet were a happy, congenial couple. They had no children but nieces and nephews were often in their home, which stands today on Andrew Johnson Highway near Jefferson City, as it was when occupied by the Senters except for two box-woods at the walk and a picket fence.

The Governor died in 1898 at the age of 64 and was buried in the Jarnigan Cemetery, Morristown, Tennessee.

ELIZABETH CHILDRESS BROWN

Elizabeth Childress Brown, First U.D.C. President of the Southern States, 1895

courtesy of
Atty. Neil S. Brown, Nashville, Tenn.

Ann Pointer Brown
Elizabeth Childress Brown

B. 1845 — M. 1864 — D. 1919

Wives of Governor John Calvin Brown

The Pointer family of Spring Hill, Giles County, Tenn. were of Virginia stock; they were socially and financially prominent and noted for their public spirit.

Ann was the daughter of Martha A. and John H. Pointer. She was a beautiful and accomplished girl. She and her sister Hattie, who married Judge Burrus in 1871, were taught by a private teacher. They later attended St. Cecilia's Academy in Nashville and Columbia Female College.

Ann was cultivated, intellectual, with graceful manners. She grew up on the plantation of her father who attained very considerable success as a planter in Giles County.

Ann was the first wife of John Calvin Brown, the son of Margaret Smith and Duncan Brown, both of whom migrated from North Carolina in 1808. They were the Blue-stocking type of Presbyterians.

John Calvin studied law with his uncle Hugh Brown at Spring Hill. He was educated in the Old Field Schools and at Jackson College at Columbia, and began the practice of law in 1839 at the age of twenty-one at Pulaski, Tennessee.

Ann died in 1858, leaving no children. After her death John C. Brown was in ill health; he went on an European tour in 1859, making a tour of Great Britain, the continent, Egypt, and the Holy Land. In 1860 he was elector on the Bell and Everett ticket. After the election of Mr. Lincoln to the Presidency and the secession of the southern states John C. Brown entered the service of his state in the War Between the States as a private, and was elected at once captain of his company, and immediately thereafter a Colonel of the Third Tennessee Infantry Regiment.

At Fort Donelson he was in command of a brigade as senior colonel, and took active part in its defense. He was captured and sent to Fort Warren; was exchanged in 1862, when he was promoted to Brig. Gen. and assigned to duty with General Braxton Bragg. He participated in the battles of Perryville, and other places in Kentucky. He was afterwards with Gen. Joe Johnston in the Georgia campaign, engaged in the battles of Chickamauga, Mission Ridge, and the hundreds days fighting to Jonesborough.

He was wounded at Perryville, Kentucky in the right thigh and was taken to Knoxville. He was unable to sit on his horse at Chickamauga as result of a cannonball shot. He was sent to Dalton, Georgia, activity was light and he was given a furlough. Here he let Cupid take shots.

The Judge John W. Childress, Major in the Confederate army and his family lived in Murfreesboro. They were now living in Griffin, Georgia as refugees.

The fifth of the twelve children of John W. Childress was the beautiful dark haired Elizabeth, who was engaged to John C. Brown. An elaborate wedding had been planned, instead, in a quiet home wedding at Griffin, Georgia in 1864 she became the second wife of John C. Brown who had a short furlough and was called back to face General Sherman.

Major John W. Childress was twice married; first in June 1831 to Sarah Williams, daughter of a wealthy farmer, Elisha Williams, who had married a daughter of Phillip Phillips of Pennsylvania. Sarah Childress was the mother of Mary, who married Col. James Avent of Murfreesboro; and James K. Polk; Elisha, who died at battle of Shiloh; John W. and Betty Brown, who was noted as one of the most elegant of young ladies; and Joseph Childress.

The next year, 1852, after the death of Sarah, he married a cousin of hers, Mary Phillips. She was the mother of William, Horace who married a granddaughter of Governor Cannon, Eloise Smith, Annie, Eugene, and Saline Childress. Sarah Childress Polk was an aunt of Elizabeth Brown.

After John C. Brown returned to Pulaski, they lived at the home on West Madison Street where Martin College stands today. They lived at Colonial Hall in Pulaski where the four Brown children grew up. The three daughters were Marie, born 1865, who became the first wife of Governor Benton McMillen, she had one son, Brown McMillen. She died December 1887. Daisy was an accomplished artist and died 1885 at the age of seventeen; Elizabeth born 1870, married John C. Burch and she died in 1904. The son, John C. Brown survived his sisters, became a noted lawyer; he was twice married, the second time to Miss Martha Roland.

Elizabeth Brown, widow of the Governor and the gallant Confederate General, at the Annual session of The National Order of the Daughters of the Confederacy held in Atlanta, Georgia in November 1905 when the name was changed to "United Daughters of the Confederacy," was made President of

the Southern States. The gavel received by Mrs. Brown; the emblem of law and order was of elegantly polished wood, cut from a tree near General Robert E. Lee's residence at Washington and Lee University, Va. The gavel was adorned with a large silver band and handsomely engraved.

She entered upon the duties as First President of U.D.C. with business capacity and zeal, presided over the organization from November 5, 1895 until ill health forced her resignation in 1896. When she assumed duties of the office there were twenty-three chartered chapters in the south. In 1896 Mrs. John Overton of Nashville called a meeting of the Tennessee chapters to meet in Nashville on January 28, 1896 for the purpose of organizing a State Divivision of U.D.C. by the widows, mothers, sisters, and wives of the Confederate fighting men. Up to this time only the states of Virginia and Georgia had completed a State Division.

Mrs. Brown in February, 1896, published an appeal to the Women of the South, "Let us prove ourselves worthy of the memory of our heroic fathers, husbands, brothers and sons." The appeal for Battle Abbey was directed by her and became the Confederate Memorial Institute edifice in the south at Richmond, Virginia.

Elizabeth Brown, prominent in the church and social life of Pulaski, Tennessee lived through Sherman's march to the sea, among elegant rosewood and mahogany furniture broken into a million fragments, china and glass strewn to the winds of heaven, a house devastated. Through it all she was a southern heroine, becoming First President of the Southern cause, a noble mother and a charming First Lady of Tennessee.

Mrs. John C. Brown, was one of the state's most distinguished women, died at her home on Eighth Avenue, South in Nashville, February 28, 1919—the widow of one of the state's most distinguished men, Governor John C. Brown.

After the war the Browns made Nashville their home, altho she spent much of her time at the ancestral home, Colonial Hall in Pulaski. She spent some time in Texas while ex Governor Brown was receiver for the Texas and Pacific Railway.

Mrs. Brown as First Lady filled her position with characteristic grace. She was prominent in U.D.C. work, one that was close to her heart. She was prominent in the D.A.R. circles. She was identified with the Ladies' Hermitage Association and the Centennial Club.

She was a life long member of the Episcopal Church, the Christ Church parish, in Nashville and Church of the Messiah at Pulaski, in which are beautiful memorials to her three daughters Marie Brown McMillen, Birdie Brown Burch, and Miss Daisy Brown.

She was a notable and distinguished figure at all social gatherings and entertained with beautiful taste, a perfect hostess.

All her life, in her home, friends recall her cordial charm and kindness, a woman who was gentle in speech, with no unkind words from Mrs. Brown's lips. No gossip was ever repeated that might injure others.

Home of Governor James D. and Susan Dunlap Porter, Paris, Tenn.

Susan Dunlap Porter

B. 1833 — M. 1851 — D. 1914

Wife of Governor James D. Porter

It was the happy fortune of Mrs. Porter to be First Lady of Tennessee, when President Rutherford B. Hayes visited Nashville in 1877, accompanied by Mrs. Hayes.

It was a warm September day when the President's train was met at the Louisville depot by a delegation of prominent Tennesseans. Governor James D. Porter and the President walked arm in arm from the train to the carriages that took them to the Capitol. As the procession moved up the streets and down to the Capitol grounds, thousands of people lined the streets to catch a glimpse of the President. After his speech on the War Between the States, and a trip to the Custom House, where the President participated in laying the cornerstone, they rested for a while at the Maxwell House where the Governor and Mrs. Porter resided, before calling on Mrs. Sarah Childress Polk at Polk Place on Vine Street.

The visitors were entertained by a six o'clock reception at the colonial Cole home on Church Street. In the receiving line Mrs. Cole stood beside Mrs. Porter, who was wearing a dress of rich gold silk material, very simply made, high neck with fine lace, long sleeves with lace at her wrists, her hair coiffured simply with a bun at the neck, held in place by a beautiful shell comb. They received the presidential party, Mrs. Hayes in a black grosgrain princess dress, square neck, perfectly fitting and relieved of its plainess by exquisite point laces. Other distinguished guests were Secretary of State William M. Evarts, Postmaster General D. M. Key, Governor Wade Hampton of South Carolina, and, among the Nashville Society, was Sarah Childress Polk, who seldom left the Polk Place for receptions and other parties.

The visiting party left Nashville the next day. Nashville had exerted every effort to entertain on a lavish scale a Chief Executive who had freed the South from the threat of Federal interference in her affairs.

Mrs. Porter, as First Lady of Tennessee, was prepared through her happy married life, her cheerful spirit, intelligence, culture and her social rank to fill the place as Governor Porter's wife and hostess.

Mrs. Porter, born 1833, Susannah H. Dunlap in Paris,

Tennessee, was the daughter of Marietta Beauchamp and General John H. Dunlap, a native of Knox County, and a granddaughter of Susannah Harding Gilliam and Hugh Dunlap born in Londonderry, Ireland, who came to America and settled in Knoxville in 1793, raising a large family of his own, besides adopting seven or eight children of his and his wife's deceased relatives. His son, Richard Dunlap, was the first male child born in Knoxville, while it was the capital of Southwest Territory.

Susannah's great grandmother was the daughter of Deveraux Gilliam, descendant of John Ellis who settled at Tuckahoe in the county of Henrico, Virginia in 1683.

James Davis Porter was born in Paris December 7, 1828, to Geraldine Horton and Dr. Thomas Kennedy Porter; his maternal grandparents were Nancy White and Josiah Horton. He was also a descendant of John and Rose Porter of Kenilworth Warwickshire, England.

Doctor Porter and Lawyer Dunlap settled in Paris, Tenn., the same year in 1823. Both families were prominent in Henry County, active in the civic affairs of Paris, both men members of the Board of Trustees of the Paris Academy.

James D. Porter was educated in the Paris Schools. He grew up with his brothers and sisters, Josiah, Ann, William, who was killed when three years old, Geraldine, who died at the age of five, Catherine, Thomas Kenedy, and W. Horton.

James Davis Porter went to the University of Nashville, where he received his B.S. Degree at the age of seventeen. In later years the University conferred upon Governor Porter the degree of L.L.D. He studied law in the office of John Dunlap in Paris. *The Paris Register* of 1851 shows that he had more than a professional interest in the Dunlap family.

On June 18, 1851, Susannah Dunlap became the bride of James D. Porter, Rev. F. C. Trimble performing the marriage ceremony.

"Mrs. Porter's father amassed a large fortune and was able to leave Susannah forty thousand dollars as an inheritance."

They began housekeeping on a farm of two hundred acres one mile from Paris on the Puryear-Murray Highway. The house was a modest white frame building located on a rolling hill, the slave quarters located behind the house.

In this home the six Porter children were born. Susannah, who was educated in private schools of Miss Fanny O'Bryan of Nashville, became the wife of Dr. W. G. Bibb.

Charles Dunlap was educated at Lexington, Kentucky, studied law at Cumberland University. Dudley was educated

184

in the public schools of Nashville, Montgomery Bell Academy and at Cecilan College near Elizabethton, Ky. Thomas Kenedy was the youngest.

The Porters had no idea of the grief and sudden deaths that awaited them. Three children met untimely deaths; the two oldest John Dunlap and Lily died about the same time in 1858 in their early childhood. In the year 1888 Dudley Porter was killed on the street in Paris, Tennessee.

The white cottage was the first of the two family homes. The second was the home of Susannah's parents, purchased at about the time of Mrs. Dunlap's death in 1893. Here the Porters lived until his death in 1912.

One of the most important questions in the life of James D. Porter from 1851 until 1861 was the growing controversy over slaves and other related problems. The young attorney had enjoyed the advantages as a boy of the upper socio-economic classes of society. His father was a slave owner, which freed him of the tasks that a boy in a small rural town would have to perform. However, his time was not spent in idleness, for he entered the junior class at U. N. at the age of fifteen.

During this tribulent period James D. Porter was willing to support the South in a long and bitter war.

His political career began in 1859 as a member of the Tennessee Legislature. In 1861 he was General Gideon Pillow's Adjutant General and assisted in organizing the troops; later he became General Cheatham's Chief of Staff and remained as such throughout the War Between the States. In 1865 he returned to his law practice in Paris, Tennessee.

He was a member of the Constitutional Convention of 1870, Judge of Circuit Court from 1870 until he was nominated for Governor in 1874. He was Governor from 1875 until 1879.

In 1885 President Grover Cleveland appointed him Secretary of State. In 1887 he resigned and he and Mrs. Porter returned to Tennessee, retiring from political life after these years in Washington, D.C.

He was responsible for the establishment of George Peabody College for Teachers, where he and Mrs. Porter lived on the Peabody campus the four years he was President of the college. He lost his fight for the retention of Peabody on the University of Nashville Campus. After his defeat, he and Mrs. Porter left Nashville on April 21, 1910 by special car, where he retired to his colonial home in Paris, Tenn. He never held a political office after his resignation as Minister to Chile in 1896.

He was suggested for President against William Jennings

Bryan. He said, "The *Nashville American* referred to me as a man of sixty years, so I am too old to run for President."

The Porters' method of life was, first, to attend to their own business — also never to live beyond their income. In this Susannah heartily agreed; her rule was never to buy anything until able to pay for it. Susannah was well off. But not for a moment was she seduced by the affluent.

She was educated at Nashville Female Academy under the direction of Drs. Lapsley and Elliot, and possessed in an eminent degree all the virtues that go to make up the good daughter, wife, mother, neighbor, and First Lady of Tennessee. She died in 1914 and was buried in Paris, Tennessee.

The love her children bore her amounts to a sublime devotion on their part.

Hundred Oaks, Marks Home, Winchester, Tenn.

Novella Davis Marks

B. 1844 — M. 1863 — D. 1906

Wife of Governor Albert S. Marks

Governor Marks married Miss Novella Davis on April 29, 1863, who was the nineteen year old daughter of Caroline Penelope Hunter and John B. Davis who lived at La Guardo, Tennessee, near Hunter Point on the Cumberland River in Wilson County.

Here she grew up with her four brothers William, Winfield, Thomas, and Samuel Davis and her sister Alice whom she and her mother nursed through smallpox during the War Between the States.

Her paternal grandparents were Betsey Williams and Thomas Davis, who was commissioned captain of the Seventeenth Regiment Militia of Tennessee in 1810 by Willie Blount, who was Governor at the time.

The father, John R. Davis, was a man of unusual character and ability; a man of splendid physique, attracting attention wherever he went, handsome with mental qualities, a bold and eloquent speaker, and a gallant soldier.

When her husband and William went to war, Mrs. Davis was left with the younger children. Her weapon of defense was a hatchet which she kept under her bed. When the Yankees were passing through Tennessee, she, her house, and provisions were spared when the Commanding officer saw Major Davis's Masonic apron hanging on the wall. He, too, being a Mason, they only took the livestock, mules, and horses.

Novella, the beautiful seventeen-year old, was engaged to the young lawyer, Albert Marks, of Colyar, Frizzell, and Marks of Winchester. He entered the Confederate army as Captain of Company E., 17th Tennessee, Regiment Infantry. This included General Zollicoffer's Command up to the death of General Zollicoffer at Mill Springs. He was later Major and still later made a Colonel.

In the Battle of Murfreesborough on December 21, 1862, he received a severe wound which necessitated amputation below the knee. (Someone later asked the cause of his lameness. He replied, "Through trifling with the Yankee Union.")

He offered, after the amputation, to release Novella from the engagement. Novella refused to be released; and they were married during the war. She followed the fortunes of war, devoting herself thence forward with redoubled affection to the happiness of her wounded lover.

She was an intelligent, superior woman, staying as near her husband as possible until the Surrender in 1865, which found her in Macon, Mississippi, with her oldest son Arthur Handley, a baby one year old who had been born at LaGrange, Georgia.

The other son, Albert Davis, was born at Winchester, Tennessee, in 1867, where Albert Marks again practiced law for two years before he was elected Chancellor of the Fourth chancery Division of Tennessee. He was re-elected in 1878 but did not serve. He was nominated and elected Governor in 1878; he served two years.

During his administration, he was concerned with railroads, the state debt, and with building up of schools and cities that were devestated by war. It was a time of peace and growth with towns increased in wealth and prosperity.

There is no record of Novella Davis Marks' education, but all records speak of her as intelligent. She was a person who furthered her own education throughout her life, as education never ends, and her accomplishments in life show she was a woman with an inquiring and brilliant mind, interested in her sons. Albert became a prominent lawyer in Nashville.

Arthur Handley entered Sewanee in 1881, a gifted young man, a poet, orator, and writer. He died at age twenty-eight and would have gone far in the literary world. He planned to become an Episcopal Minister but his life was cut short by typhoid fever.

He was in the Consulate Service to Germany and England during President Grover Cleveland's Administration. Mary Hunt of Nashville was touring the Continent of Europe, and they were married in Sterling, Scotland, in 1888. He resigned and they returned to Winchester, where they remodeled the Governor's Mansion. They used cheap labor and the red clay soil of Franklin County and copied the castles they saw in Europe.

The library was an exact replica of the Walter Scott library in Kensington Palace in Edinburg, Scotland; it is still standing, a place of beauty in Winchester. Mary Hunt and Arthur Marks had one son, Albert Smith, and Lawyer Dempsey Marks of Clarksville, Tennessee is a grandson.

Mrs. Louise Hunter Marks of Clarksville says of her husband's grandmother, Novella Davis, "She became a member of the Board of Directors, and Vice Regent until 1898. She was responsible for procuring State Appropriation for L. H. A. and instrumental in bringing the chair of Law to Cumberland University at Lebanon. She was a member of the Presbyterian Church and the United Daughters of the Confederacy and a Daughter of the American Revolution. She was a great-granddaughter of Evan Davis, who fought at the Battle of King's Mountain. She was also a direct descendant of John Williamson who fought at the age of fifteen in the Revolutionary War under General Green, and a great grandniece of Colonel Thomas Williamson, who served with General Andrew Jackson at New Orleans."

Novella Davis died March 24, 1906, at Lebanon, Tennessee, and is buried beside the Governor in Winchester, who preceded her in death in 1891. He died at the Maxwell House in Nashville with Novella at his side.

"Mrs. Marks combined the elements of a perfect lady, noble in person, a fine scholar, a brilliant conversationalist, an ornament of society; yet she was domestic and practical in the management of her home. She was nowhere out of place; but whatever she undertook to do, it was as though that alone had been her life's occupation."

While her husband was necessarily absent from home, she managed the farm with the skill and energy of a first rate farmer.

Novella Davis as a First Lady is given a distinguished place among the First Ladies of Tennessee. She was recognized in her day as a perfect type of grandeur with which the Southern ladies rose to the emergencies of the war and its consequences and without ceasing to be refined and cultivated, self sacrificing, and a practical woman in coping with adversity and calamity as shown in her diary.

"She will be remembered for this or that," as remarked by a friend. "I met her accidentally, and my first thoughts were, 'What a beautiful young lady.' She was beautiful and the coming years did not make her less so. Here was a woman with beauty without vanity, intelligent without egotism — I say, 'No wonder Colonel Marks fell in love with her at first sight . . .' He offered to release her after he lost his foot, but instead of warping her affections, it intensified her love for him. No two people were more suited, and none could have loved each other more. He was above the average man. It does me good to praise them. They were ever good and kind to me."

— Writer Unknown.

MY RETURN FROM DIXIE

The following very interesting story is written by Mrs. Albert S. Marks, whose husband was Colonel of the 17th Tennessee Infantry during the War Between the States and later an eminent Judge in Chancery and Governor of Tennessee. Mrs. Marks resided at Lebanon, Tennessee when the article was written for Confederate Veteran Vol. 14:

"The signal of Lee at Appomattox that the War Between the States was at an end found me boarding in the cultured and charming family of Dr. Lyles at Macon, Mississippi, where I had passed the last six dreary months of refugee life. The supply of provisions was well-nigh exhausted. The late overflows had ruined much of the growing crops; the enemy had conquered; Lincoln had been insanely murdered, uselessly inflaming the Northern hearts to hatred and revenge. The very air was heavy with gloom; and the dismal, daily croak of the swamp frog was a fitting chime to the hopelessness that filled the land.

My husband must wait for the capitulation of General Dick Taylor; and with affairs in this desperate state, it was decided that to go as far as possible on Confederate money, I should start at once for Tennessee, with my baby boy of thirteen months, a small negro boy who had fallen into our hands by the death of his young master, and my sister-in-law, who was nearby at a boarding school. On the first day of May, my husband accompanied us to Meridian, where with feelings of anxiety and wretchedness, but desperate determination, we bade him adieu, and with my young party (myself a little more than a school girl) I set out by rail to Jackson, Mississippi. No incident worthy of note occurred until we reached Grenada. Here we found Major Mellon, a distant relative, though a stranger, to whom we bore a letter of introduction from my husband. It was difficult to get lodging; but with his aid, we finally succeeded, paying out our first greenbacks at extravagant prices. The Major had on hand a lot of commissary supplies; and, not knowing that he could do better with them, gave us a small sack each of sugar and coffee. I took them, not knowing what I could do with them.

We were getting so near the enemy lines that good coaches were not sent north of Grenada, but we were glad to have the comfort of even the roughest. These ran only to Yackney River, where the bridge had been burned, and here we had to take an ordinary flat car drawn by mules. Just after we had boarded the train at Grenada, some kind hand offered my boy a broad stick of white cream candy. The little fellow, though usually very friendly, turned away, showing his lack of acquaintance with such luxuries; and it called forth at once the remark, "I know you have been in Rebeldom."

As we approached nearer the Enemy's lines the feeling of not knowing what to expect increased with every mile we traveled. The first night out from Grenada we passed at a farmhouse, where we were comfortable and paid our fare with sugar and coffee, which we thought fortunate, as prospect for the means of transportation grew more uncertain. We started with fresh hope next morning, finding ourselves in quite a party, each bent on some point north. Four persons I remember—two gentlemen from Memphis, Mr. W. and Mr. G. and two ladies, Mrs. M. Miss Gibson, the latter from Alexandria, Virginia, but recently a teacher at Marion, Alabama. She was wearing mourning for a dead lover, a Confederate colonel, who fell in Atlanta. She had several times made the journey north through the Federal lines, and her knowledge of the route naturally made her our leader.

The Southern sun poured its burning rays upon us on that open car and sometimes seemed more than we could bear; but in absence of umbrellas, the gentlemen thatched our heads with bushes from the roadside, adding much to our comfort in this novel ride. When we came to a downgrade, our mules had to be detached. The car, propelled by its own weight, ran at a rapid speed; and on reaching the level again, we had to wait for our mules to come up. A few miles past Sardis our driver was panic-stricken by being hailed with the news that the Federals were just ahead, taking all the horses and mules to be found. With this he quickly changed the mules to the other end of the car and started southward. Continuing in that direction until night closed upon us at Sardis, finding us but little in advance of the point that we had left in the morning. This was a depressing step for several reasons, the most important one the spending of our little stock of money in an unnecessary delay. The Federals were all about town. The night was an anxious one; and when it was over, a good many of my good dollars were gone.

With renewed courage, we started northward again next day and traveled without special incident until after we passed Como. Some miles beyond rumors of trouble about our mules again reversed our direction, and night coming on as we reached Como, we halted, perplexed, not knowing where to pass it. Another day almost wasted. Mr. G. of Memphis kindly came to our relief and proposed to go to an acquaintance who lived in a stately mansion just in sight and procure lodging for Miss Gibson and my party. Our hearts leaped for joy, and we embraced him for his goodness when he returned with a favorable answer. Though forty years have gone by, memory brings vividly back the grounds, the genial old gentleman who gave us friendly greeting, the dark paper, and hangings (giving the parlor a dismal look), the cool broad halls, the luxurious beds, and handsome furniture of the room assigned to us, the comfortable breakfast, but no word of welcome from the hostess. When we passed out the next morning, though we had been sumptuously entertained and left none of our gold for it, it was an indefinite feeling if injury, knowing for ourselves that the cup of cold water must be given in a Christian spirit of its mission be perfectly fulfilled and that high bred women sometimes forget, or neglect, to be womanly.

Without further interruption, we arrived next day at Senatobia, the end of the mule line. By advice of Miss Gibson, we passed the night here at the house of the man who owned and drove the hack to Memphis, distant a little less than forty miles. As we crossed the Cold Water Bottoms, we saw here and there evidence that war was in the land; and as we neared Memphis, more often still a lonely chimney in a yard overgrown with weeds and brambles spoke plainly the story of devestation and destruction. We were told that we must pass the picket guard around the city before sunset, for at that hour a signal was fired, after which no one was permitted to pass the line.

Just as we drove in sight a gun rang out on the evening air, and we knew we were too late. Vexation of vexations! What were we to do? Miss Gibson assumed the lead and proposed a personal interview with the captain of the guard. What passed we did not know, as we remained in the back while she, accompanied by one of the gentlemen, went to his quarters. However, she maneuvered us through; and with feelings of oppressed relief, we entered Memphis as a city of refuge, each one to go his or her way.

With my party I drove to the Gayoso House. When the old negro porter came forward to assist us out, I, being in a friendly mood, addressed him as uncle. At this M. nudged me on the arm and whispered in bated breath: "Sister, remember it is no longer uncle!"

The hackman was to call at my room after tea for a settlement. Having been a Confederate soldier, I expected to find him brave and chivalric. I knew that his charges from Senatobia to Memphis were thirty-five dollars in greenbacks, which were then selling two for one in gold. Regular rates would take the larger part of my money I had left, so I determined to throw myself upon his chivalry and see if that could affect anything for me. I laid my gold in his hand, told him how far from home I was, that we were the family of a Confederate soldier and that I wanted him to take such part as he thought would be a compensation and leave me enough for the rest of the journey.

His avarice only responded, and the shylock took seventy of my one hundred dollars, making my trunk half rate. I was too much absorbed with my journey to think much of his lack of generosity, which only made the need of pressing forward the greater.

The next morning the first thing to be done was to see a newspaper to learn when a boat started up the river. To our joy the St. Patrick was advertised for Louisville at four o'clock in the afternoon. But General Washburn must be seen and passes secured. These we obtained without trouble for any boat. We found Captain Hart a gentleman and his boat a model. Nearly all on board were Southern people, and we not only enjoyed the sumptuous fare but the genial people who soon made a hero of our little boy, whose petting and overfeeding resulted in making him sick, just as well-meant kindness often makes harm.

The day was a delightful one on the broad Mississippi; and looking back on it now, I can well believe the law of compensation when I contrast the mule car and ambulance hack with that magnificent packet and its agreeable company. Two nights and one day out brought us to Smithland, at the mouth of the Cumberland. Here we met a cold wave, cloaks and good fires being necessary, and a cold wave for our hearts also in the form of Federal Blue. The town was filled with soldiers, who abounded at the Hotel where we spent the day. The fish was not so savory as that on the St. Patrick, and we ate in oppressed silence. The Cumberland was getting low, the boats to Nashville becoming infrequent. There was terror in the thought that we might have to lie here for days; but not so, for fortune favored us. The Emma Floyd landed, bound for Nashville. We hastened at once to take passage; but as we were going from the wharf boat, a negro guard, whom in our hurry I had not noticed with his white-gloved hand tapped my arm and demanded passes. With satisfaction I drew out the pass from General Washburn; but to my horror, he replied that that would not do, and I must have a pass from the commandant there.

Where was he? The boat was about ready to depart, and I

must see Captain Hildreth and ask him to wait for me long enough to go to the commandant's office. Depositing baby and nurse with him, my sister and I hurriedly sought the office of the commandant. Calling for him, we were told that he was out of town. Then we must see the adjutant, but he was also absent. Here was another dilemma.

Perplexed and worried, we asked: "What can be done?"

Again the goodness of human nature came to the surface. The Quarter Master agreed to sign our passes, which he did; and with light hearts, we hastened back to our boat.

The Cumberland was narrow and insignificant to the grand, proud, rolling Mississippi and the beautiful Ohio; but its laughing waters made music to my heart, for it was the river of my childhood, and I gazed upon its rugged banks with sweet satisfaction as I quietly glided home over its glassy bottom. Fort Donelson must be passed, and I must go back in memory to that day of wild suspense when dear ones had learned the first hard lesson of war in characters of blood. And the sad sequel of prison life eked out at Johnson's Island, Camp Morton, and in Boston's dreary harbor. Even then in the tumult of the hour I felt that that experience must be laid away with the sacred things of the past, and we had come to the lesson of rehabilitation and learning to live in peace with our enemies.

Captain Hildreth was most courteous and accomodating. He was making an excursion trip with a party chaperoned by Mrs. Rice from Cincinnatti, who proved a Southern sympathizer.

The time glided pleasantly enough with our little coterie, composed as it was with Northern girls, whom we could not regard but foes; Northern papers, drunken with rage and victory, teemed with anathemas against Jefferson Davis and his confederates.

The change of simple food of the confederacy to bonbons made havoc of my little boy, who was now sick in bed. Mrs. Rice, with her sweet mother kindness, weighed and gave him medicine from her own chest. 'You should have medical advice, if you have no money to pay for it. I have, and you can repay me in the future, if you have it, if not, it will make no difference.'

I had a few dollars left. I sought the Captain and asked for a physician as we were nearing Clarksville. Upon learning of the nature of the illness, he gave a cordial, made by himself; and soon my baby was healed.

One more ordeal awaited us — the searching of our baggage; with this closed, the conflicts of my trip, except the annoying conduct of the negro boy, he was utterly demoralized by his new-found Yankee friends and was so dazed and beyond my control, I dropped him at Nashville to cast his lot with them.

After he was grown, one day he rapped on my door with the greeting that he had come to live with Marse Albert.

In Nashville we were kindly entertained by old friends, Henry Vaughn, a hospitable breakfast and a carriage to send us home but a few miles away across the river. Passing the plantation of my uncle, whose blacks still remained there as usual though he was absent in the South, the excited halloes of welcome and delight that met us, gave me the last taste of old slavery days.

Home at last we dined on Tennessee fried chicken and Aunt Dinah's hoecake, ruin and desolation about us; but we looked forward never more backward, 'There was life in the old land yet.'"

Governor Hawkin's Home and Law Office, Huntingdon, Tenn.

Governor Alvin and Justina Ott Hawkins and Family.

Justina M. Ott Hawkins

B. 1826 — M. 1847 — D. 1901

"A Beautiful Life"

Wife of Governor Alvin Hawkins

"Alvin," said Ella Hawkins, "my sister from Murfreesboro will be downstairs in a few minutes. I want you to meet her."

Alvin sat down, rocking in one of the big, old chairs in the Isaac Hawkins' parlor and thinking of the new case of the horse theif coming up in court on the morrow.

He heard the footsteps and swishing of silk. There in the doorway in orange taffeta stood a beautiful dream, his sister-in-law's sister, Justina Ott.

"This is the one I've been seeing in my dreams," thought Alvin: "Beautiful as a Dream."

Days later:

It was a lot easier to be with Justina, strolling in the vineyard with the succulent, purple grapes overhead or in the gardens of his younger brother, than in the courtroom with horse thieves.

Justina, who possessed a beautiful face and a graceful figure, with a sweet retiring, modest demeanor, decided she liked what she saw of this big, handsome gentleman with his gift of persuasion in his profession of law; he was losing no time in winning this case of hearts.

It was August 17, 1847. . .at the appointed time, the beautiful strains of the organ announced the coming of the wedding party. Justina Ott became Mrs. Alvin Hawkins, and according to fate, would one day be a First Lady of the State of Tennessee.

Alvin found his beautiful dream Justina a strong, uplifting character, overflowing with the virtues of young woman hood.

He was five years older than Justina; he was born in Bath County, Kentucky, December 2, 1821. His father was a farmer and a gunsmith. He came to Tennessee from Kentucky in 1826; he first settled in Maury County and later Carroll County. His grandfather, John M. Hawkins, was of early English descent, whose ancestors were prominent in the history of England. Polly Ralston Hawkins was the mother of thirteen sons. Alvin was her eldest, but all were prominent in the public affairs of Tennessee.

Such mothers were rare. The physical events were many, but she found time to help her children with their education. Alvin attended the public schools, such as they were. At eighteen he attended Bethel College; two years later he entered the office of the noted Honorable Benjamin Totton and studied law. After a year, he was admitted to the bar in Huntington and became a partner of his cousin, Isaac R. Hawkins.

In 1843 he opened his own law office. Ten years later he was elected to the Tennessee Legislature, the beginning of his political career, along with raising and educating six children, two growing to manhood, Ernest and Alonzo.

During the time when the war years were brewing, Alvin Hawkins was an uncompromising Union man. He made every effort to keep Tennessee from seceding.

He was formerly a Whig, then a Union man, and ever afterward a Republican.

By proclamation from President Johnson, he was elected to Congress, but was not allowed to serve. He took no active part in that Congressional session but was President of its sessions. In 1864 he was appointed United States Attorney for West Tennessee.

He resigned as U. S. District Attorney in 1865 and was appointed one of the Supreme Justices of Tennessee. The constitution of 1870 displaced him, and he returned to Huntington and resumed his law practice.

Every day scenes acquired a new meaning; it seemed a pleasure to be a devoted family man with Justina and the children, to go fishing in Beaver creek, giving his personal attention to his garden and orchard, attending the Methodist Church where he was one of its laymen.

For ten years he enjoyed private home life; but in 1880, he was elected Governor on the Republican ticket with a majority of votes. He was fifty-five years old when he was inaugurated in 1881, holding office until 1883. Governor Hawkins was a large man with fine personal appearance. As a public speaker, he was forceful, logical, and convincing.

His administration was in the midst of events and associations that besmirched many men. Through all of it, he passed with a clear record, and is a striking example of the fact that public life does not corrupt a patriot.

Ernest Hawkins, who was private secretary during his fathers term of office, had married Lula Mae Cochran. She died leaving a year-old daughter, Love, who was born at a critical period in the history of the state, when education had been interrupted by the War and Reconstruction period. Her grandmother graciously welcomed the child into her home and loving care. Justina had profited her time with Dilworth's speller, the New Testament, learned genders of the nouns, could read and write well for her day. She taught Love at home, and when she entered the public schools of Huntington, she was ready for the fourth grade. She graduated in 1892 and taught school until 1932. In the meantime she had married Olgha Mebane in 1918.

While Governor, Alvin Hawkins and his son Ernest lived among the beautiful antiques in the old Maxwell House Hotel. Justina and the other children stayed home. Hotels were no place for children. Among her own treasured antiques, she kept the home fires burning. She was a woman who placed cultural, spiritual and academic values where they belonged.

Ernest Hawkins married Josephene McCall, a descendant of Revolutionary soldier, John McCall, about 1884. They were the parents of Elnora Childs, Mary Hawkins Edwards, and Helen H. Morford, a past State Regent of the Daughters of the American Revolution.

After the death of Justina, Ex-Governor Hawkins made his home with Dr. Ernest, who was a druggist and his wife Josephine in Huntington. Their oldest boy was a constant companion of his grandfather and young Alvin was also a favorite of his grandfather.

The other surviving son at that time was Alonzo, who had been a law partner of his father. In 1878 he married a Miss Lucy Ramsey, daughter of Doctor and Katherine Kendresh Ramsey in Huntington at the Cumberland Presbyterian Church.

An old, faded love letter from President Martin Van Buren to her mother Katherine is preserved in a Hawkins' family scrap book. Van Buren was called the "Fox of Kinderhook." He was a handsome man who lived at the Van Buren estate, "Linden Wald," at Kinderhook, New York.

Alonzo and Lucy Hawkins had six children. Two little girls, Kitty and Lisa, died in infancy. The four sons were Raymond, Ivan, Gordon, and Landis, who is the only living grandson of Governor Hawkins. He and his wife, Ethel, live in Bowling Green, Kentucky. They have one daughter, Love, and two granddaughters living in Memphis, Tennessee.

Governor Hawkins was stricken with pneumonia at the age of eighty-four. He passed away April 17, 1905. Justina preceded him on June 17, 1901. She was loved for the beauty of her life in its benign home influence on the lives of all who came in contact with her. It was far-reaching in its effect for good, even with her remarkable, retiring nature.

A beautiful woman, strong, real, and uplifting, her seventy years were jeweled with kindness and good deeds. She grew up in the Presbyterian Church, but later became a Methodist. She was a strong Christian character and a tower of strength to others.

In her obituary are these words:

"A beautiful life has closed; but its influence will live on while the sainted soul is at the feet of the great White Throne, reaping the rewards of those who love Him and keep His word."

The 1850 Home of Julia Peete Bate, Huntsville, Alabama.

Julia Peete Bate

courtesy of
Julian Mastin, Fort Worth, Texas

Julia Peete Bate

B. 1856

Wife of Governor William B. Bate

"A Harbinger of good fortune through William Brimage Bate's life:"

Huntsville, Alabama, is a town of old pillared mansions, blue sky, red earth, green grass, and white magnolia blossoms, where Julia Peete became the bride of William Brimage Bate, a future Tennessee Governor, on January 17, 1856.

Julia was the daughter of Susan Pope and Colonel Samuel Peete, who were married in Madison County, Alabama, on August 6, 1833. Susan Ann Pope was the daughter of Eliza Wyatt and Benjamin Pope of Delaware. Julia's great-Wyatt and Benjamin Pope of Delaware. Julia's great-grandfather Pope was a Lieutenant-Colonel in the Revolutionary Army.

Mrs. Peete died when Julia was three years old and her baby Mary was five months old. They were reared by the grand-parents Pope and three aunts. When Julia was sixteen, she lived with her aunt Eliza Mastin at the Mastin Mansion in Huntsville, Alabama; Julia was sent to school in Philadelphia and on her return home, her father gave her a handsome residence in Hunstville.

Julia was a woman of much intellectual culture, fine social character, with a face fascinating by sweetness and innocence of expression. She was much like her father, Samuel Peete, a lawyer of great ability and success. He practiced in Alabama until he was near fifty years old. He had come to Huntsville from Sussex County, Virginia, in 1819 and owned a large plantation. They brought their servants with them, who were greatly attached to the family. Colonel Peete was a graduate of William and Mary College, very refined and dignified. He was well-versed in literature.

William B. Bate always regarded Julia as a most unusual lady, even before she became a First Lady of Tennessee. And his marriage by far the happiest and most fortunate event of his life.

His attachment to and reverence for his attractive Julia was unbounded, and their forty-nine years of married life was very beautiful and unbroken. Governor Bate, by reason of his natural affection, often referred to the date, January 17th, as his "lucky day" for on that date he married the beautiful Julia under the orange blossoms, and twenty years later one of the four daughters was happily married. On January 17, 1885, the result of his second elevation as Governor of Tennessee, was declared by the General Assembly, and on January 17th, 1893, and also 1899 he was elected to the Senate. He liked to think that his happy marriage was a harbinger of good fortune through life.

William B. Bate was reared at Bledsoe Lick, now known as Castalian Springs, a locality eight miles east of Gallatin, Tennessee. His father, James Bate, died when he was fifteen years ago. He began his education at Rural Academy, a log house which burned and was replaced by Bledsoe Academy, where he continued his education with alteration of work on the farm until he was eighteen. He went as second clerk on the steamboat Saladin, plying between Nashville and New Orleans; here he showed his heroism by saving the lives of several passengers who had been thrown into the Mississippi River by the collision of two boats. He enlisted in the Mexican War and was the first Tennessean to reach enemy country. On his return to Castalian Springs, he established the "Tenth Legion," and became editor of a Democratic paper.

At the age of twenty-three, he entered politics as a state legislator. He was active in the support of a bill for the betterment of public schools.

In 1852 he graduated from Lebanon Law School and became a member of the Gallatin Bar. Then in 1854 he was elected Attorney General of the Nashville District. By 1860 he was a Brickenridge-Lane elector.

The day after the firing of the first gun at Fort Sumpter in the War Between the States, he entered and mustered as a private soldier in a company being raised at Gallatin, Tennessee. It became Company I, Second Tennessee Infantry of the Confederate States; he was made Captain and later elected Colonel of his regiment.

In 1861, Colonel Bate was a devoted family man in the society of his wife and the little girls; he was very much attached to his home, but left all to offer his life for the cause on the battle field. Four years of battle included Bull Run, Bentonville, and other engagements with the enemy.

The Second Tennessee Infantry became known as one of the crack regiments of the army; it remained with the army of North Virginia during the summer, fall, and winter of 1861-1862. Before the conscript law was enforced, the Infantry re-enlisted and was armed with Minie Rifles—Colonel Bate and his regiment were sent to General Albert Sidney Johnson, whose headquarters were south of the Tennessee River. Five hundred of these men whose unexpired furloughs were in their pockets voluntarily joined the army near Corinth, Mississippi, charged through the murderous cross-fire and Colonel Bate had his leg broken by a minie ball.

The field of Shiloh was strangely fatal to William B. Bate; his brother Humphrey Bate, Captain Tyre his brother-in-law, and a cousin James McDaniel were all killed, and a cousin Doctor Humphrey Bate was severly wounded. Three killed and two wounded, a family scene perhaps without parallel in the annals of the War Between the States.

During a lull in the battle, the two brothers met; as they were in conversation, Colonel William B. asked brother Humphrey for a light from his cigar. In the act of lighting the cigar, Capt. Humphrey received the wound from which he died. Colonel William B. Bate was often seen with a cigar, but never lighted one again as long as he lived.

In this battle the bones and arteries of William B. Bate's left leg were severed. He refused to have his leg amputated—refused to take any drug that would cause him to lose conciousness for fear the Doctors would amputate. He kept a pistol under his pillow, if they should offer to do so.

He was removed in a wagon to a point within the Confederate lines, and his ever faithful Julia met him on the way and accompanied him. She had found a copy of "Gil Blas;" it furnished the wounded General great satisfaction to have his belove wife sit beside him and read to him from the book about doctors. He lingered for over four months before he could use crutches.

On crutches he offered his services in the field. He was promoted to Brigadier General on Octobrr 3, 1862, by President Jefferson Davis. He was not able to be present at the battle of Perryville and Murfreesboro. At the battle of Hoover's Gap on June 3, 1863, he rode up and down the line during the time of fighting, using his crutch instead of a sword and calling his men to fight to the last.

It was after the battle of Shiloh that President Davis toured the "Field of Death," trees torn, the dead lying everywhere, a horse dead with officer's trappings on. He asked, "Whose horse?"

The guide replied, "Brigadier General Bate's of Tennessee."

Three hundred yards there was a little black mare with officer's trappings, again the question, "Whose horse?" and again the reply, "It is Brigadier General Bate's of Tennessee."

When they reached the front, where Bate's Brigade took the Federal works on Sunday, they saw the mouse-colored horse lying close to the breastworks, again the question, "Whose horse?" and for the third time, the guide replied," Brigadier

General Bate's of Tennessee."

President Davis remarked, "The General must be a dashing officer."

The Eufaula battery of General Bate's brigade is said to have fired the first and last guns of the battle of Chicamauga. After the battle, he was offered the rank of "Major General of Cavalry," which he refused, but accepted the rank of Major General of Infantry. He was also offered the Governorship to succeed Governor Isham G. Harris, but he quickly replied, "I shall accept no civic honor as long as an enemy desecrates Tennessee soil."

After the war, he returned with Julia and the girls to his old home at Castalian Springs in Sumner County. He was almost a cripple with little money, just the old farm. After some months, he opened a law office in Nashville. His large earnings paid off $30,000 debts for persons unable to pay their security debts to him before the war, and he was able to give his family a comfortable home and educate the two living daughters, Susie and Maizie; Jennie Bate died at the age of fifteen, and Bell at the age of six.

His law firm had the largest practice in Nashville when he was inaugurated Governor in 1883. During his administration 1883-1887, it is said that it stands in public estimation as one of the most honest, competent, and thorough administrations in the entire history of the state.

William B. Bate lived in the age of great railway and steamship transportation, telegraph and telephone, War with Mexico, The War Between the States, the Reconstruction Period, also when the South was looked upon as the "Bloody Shirt Period."

"He was a child of Tennessee's bosom, nurtured in his boyhood on her generous lap; he served her in his early youth and ripe manhood, mingled in her strife—He loved her rocks and rills, her woods and templed hills."

He was opposed to rudeness. After the war he was in a Federal office in Gallatin, Tennessee; a blustery Federal agent for the government called a Sumner County lady, who was talking about a war claim, a liar. Out of a clear blue sky the fiery, bluster, fighter Captain received a stunning blow on the cheek from Bate's open hand, with the invitation, "To help himself if he did not like it."

Governor Bate was a simple, plain man devoid of conceit, unusually blessed in his home relationship; while Governor, they lived on Russell Street in East Nashville from 1883-1887; here he found his happiest hours around the family hearthstone with Julia and the girls.

On one occasion, when some public ceremonial compliment was paid to Julia Peete Bate, Governor Bate responded, "I thank you for the compliment to my wife, and I challenge any man t feel more kindly and lovingly to the beautiful and charming women of Alabama than I do. You will pardon the personality when I say that in the long ago, and it seems but yesterday, it was in the beautiful city of Huntsville, Alabama, nestling at the foot of Mont Sano—overlooking a valley that smiled with. delight that I was given under the orange blossoms, one of all the sweet girl flowers that grew and blossomed in the refined and cultivated social gardens; she has been for more than forty years my companion and comfort through war and peace, through weal and woe, through good and evil fortune, and although she has gone through motherhood, and grandmother hood, still she is my cheerful companion and my faithful comforter. So I feel that I can challenge with impunity the right of any man who was not born under Alabama's aegis and who does not live on Alabama soil to feel nearer and dearer to Alabama than I."

Socially William B. Bate made little distinction between Democrates and Republicans, for both parties held him in high esteem and personal respect.

As a Senator, with a severe cold, he deemed it a pleasure and sense of duty to attend the second inauguration of Theodore Roosevelt on March 4, 1905. He sat an hour on the cold platform in front of the Capitol. He returned to the Ebbitt House where he and Julia resided.

On March 9, 1905, he died in the morning. He conversed wife his beloved wife—on his death bed he recited the Lord's Prayer. He said, "Julia, take me back to Tennessee; I want to be buried at Mount Olivet, with my kindred."

MEMORIAL ADDRESS OF MR. STANLEY OF KENTUCKY

"I could write upon the tomb of William B. Bate with truth and sincerity the motto of the Prince of Wales and the dead Bohemian King, 'I serve.' One single incident in his life portrays in rare and radiant colors his flawless devotion to duty. Wounded at Shiloh, his horse shot from under him at Chicamauga, wounded again in Atlanta, ragged, emaciated, racked with pain, with pale face and thin lips, you see this heroic figure on his crutches amid his companions in arms. It was at this time that there came to him the tempting offer of civic honors, "Governor of his state," of ease and wealth and fame. Unsolicited, a grateful and trusting people laid at his feet the chief magistracy of a sovereign state. The old soldier was immovable. Setting his face like a flint toward the foe, who he knew was destined to ultimate victory, he took in his manly arms his wretched companions and sent back to those who would tempt him with office of power that message which shall thrill Tennesseans in the centuries to come:

'I shall accept no civic honor as long as an enemy of Tennessee desecrates her soil."

After the wishes of Governor Bate had been carried out, "Take me back to Tennessee," on the train to Nashville, Julia remarked to a friend, "In all the years of travel, this is the first free ride on a train as a servant to his state and country that William Bate has ever had. He always paid his own transportation wherever he went."

Julia was now seventy years old. She did not need to live alone. When Mazie and Thomas Mastin returned to their home in Grandview, Texas, she went along to make her home with them and the four grandchildren.

She told the children of her early life in Huntsville, Alabama, living in the antibellum house, her life in Philadelphia, how she met William B. Bate while visiting a girl friend in Tennessee, that the Bate family were originally from Yorkshire, England, the great, great, great, great grandmother came in the colonial days, and first lived in Bertie County, North Carolina, Sarah Legate, and died at the age of one hundred in the year 1800. William's grandfather Col. Humphrey Bate came to Tennessee in 1803. His wife was Elizabeth Brimage of Bertie County, North Carolina, one of her five children was James Henry who married Amanda Weatherford in 1825, and William Brimage was born October 7, 1826."

Julia Bate was #48912, a member of the Daughters of the American Revolution through her ancestor great grandfather Charles Pope, born 1748, in Smyrna, Delaware and died in Savanah, Georgia, in 1803. His wife was Jane Stokely.

Julia was a devout Methodist and nothing except extreme sickness kept her from driving her gentle old "Smithz" hitched to the buggy every Sunday morning to Grandview Methodist Church, where she taught the Julia Bate Bible Class, which still has the name. She gave this church its first Pipe Organ. She was a woman of fine Christian qualities; she had read her Bible through many times and could quote with authority any verse. In her late years, she had cataracts that made reading difficult for her. Maud Ackers of Grandview came frequently and read to her.

Julia's grandson, Attorney Julian Mastin of FortWorth Texas, says he adored his dear grandmother Julia Peete Bate and his recollections go back in happy repose, "after Sunday School was over at the Presbyterian Church he would hasten over to the Methodist Church for the short sermon, then sit beside his beloved grandmother who would let him drive old "Smitz" home. He would unharness and feed the horse and with his gun and dog be out in the field as his father and mother and the two brothers and sister were singing the last hymn at the Presbyterian Church. The real magnet that drew him to the Methodist Church was grandmother Julia."

"Julia Peete Bate will be remembered as kind, reverent, thoughtful, with grace and beauty and like her father Samuel Peete, a very cultured and beloved person. She was never known to raise her voice or to speak an unkind word about anyone."

Robin Roost, Home of Gov. Bob Taylor, Johnson City.

courtesy of
Sue Brown

Bob Taylor Birthplace.

courtesy of
Lelia Taylor

Sarah Baird Taylor.

courtesy of
Atty. Robert L. Taylor

Sarah Baird, Alice Hill, Mayme St. John

Wives of Robert Love Taylor

When Bob Taylor was Governor, 1887-1891 - 1897-1899, he was accused of using his pardoning power to excess.

Sam Jones criticized him one time in one of his sermons for abusing his pardoning power. Bob's reply to Sam was, "If it hadn't been for the pardoning power of God Almighty, you, Sam Jones, would have been in Hell long ago."

A Governor's pardoning power or use of it rarely ever hurts him with the people. The masses of people believe in pardon.

Sarah Baird had been the wife of Bob Taylor for nine years when he became Governor in 1887. He was twenty-eight years old when he brought Sarah as a bride to Happy Valley from Asheville, North Carolina.

That same year he was admitted to practice law. Young Bob, in his first venture into politics, defeated the Republican nominee, Major August H. Pettyjohn, of Greenville in 1887. Pettyjohn was a Civil War hero and a leading G.O.P. figure at the time.

Taylor's victory was attributed largely to a split in the G.O.P. ranks—led by his older brother, Alfred Alexander Taylor.

Bob Taylor was the son of Emaline Haynes, granddaughter of George Haynes and Miss McInruff. Her parents were Rhoda Taylor and David Haynes. His father, Honorable Nathaniel Taylor, was the son of James P. Taylor and Mary Carter Taylor. His great great grandfather was Nathaniel Taylor, and he was a son of Andrew Taylor from Rockbridge County, Virginia.

Bob Taylor's brothers were James P., Alfred A., and Hugh Taylor; the two sisters were Eva Jobe and Rhoda Taylor Reeves.

Mrs. Emaline Taylor was a deeply religious woman and led a pious life, free-hearted, and a river of charity of kindness to her nighbors, with sympathy for the sick and unfortunate. As an entertainer in her home, she was incomparable.

The home was a favorite gathering place for young and old, and a resort for all the preachers of all denominations, who greatly enjoyed the musical feasts with Mrs. Taylor at the organ and the fried chicken Mrs. Taylor and her cooks so richly and abundantly supplied. Robert Love Taylor, when asked where he was born, replied, "In the mountains of East Tennessee, which

213

are so tall you can stand on the top and tickle the feet of the angels."

One of the beautiful features Sarah Baird found in her husband was that his love and charity began at home. No man ever loved his family more devotedly, and according to his means and the dictates of prudence, provided for them more amply and abundantly than Bob Taylor.

Although a layman, making no formal or conspicious profession of religion, yet his whole life was a practical sermon and a beautiful example of deeds of charity, compassion, and love, like his mother toward his fellowman. He loved his neighbor as himself and by the same token, we cannot but believe he loved God supremely.

Bob Taylor was struggling with poverty as editor of "The Johnson City Comet" in 1884. Old brother Barlow was an active member of the Methodist Church and a great friend of Bob Taylor. He was not too highly educated. He was a unique character, saying things in quaint and striking manner.

One morning in the darkest hours of Bob's struggle, with the wolf barking at his door, Sarah was indignant at the loud rapping at the door in the cold, wee, small hour in the morning. Bob, in his long handles, unlatched the door, thrust his head out and greeted Mr. Barlow in the most cordial manner as if four o'clock was a nice hour for callers.

"Good morning, Robert," said Mr. Barlow. "I hope you are right pert this morning and ready for your rashions—if you've got on hands."

"Robert, I'm in distressful need of help, and I thought I'd come around and see if I couldn't arrange with you on a little matter of finance. That's a big meetin' startin' day after tomorrow in the Crab Orchard, up in Carter County, and I must be thar; but I find I haven't enough money to take me thar on the Narrow Gage Railroad; Robert, I need three dollars, and I have come to you for that amount. Can you furnish it?"

"Why, Uncle Barlow," said Bob. "I haven't a red cent to save me from hanging. If I had, you know you could get it, if I had to hang."

"I'se a feared this mout be the case with you this mornin', Robert, and so I'd take time by the forelock and come and give you notice. I don't have to be thar til tomorry morning, and I'll give you til then to get it up. Now Robert, don't fail to have that money. If you do the Lord's work is gyne to suffer."

"I'll do my best," said Bob. And he did, for he went and borrowed the money from a friend.

Robert L. Taylor became U. S. Pension Agent and moved to Knoxville in 1885. No jollier man sat around the fireside.

214

With Sarah quietly knitting, the boarders, Nathan Gregg, Frank Dosser, and Judge C. J. St. John at the end of the day listened to Bob's funny stories and his singing to the children, Em and Ret, sitting on his knee.

Later they were the parents of Kathyrn, David Haynes, and Robert L.

Mrs. Kathyrn Taylor (Mrs. Hilsman) said of her mother that Sarah Baird was a woman of beauty, warmth, and charm; and of all the things written about her father, her mother had never been given the credit for keeping the home fires burning and a woman of great strength of character, loved by all who knew her.

Mrs. Hilsman Taylor was a refined lady, gracious, friendly with the most charming, lovely voice.

In 1886 Robert Taylor was urged to make the race for Governor on the Democratic ticket. The republicans had nominated his brother, Alf A. Taylor.

The Convention met and wired to know if he would accept the nomination. He wired his answer:

"A seedy individual once appeared at my mother's home and said, 'Emarline, if you don't believe I can carry a ham home, just try me.' " signed Robert L. Taylor.

That night he received a telegram saying that he had received two-thirds majority vote.

During the famous war of the Roses, Republican Alf, took the red and Bob, the white. You could tell a man's politics by the color of rose he wore while the brothers rode together, slept together, and discussed the tariff and the navy and National aid to education and purely U.S. affairs; about the only state question was the penitentiary lease system. The brothers attracted more attention than any two candidates in America.

This ended it for the Democrats. Bob won as Governor. He was elected three times, serving from 1887 to 1891 and 1897 to 1899.

After the death of Sarah Baird, the children lived in the home of Alf and Jennie Anderson Taylor, Governor Bob married Alice Hill of Tuscaloosa, Alabama, a marriage which was of short duration.

In 1904 he married Mamie L. St. John, the daughter of Noah St. John of Marion, Virginia. Her father was a widely-known lawyer and member of the Virginia General Assembly.

Mrs. Taylor lived in Washington after the death of Senator Taylor in 1912. She was one of the founders of the Congressional Club, a Washington organization made up of wives of Congress members. She spent her last years in Bristol. She died in August, 1962, in an Elizabethton nursing home. She had one sister, Mrs.

Toe Thomas of Bluff City.

Mrs. Taylor was a cousin to Bob and Alf Taylor and also Lorena Butler, wife of Governor John I. Cox.

Doctor W. S. Neighbors at the last rites for Governor Bob Taylor, said:

"If you never knew Bob Taylor in his home, much of the best and most remarkable in him you never knew. No one set of words can adaquately describe him here. He was the liveliest of the lively, the greatest of the great, the saddest of the sad, and sickest of the sick, according to the conditions that obtained at home.

If every member of his family was happy and strong, he was the jolliest boy there—into every kind of prank, a perfect child among the children—but, if any member of his family was sick, the whole scene was changed. He was the sickest of the sick: I have seen the dear sensitive soul walk the floor in agony, face all pinched and drawn over the suffering of any member of his household. I have seen him again when the Doctor had announced that the patient was out of danger, stir the whole household with laughter almost before the tears of grief were gone from his face."

Church was sacred to Bob Taylor. He would never lecture in a Church. "No, no," he would say, "Let me speak in the warehouse, or a barn, or out under the spreading oaks, but not there. That is the house of God."

A few days before he died, he was in a friend's house. The children gathered around him and asked him to sing for them. He sang several little songs that amused them. Then he said, "Children, I want to sing one more song." He then tenderly sang, "Jesus, Lover of My Soul, Let me to thy Bosom fly."

"Senator Taylor, this state's standard bearer, fell in the thick of the fight, the other day, with his face to the foe. O! Tennessee! Thou who didst give to this Nation such a gifted son, hast the right to march in the front rank of states."

Life of Bob Taylor, "Our Bob"

Governor John Price Buchanan

Used the Upper Story Porch as a Platform to

Speak to His Friends and Neighbors

After the convention of 1890 that had nominated *HIM*.

The home is shown as it looked before it was razed. It was built in 1873. By the young Buchanan, former Confederate soldier, and there he took his wife, Frances McGill to live.

Miss Rebecca Buchanan recalled the night in 1890: "A string of carriages bearing a crowd of gay people, some shouting and others blowing horns, traveled up the hill toward the two story frame house set in a clump of trees, where John Price Buchanan, Rutherford county farmer and former Confederate soldier, began to speak to his friends in a few simple words of thanks. He was tired from the long days of battle in the State Democratic Convention that had chosen him as the party's nominee for governor."

Since 1873, John and Frances McGill Buchanan had lived at this home, which they had christened, The Big Creek Stock Farm.

John Buchanan born in Williamson county in 1847, had volunteered for the Confederate army at the age of sixteen and had served in Alabama under General Nathan Bedford Forrest. Four years after the close of the war he went to Rutherford County and married Frances whose father was an older Confederate Soldier and landowner, on the McGill property they built the home.

The Farmers Alliance, with John Buchanan as its president had dominated the State Democratic Convention of 1890. Buchanan was nominated after several days deadlock between four candidates- Capt. Josiah Patterson of Memphis, whose son Malcolm R. Patterson later became governor, Judge John M. Taylor of West Tennessee, Col. Jere Baxter of Nashville and Buchanan.

Miss Rebecca who was fifteen years old at the time, recalled that her father was introduced by former Governor Bob Taylor and that the latter made reference to the "hayseeder" who was to suceed him.

Governor Buchanan was defeated by Peter Turney in 1892, after withdrawing from the Democratic Convention and making the race as an independent.

He returned to his farm where he remained until he moved to Murfreesboro. He never again was active in politics, but retained an interest in state and National affairs.

Home of Governor John P. Buchanan, 1873, Murfreesboro, Tenn.

Frances McGill Buchanan.

courtesy of
E. Buchanan Worley

Frances Louise McGill Buchanan

B. 1848 — M. 1873 — D. 1927

Wife of Governor John Price Buchanan

At the inauguration of Governor John Price Buchanan, January, 1891, Frances Louise McGill Buchanan, with the three older children, Rebecca, age fifteen; Thomas, and John attended the ceremony in the Hall of Representatives in Nashville.

Dressed in a black grenadine dress trimmed with jet beads, with a black cape and little black hat trimmed with a taffeta bow, a black bird wing, an ostrich plume fastened with a small black velvet ribbon and a tiny brilliant ornament, Frances sat with the spectators.

Living on a farm on Manchester pike, nine miles from Murfreesboro, one of the servants had driven them to Murfreesboro in the two horse surrey on the day before, where they took a train to Nashville. On arriving there, they went to the Maxwell House and spent the night with Mr. Buchanan.

Mrs. Buchanan was the daughter of Amanda Norman and James McGill of Rutherford County, Tennessee. She was born October 30, 1848.

She attended the country schools of Rutherford County, growing to young womanhood. She was sent to a girl's school at Woodbury, Tennessee. Here she met the young farmer from Williamson County.

He was a member of a family famous in the history of the state. His parents were Margaret Sample and Thomas Buchanan. His paternal great great grandparents were Major John and Sallie Buchanan, the pioneer companion of James Roberson in the settlement of Nashville in 1779 and the founder of the celebrated Buchanan Station in 1782.

John Price Buchanan received a good common school education. He became a prosperous farmer and stock raiser of Rutherford County and was one of the few farmers to become a Governor of Tennessee. He was elected to the State Legislature in 1886 and again in 1888, a leading spirit in protecting the farmer profits as President of the Farmers' Alliance.

The farmers had hope of the unreasonable and impossible change in the management of State affairs when he became Governor at the close of Bob Taylor's administration.

He was unable to do much for the farmers, but was credited for the passage of a secondary school law including the study of Tennessee History and Civics.

In 1891, public school teaching did not go higher than the primary level. His administration was marked by labor unrest and reform. He was responsible for granting Confederate pensions.

While her husband was Governor, Mrs. Buchanan spent part-time in Nashville with her husband; the other part she spent at the farm home, looking after the management of the stock, the planting, and harvesting, and caring for her eight children.

The four boys were Thomas, John Price, Jr., Robert Norman, and James McGill. The four girls were Margaret David, Susan Mathews, Frances Louise, who is now Mrs. Webb of Murfreesboro. She attended public schools and Ward Belmont; Rebecca Jane, fondly called Janie, died at the age of eighty-nine, on June 23, 1965. She was a beloved instructor at Middle State University at Murfreesboro, Tennessee. A Club was named in her honor, "The Buchanan Dramatic Club." She was educated in the best of schools in Nashville. She was a teacher at Bethel College, McKenzie, Tennessee, Belmont College in Nashville, before going to M.T.S.U.

Mrs. Louise Webb says of her other sisters and brothers: "Thomas, a Cumberland Presbyterian minister, was killed by lightning in 1908. John Price died in 1958. Margaret died while a student at Soule College. Susan died in 1928, the wife of Reverend Cliff M. Epps. Robert Norman is a Doctor, living near Gallatin, Tennessee."

In 1926, the Buchanans moved from the farm to Murfreesboro where Mrs. Buchanan died November 30, 1927, Reverend Kenan Mathews, a nephew, and a missionary from Japan conducted the funeral services held in the Buchanan home.

At the Cumberland Presbyterian Church, Ex-Governor Buchanan could be seen sitting in his "rocking chair" at Sunday services. He lived until May 14, 1930, and is buried in Murfreesboro, Tennessee.

Mrs. Webb says, "Mother had no hobbies; she made the children's clothes and did her shopping in Murfreesboro and Nashville. She entertained many guests at Nashville and at our farm home. She took the children to Sunday School and Church regularly. She was interested in all phases of her Church. She belonged to the Missionary Circle. She was church pianist, a Bible teacher. She was an Elder and a clerk of the Sessions in Mount Tabor Church for over forty years. Mrs. Buchanan was baptized in the Cumberland Presbyterian Church, and in early life became a faithful member, at every stage of her existence she was pervaded by a deep religious sentiment and the Bible was her constant companion. For her neighborly and charitable

221

nature, she was proverbial.''

This estimable lady was in life more truly than put into words, a wife, a mother, a First Lady, and a Christian — self was forgotten and the good of others alone remembered. She was esteemed and loved by all who knew her.

Spot where Governor Peter Turney was born, Jasper, Tenn.

Casandra Garner Turney
Hannah Ferguson Graham Turney
Wives of Governor Peter Turney

Casandra Garner was the first wife of Governor Peter Turney. She was the daughter of Elizabeth Wadlington of Kentucky, and Thomas A. Garner of a North Carolina family. He was a wealthy farmer in Franklin County and a representative of Tennessee State Legislature. He died in 1881 at the age of eighty-five.

Casandra's grandfather, Thomas Garner Sr., was a pioneer settler of Franklin County. He died at the age of ninety-five, a well-read man of a strong, quick mind, aspiring to nothing more than responsibility and industry.

Casandra's life span was not like her father's or grandfather's ; it was of short duration.

On June 10, 1851, when she became the bride of the future Governor Peter Turney, she was a beautiful fifteen year old girl. He was a young lawyer in his father's law office in Winchester Tennessee, where they lived until her death March 28, 1857, leaving three children, Thomas Turney, who died March 4, 1874, Virginia and Hopkins L. Turney.

It was three years later on April 27, 1860, that Peter Turney married the twenty-four year old Hannah Graham of Marion County. She was born in 1835 in Jackson County, the daughter of Aletha Roberts of Davidson County and John Graham, who came from Pennsylvania to Tennessee. He became a large land owner located on the Tennessee River near South Pittsburg in Marion County.

Peter Turney and Hannah Graham were the parents of nine children; twin daughters Teresa and Aletha, Samuel, Peter Jr., Lowndes, James, Hannah, Woodson and Miller France. Mrs. Turner was related to the Buchanans, of Davidson County, and the Ridleys of Rutherford County.

Judge Peter Turney was the son of Teresa Frances, who was the daughter of Hannah Henry and Miller Frances. She was born in Rhea County in 1809. She died in 1879; a woman of ability and mind to manage the farm while her husband Hopkins L. Turney, Legislator, Congressman, and United States Senator, was away from home.

Hopkins Turney was born in Smith County in 1797; he was married in 1826 and died August 1, 1857. He was in the War of 1812.

Peter Turney, a man who came from sturdy ancestry became Governor of Tennessee in 1893, serving until 1897.

Hannah Graham had been dead five years. The twin girls Teresa and Aletha were hostesses during their father's administration. A very dear friend of Miss Emily Mosley of Winchester who recalls many remeniscences of their days together in the past.

During Governor Turney's administration the Southern Railway began operation, a lease system of prisoners was changed, and nine thousand acres of coal land were purchased in Morgan county. A new penitentiary was built at Brushy Mountain and the first coal was mined in Tennessee.

Hannah Graham was attractive, well built; a good-looking girl. She spent her early girlhood on the farm with her brothers; Hope, John, and Dr. Michael Graham, Her three sisters were Wilma Graham, Martha, who married J. W. Reynolds, and Nancy, who married Captain W. E. Donaldson, a prominent lawyer of Jasper, Tennessee. He served as captain in the Confederate army under his brother-in-law Peter Turney's First Tennessee Regiment.

Mrs. James E. Thorogood of Sewannee, Tennessee tells of the ardent Confederate Peter Turney who formed the "First Tennessee Regiment" and was already in Virginia when Governor Harris proclaimed that Tennessee's ties with the United States were dissolved.

It was the first day of May, 1861. Colonel Turney was on his horse at the head of his regiment ready to give the signal to march for Decherd from Winchester. The regiment was to entrain for Virginia. A runner dashed across the square and rushed to the Colonel with a note in his hand. Turner read it, threw back his head and laughed. It was a summons from Aunt Annie Finch, a fierce secessionist that lived on the Tullahoma Road. The note to Colonel Turney read: "Peter - march your men here before you go to war with them. I want to sing them a song."

Colonel Turney gave the command. The regiment wheeled and followed its leader out the Tullahoma Road. Word ran through the ranks that they were marching out to Aunt Annie's to have her serenade them. They whooped in glee. Followed by carriages full of Winchester citizens, they reached the old colonial house among the pines.

' Aunt Annie hobbled out to meet the boys, her old eyes burning with excitement. She had her platform ready; two boxes and a chair rested precariously on the top. The soldiers filled the yard and an expectant hush fell.

"Peter," Aunt Annie quavered, "you had better come and help me up—and then you had better hold me, too; I might fall." Colonel Turney climbed up and threw a steadying hand around

her. She cleared her throat and in her ancient reedy voice sang:
> "Hail Columbia, happy land,
> Hail ye heroes, heaven born band."

"That's all I know, Peter."

Turney lifted the old lady down. His soldiers cheered madly. Aunt Annie kissed the Colonel. Turney gave the command, and the regiment marched off where they saw service on many of the bloody, storm-rent fields of the South. Turney led his regiment to victory. He fought in the battles of Seven Pines, the Second Battle of Manassas, Cedar Run, Harper's Ferry, Antietam, Sharpsburg and Fredericksburg.

Colonel Turney was acting brigadier-general, after the death blow to Hatton at Seven Pines. At Fredericksburg on December 13, 1862, he received an almost fatal wound, when his fine horse, Tom, saved the day for the Confederate forces as well as the life of Colonel Peter Turney.

Stationed at the weakest point for the Confederate defense, for the lay of the land as well as the protection of heavy wooded land favored the Union attack, the first assault of the day's fighting was made against Archer's brigade of which Turney was in command. A flank was broken in the first attack; Turney rallied his forces and made a difficult flank-to-flank charge, checking and driving out Union assaulters under General John Gibbon. In the midst of this charge, a slug of lead struck Colonel Turney in the mouth, passed through his throat, taking half his tongue. The slug barely missed the jugular vein and lodged in the left side of his neck. He was flung from his horse and lay unconscious. The counter charge wavered and Turney's men fell back. The riderless Tom followed the soldiers in their retreat. The Union troops pressed forward eagerly. Then Turney's horse, stopped and neighed loudly, as if sensing disaster, turned and galloped back to where his master lay. The Tennesseans, seeing gallant "old Tom" going back into action, rallied, followed him and drove off the attack, making old Tom a deciding factor in the defeat of the Federal army at Fredericksburg.

Peter Turney was taken up in a blanket by four of his soldiers. An exploding shell wounded and killed all four and the Colonel was dropped heavily to the ground. After that an order was given to let him alone and take no more risks, but Sam Estill, a comrade from Winchester, crawled out under fire and turned him over, saving him from choking on teeth and blood.

Later he was taken to Field Hospitals, but the slug was too close to the jugular vein for surgeons to operate. As soon as he was able, he was sent home to be nursed by his mother and wife Hannah.

By the spring of 1863, he had gained strength and reported for service. He was sent south to a more favorable climate and soon was given command of troops at Lake City Florida. Hannah and the children followed him south to Monticello, Florida. While they were residing here, their home was burned by the Federals under General Rosecrans, enroute to Chattanooga after the battle of Murfreesboro.

A detachment of Federal cavalry rode up to the Turney house, which was tended by Negro servants, slaves of the family. The leader questioned old Aunt Sally Turney, who had nursed Peter to manhood and lived to be 120 years old, "Who lives here?"

"Dis heah is Colonel Turney's house," Aunt Sally eyed him sullenly.

"Where is Colonel Turney?" the officer demanded.

"He gone souf to fight the Yankees down deah," she said frowning.

"How many men in the family?" Sally was becoming aroused.

"Dey is jest three," she responded proudly and austerely, "all in de army—and ole mis' (Turney's mother) says she wish to Gawd huh had thirty—and all of 'em a fighting de Yankees."

They burned the house with all its contents. Today the remains can be seen near Cowan, Tennessee.

Turney's First Tennessee surrendered at Appomattox. It was less than a hundred of the boys that returned at the close of the war.

Peter, Hannah, and the children returned to Winchester without means except for a house and lot. He resumed his law practice and attended the Protestant Episcopal church and the masonic lodge which he joined in 1857. He was also a Knight of Pythias and a Knight of Honor.

Turney remained dangerously ill from his war wound. It was obvious that he was being seriously poisioned from it, although he had been taken to the best surgeons all over the south. All refused to operate and extract the imbedded slug so perilously near the jugular vein. Colonel Turney's brother-in-lae, Dr. Michael Graham, a physician, was entreated to operate by the whole family, but he feared to do so.

Finally, Hannah Graham, Turney's wife became desperate. One night she quietly announced that she intended to extract the slug herself with an instrument of her own. Doctor Graham, declaring that he could not bear to see the Colonel die at the hands of his wife and seeing his sister was determined to do what she planned, operated at once.

227

The Colonel improved at once and lived nearly forty years after the War ended. He practiced law until 1870 when he went on the Supreme Bench at a salary of forty thousand dollars a year.

He became Governor of Tennessee in 1893, serving until 1897. The determined Hannah had lain in the cemetery at Winchester since 1887, remembered for her devotion to family and husband.

Colonial Hall, Home of Governor John C. Brown, Pulaski, Tenn.

courtesy of
Helen Zucarella

Marie Childress Brown McMillin

B. 1865 — D. 1887

Wife of Governor Benton McMillin

Marie Brown, born on October 30, 1865, was the first wife of Governor Benton McMillin. She was the daughter of Governor John C. and Betty Childress Brown of Pulaski, Tennessee. They lived at Colonial Hall where Marie attended the schools in Pulaski and the Episcopal Church, along with her brother John, her sister Daisy, the family artist, and Elizabeth.

Her paternal grandparents were Margaret Smith and Duncan Brown, who were Virginia Revolutionary stock and blue-stocking Presbyterians.

The Browns migrated to Tennessee and settled in Giles County. They were the parents of another Governor, son Neil Brown, who was seventeen years older than John C., Marie's father, a Captain in the Confederate army. He rose to Major General and on to Governor of Tennessee from 1871 to 1875.

Her maternal great grandparents were Elizabeth Whitsett and Joel Childress of Rutherford County, and she was also a great neice of Sarah Childress Polk.

Benton McMillin was born in Monroe County, Kentucky, the third of six children of Elizabeth Black and John McMillin. He attended Philmath Academy in Tennessee and the Kentucky Agricultural and Mechanical College at Lexington, Kentucky.

He studied law under Judge E. L. Gardenshire in Carthage, Tennessee. He opened his first Law office in Celina in 1871, and in 1875 he represented Macon, Clay, and Jackson Counties. In 1879 he was elected to the United States Congress. He was re-elected continously until 1898.

Marie Brown McMillin was the mother of Brown McMillin. She did not live long after his birth; she died in December. 1887 Her monument in Pulaski cemetery is inscribed:

Marie Brown
wife of
Benton McMillin
Born, Oct. 30, 1865; Died, Dec. 7, 1887
A dutiful daughter—an affectionate wife
a fond mother
She adorned every station of life—
And died as she had lived,
a Christian

On January 16, 1899, Benton McMillin was inaugurated as Governor. Bob Taylor made a speech that was meant to be his farewell to politics. There was a touch of bitterness in his words:

"I am about to shuffle off this moral coil of politics and fly away to the heaven of my native mountains, where I may think and dream in peace, safe from the sickening sting of unjust criticism, safe from the talons of some old political vulture, safe from the slimy kiss and the keen danger of ingratitude. . . . . . . while I believe the good in politics outweighs the bad, yet how thorny is the path and how unhappy the pilgrimage to him who dares to do his duty! There are no flowers except a few bouquets snatched from the graves of fallen foes. There is no happiness except the transient thrill of cruel triumph, which passes like a shadow across the heart. Every honest man who runs for office is a candidate for trouble, for the fruits of political victory turn to ashes on the lips."

Turning to the Governor Elect, he concluded with these words, "And now, Benton McMillin, you have given your hand and heart to Tennessee. I now pronounce you man and wife and may the Lord have mercy on your soul."

Louise Foster McMillin.

Lucile Foster McMillin

Wife of Governor Benton McMillin

A chief feature at the Old Folk's Concert given at the Rayman Auditorium under the direction of Nashville Chapter U. D. C. on April 15, 1905, was the appearance of Lucile Foster McMillin, who for the first time since her residence as First Lady in Tennessee gave a public reading for this worthy cause. The dress worn by her on this occasion was once worn by Mrs. Andrew Jackson to a court hall in Berlin, Prussia, during Polk's Administration. Her ornaments included a miniature locket of Lewis Randolph, Jefferson's grandson, an old gold locket bracelet, and a beautiful miniature bracelet of Lieutenant D. S. Donelson of the Confederate Service, which is a painting of the celebrated Taulsier, bearing the date 1848.

In 1888 Benton McMillin married Lucile Foster, as his second wife. They were the parents of one daughter Elinor. Mrs. McMillin was an outstanding Tennessee woman in national life.

One of the best-looking, best dressed women in Washington, Mrs. McMillin held her first position in public life, Civil Service Commissioner. She was once asked if that was her first public job? She replied, "The first one I have ever been paid for." She held the highest official job of any Tennessee woman.

Lucile Foster McMillin's association with men in public life began in her early childhood home in Shreveport, Louisiana, where every one of importance was entertained. Her father, Captain James Foster, was one of the largest and wealthiest cotton planters in Louisiana. He never ran for a public office himself but placed others there. Such a power was Captain Foster that he was called, "Warwick, the King maker," after England's Warwick of old. His state honors were his resolute fight against "carpet bag" rule and the Louisiana Lottery.

Her mother, Mrs. James Foster, was outstanding too; she was one of the first suffragettes in the South and was the first president of the first Woman's Club organized in North Louisiana.

Lucile's sister, Mrs. Foster Comegys, was a professional dramatic entertainer, filling brilliant engagements and often visiting her in Nashville.

The Foster family were leaders in all activities of Louisiana; their daughter Louise's life continued along lines marked from the beginning. She had always moved in a natural sphere. As a child she had a French Governess. She later added Spanish which was easy, as she spoke French fluently.

After graduation from Mary Baldwin's Seminary, she took diction in both New York and Paris, little realizing then how well this was to serve her in later years in political campaigns, dramatic readings, lectures, and country-wide speeches she made in connection with her job as Civil Service Commissioner. President Roosevelt appointed her to this position.

She was a member of C. S. C. from 1933 until she resigned on account of ill health in 1946. She died in Washington February, 1946. After services there, she was later brought to Nashville and buried beside her husband, Governor McMillin, who preceded her death January 8, 1933, at the age of eighty-eight. Five living governors were pallbearers. Governor McMillin made one of the best governors Tennessee ever had and was among the last of the old type statesman who regarded a public office as a public trust in the strictest sense.

Governor McMillin was a Congressman for over twenty years. Tariff reform was his great objective, and it was he who wrote the income tax provision in the Wilson tariff bill. Although he was always a power in Congress, he resigned soon after their marriage, because he was elected Governor in 1898 and re-elected in 1900, serving until 1903.

His beautiful young wife was hardly more than a girl who devoted all her talents with marvelous tact and sparkling enthusiasm to her new role as First Lady of Tennessee, while her husband was bringing about the final establishing and marking the boundry line between Virginia and Tennessee. He also brought about economic reforms that would enable the payment of state debts, uniform text books for schools, and the appointment of Morgan C. Fitzpatrick as State Superintendent. The Text Book Commission made five-year contracts for books.

After leaving the Gubernatorial chair, he engaged in the insurance business in Nashville. He ran for governor against Poston and Ben Hooper in 1912, and he was defeated by Ben Hooper. Benton McMillin's son, Brown McMillin, died October 25, 1912, and he did no more campaigning after Brown's death. The Nashville Tennessean said, "It is impossible to tell how much effect this had on the election returns."

President Wilson appointed Governor McMillin as Minister to Peru, where he and Mrs. McMillin remained for seven years in the U. S. Legation among the cool splashing fountains and romantic gardens.

Louise was at home in the Latin American atmosphere. She

learned Spanish so well she could translate the Minister's speeches when he needed to use their language.

She also made a study of Spanish plays and cut and presented them when she returned to the United States.

She enjoyed the colorful life, even riding mule-back in jungles that no woman had before explored. They led a gay and full life attending Opera, she being a delightful hostess and ambassadress.

The McMillins returned to Nashville after seven years in Peru and two in Guatemala. She had campaigned in political campaigns and now she engaged in club work and politics on her own. She often lectured on Spanish Drama and Dramatics—"Unusual Experiences in Unusual Countries," "What Women Can Do With the Vote," "Citzenship," and others.

She was active in "Little Theater" and gardening. She was State President of Tennessee Federation of Women's clubs. She was the first National Committee Woman from Tennessee, Regional Director of Democratic Women of Southern States appointed by Cordell Hull. Here she had women of eleven states under her.

Mrs. McMillin gave the baccalaureate address to Lincoln Memorial University at Harrogate, where the honorary degree of Doctor of Human Letters was conferred on her.

She made the Alumna Address at Wesleyan College, Macon, Ga. on its celebration of one hundred birthdays. She was principal speaker, "Woman in Government" to the Pan-Hellenic Association at Mayflower Hotel Luncheon. "Women are needed in government; they are born agitators; they are the natural economists of the nation. Women are extra-ordinarily willing to accept responsibility."

While Commissioner she was asked, "Aren't the irregular hours wearing?" She replied, "I go to bed regularly every night. I go to the office regularly every morning.

Her work was a tireless task; she had many obligations, but she arrived early and worked late, carrying her accessories with her for after five teas and cocktail parties.

The National Botanical Gardens named an azalea, "Lucile Foster McMillin," in her honor.

She was a woman of wit and spontaneous gaiety, and she found the full expression of her talents and brought all her power of an understanding heart and mind to help others in her work.

Louise Douglas Keith Frazier.

courtesy of
Congressman J. B. Frazier, Jr.

Louise Douglas Keith Frazier

B. 1860 — M. 1881 — D. 19

Wife of Governor James B. Frazier

Louise Douglas Keith was the daughter of Sarah Ann Penelope Foree and Alexander Hume Keith, a prominent attorney, wealthy planter, and a veteran of the Seminole and Mexican Wars. Louise was born on August 5, 1860. Her 'father was the son of Charles Fleming Keith, Judge of Circuit Court at Athens, Tennessee, for twenty-four years, and her great grandfather Alexander Keith was an aid to General Goerge Washington during the American Revolution.

Louise Keith came of a long line of Virginia ancestry and was a direct descendent of William Randolph and Captain William Douglas.

"Louise as Mrs. James B. Frazier became a First Lady of Tennessee in 1903. She was the mother of four children, whom she taught to say, 'Cousin George Washington, Cousin Thomas Jefferson, Cousin Francis Key, and Cousin John Marshall'."

Marshall's mother was a sister to her grandfather Alexander Keith. Thomas Jefferson's mother was a sister of Thomas Randolph of Tuckahoe, and George Washington's mother, Mary, was a sister to Hannah Ball, another of Louise's grandmothers.

The raven-haired, blue-eyed, beautiful Louise grew up in Athens, Tennessee, with her brothers Augustine, Alexander, and Charles Fleming , her three sisters Anne, Cornelia, and Kate. They attended Athens' schools and Tennessee Wesleyan College. Louise was also a student in Staunton, Virginia. She was highly gifted in mind with powers so vast and such quick and clear perception that she was superior to the general run of females of her day.

The reminiscences of her life carried her back to the period of "tales of early settlement of Tennessee" as told by her grandmother, Elizabeth Douglas Heale Keith.

Elizabeth and Judge Charles Fleming Keith came to Tennessee from Warrenton, Virginia, in 1820. Prior to this, the family came from Scotland in 1700. They first settled at Jefferson City, Tennessee. In 1819 they moved to Athens, where the family lived in a log cabin until the Plantation Home, "Elmwood," was built on the Elmwood estate.

Living in the Indian Territory, the Monroe Massacre was impressed upon their minds. Mrs. Keith looked up from her sewing horrified to see their high staked fence surrounded by war-painted Indians. This brave pioneer, Mrs. Keith, walked calmly into her kitchen, picked up a large basket of tea cakes just out of the oven, motioning for her servant to follow with a basket of apples. They went to the fence and gave each Indian an apple and a tea cake saying in Cherokee, "Osee-u" (Good-morning.) Then she returned to her sewing calmly as if nothing had happened. This was an every day occurrence. Soon she saw the Indians single file walking away through the forests. The Indians were friends of Sarah Foree, Louise's other grandmother. When time came for them to leave on "The Trail of Tears", they came weeping over leaving Doctor Foree and gave them nice gifts.

Louise Keith, prior to her marriage, had led an exceptionally happly life. She had been the recipient of distinguished attentions, including the meeting of James Beriah Frazier in Chattanooga.

On January 10, 1881, in Keith Memorial Church in Athens, she was united in marriage to the young lawyer, who had just graduated at the University of Tennessee at the age of twenty-one in 1878.

The very tall, handsome, young man had spent his boyhood on the farm of his father, Judge Thomas N. Frazier, near Nashville. He also studied law in his father's law office, who was for many years Judge of the Criminal Court of Davidson County.

After his marriage James B. Frazier began the practice of law in Chattanooga. In her new home with a desire to please and a willingness to be pleased, Louise Frazier was popular in Chattanooga Society and was to her husband a support and friend.

In 1900 he was made Presidential elector for the state at large on the Democratic ticket. His campaign speeches were noted for their vigor, eloquence, and their fairness. By them Mr. Frazier did much to win the confidence and esteem of the people who afterward made him Governor.

In 1902 he was nominated and was inaugurated on January 29, 1903. In November 1904 he was re-elected to the same high office. His administration was one of wise managment and great prosperity for Tennessee.

While Governor, they lived at the old Tulane Hotel in Nashville. In 1905 Ann Keith Frazier had the honor of christening the ship "Tennessee" at the launching at Hampton Roads, Virginia. It was one of the outstanding occasions for the fourteen year old, her father, mother, and the Governor's entire staff who went to the affair.

Keith Sommerville says, "The Confederate Veterans met in

Nashville. My mother decided to give an affair in the state Capitol, since it was a huge affair; and we lived in the Hotel. The Capitol was so dirty that mother got the prisoners from the state penitentiary, equipped them with soap, mops, and brooms; they made it spotless under her directions. That night she and the Governor shook hands with five thousand and fed them. Mother was always a great party giver."

Many receptions for Tennessee Legislature and State officials were held at Tulane Hotel.

James B. Frazier resigned the Governorship in 1905 to fill the vacancy in the United States Senate, caused by the death of Ex-Governor, William B. Bate. The Frazier family moved to Washington, D. C., where he served until 1921.

The Saturday Evening Post, in an article about Senators and their wives, said, "Senator and Mrs. Frazier were the handsomest couple in Washington."

William Jennings Bryan once remarked, "Louise Keith Frazier is not only the most beautiful woman I have met in my travels about the United States, but the wittiest."

Mrs. Frazier was interested in history and genealogy. She started the Keith family tree which her daughter Keith Sommerville finished and spent a summer in Scotland, visiting the Earl of Kentmore at Keith Hall—a Castle of seventy-five rooms, built in the year 1200.

Mrs. Frazier was always admonishing the girls, Louise and Keith, that "One piece of polished silver was an ornament to a house, but a wagon load of dirty silver was a disgrace."

She was interested in her church work, a Sunday School teacher, member of Colonial Dames, the Daughters of the American Revolution, The United Daughters of the Confederacy. She organized and was President of Elmwood Garden Club in Chattanooga and other worthy organizations.

It was often said by Tennesseans that James Beriah Frazier was born for Statesmanship. In appearance, in background, in dignity, and in qualities of mind, and heart rarely seen in the State, which itself has been a source of Statesmanship.

Tennesseans know likewise that Governor Frazier married a woman who seemed to be born to be the wife of a statesman. She commanded admiration and respect by her womanly accomplishments and dignity in Nashville. She knew government and was interested in it; she knew social life and her beauty, her mentality as well as her ancestry fitted her for it.

Senator James B. Frazier, Jr. says, "My mother was very outstanding, exceptionally good-looking, a brilliant conversationalist, the best informed woman I have ever known on all subjects, and the most gracious, lovely, kind, and interesting person I have ever known."

Constantly at her husband's side, always a helper and giver of strength, whether at the family home in Chattanooga or Governor's Lady in Nashville or in Washington Society, she graced every occasion, and James B. Frazier leaned heavily on her unfailing tender ministry and counsel.

Mr. Will Shepherd in his personal column gave an outstanding account of the death of Louise Frazier, November 18, 1942:

"The death of the wife of the late Governor Frazier recalls to mind, 'Life in this community and state of a period long since passed in review.' Along about the turn of the century and some years following was the period in which Senator and Mrs. Frazier were in the heyday of their brilliant careers: one be Governor of a great State, later Senator with dignity and brilliance; the other, his wife, presiding with dignity and charm to the duties incumbent upon her high station in the political and social life of the period.

"Both were of distinguished lineage. The Senator commanding in appearance, and master of oratory. Throughout his career his wife played a conspicious role. She fit the picture as the wife and chief aid to her distinguished husband as no one else could have filled it.

"I grieve over the death of this most estimable lady, of the old South, prominent and active in every worthwhile effort of the day; she was just as much a part of life of the period as was her Governor husband.

"Her death removes about the last of the element of citizenship that predominated the period when a distinguished Governor in silk hat and Prince Albert coat rode to State receptions in Landeau behind a pair of spanking bays or sorrells. This is the part the distinguished but now lamented couple played in the life of the day. The Frazier home on Oak Street, Chattanooga, where the prominent people lived in the downtown residential area, was the center of activity.

"Few sons and daughters of truly great and illustrious men and women have reflected honor upon their parents as Brigadier General Thomas H. Frazier, United States Attorney James B. Jr., Louise Douglas Fort, and Keith Sommerville. Let it be a source of joy rather than regret that they won high places in life and in homes that attest the fullness with which Mrs. Frazier's life carried out these principles."

"The heart of her husband doth safely trust her,
So that he shall have no need of spoil.
She will do him good and not evil, all the days of her life.
She openeth her mouth with wisdom;
And in her tongue is the law of kindness.

Her husband is known in the gates where he sitteth among the elders of the land.

She looketh well to the ways of her husband;
Her children rise up and call her blessed."

—Proverbs: 31

Lorena Butler Cox

B. 1870

Wife of Governor John I. Cox

Lorena Butler was born in Verona, Kentucky, in the year 1870. She was the daughter of Mary Theresa Dulaney and Dr. Mathew Moore Butler of Medical Grove, near Blountville, Tennessee. The home was called "Medical Grove," because all the Butler sons were physicians.

Lorena married John I. Cox of Bristol, who became Governor of Tennessee in 1905, when James Beriah Frazier was elected by the Tennessee Legislature to fill the place vacated by the death of Governor William B. Bate who was United States Senator, John I. Cox was speaker of the Senate and automatically became Governor to fill out Governor James B. Frazier's unexpired term.

John I. Cox was born in Sullivan County, November 23, 1857. His father, Henry W. Cox, lost his life in the Confederate Army when John was seven years old.

The Cox family was among the pioneers of East Tennessee. There were eleven brothers who came from Bristol, England, and cast their lot with the Jamestown settlers. Four of the brothers, John, William, Isaac, and Abraham were signers of the Watauga Compact, the first written Constitution of the Western World.

John I. Cox was educated in the old Field Schools of Sullivan County, such as they were after the War Between the States.

At the age of ten, his mother hired him to a farmer for twenty-five cents a week, that he might learn to work and that the pittance might go to support the family.

He remained on the farm until the age of twenty-one. At the age of sixteen he became a Star Route Mail carrier. At eighteen he was appointed Road Commissioner. In the meantime he went to school when he could, working his way through Blountville Academy and studying law with Judge W. V. Deadrick, whose daughter (Tennessee history says) he later married. He practiced law in Blountville, became County Judge and afterward County Attorney.

In 1889, when he moved to Bristol, Tennessee, he became City Attorney, Representative of the Legislature. In 1900 he was elected to the State Senate. He continued in the Senate until he became Governor in 1905.

During his Administration, the Tennessee State Flag was adopted. The public schools were also improved by good legislation. Old Soldiers' pensions were increased; it was a period of thrifty activity.

As First Lady Lorena Butler Cox lived in a rented Mansion in Nashville, giving many receptions for notable figures of the day. She enjoyed the good times and entertaining and was a loving, sunny hearted, unselfish person.

She was the grand'daughter of William F. and Elizabeth Gaines Butler and Mary Taylor and Doctor Elanah Delaney. She was a direct descendant of the Revolutionary soldier, Andrew Taylor.

Among the second wave of settlers in Watauga Valley, there came men of substance, culture, education, men with a love for the beautiful. They made their homes to conform to the mode of living in the far away American Colonies.

One of these men, Andrew Taylor, was the great grandfather of Bob and Alf Taylor, also the great, great grandfather of Lorena Butler Cox; he came from Rockbridge, Virginia, and raised his roof tree in Watauga Valley, afterward known as "Happy Valley."

His son built Watauga Point in 1815. This Nathaniel Taylor married Mary Patton of Rockbridge, Virginia. Her sister-in-law, Mary Keen Patton, was noted for making the powder with which John Sevier's men won the Battle of King's Mountain.

The Taylor Ancestral Home's main entrance hall had wooden sheathed walls, fish wainscoating and carved cornice in dental design. The doors gave off to the right and to the left to the big dining room with a carved mantle of rare beauty. The legend is that General Taylor and Mary Patton showed their patriotism by using white walls, blue wainscoating, and red moulding.

Here at this home, the daughters of the family were married; Anna married Thomas Love; Lorena became Mrs. Jacob Tipton; Mary married Dr. Dulaney; their daughter Mary became the mother of Mrs. John I. Cox.

In 1875, when Lorena was five years old, her parents moved from Verona, Kentucky, to Anderson Street, Bristol, Tennessee. Her father was one of the leading physicians of Bristol, where he died in 1913.

Lorena Butler's early advantages were in keeping with her elevated position as a Governor's Lady; she attended schools in Bristol, Maryville College, Centenary College, Cleveland, Tennessee, and Sullins College at Bristol.

She enjoyed the leisure and opportunity of development of all characteristics which adorn humanity and render life attractive. She was of slight build, with auburn hair and penetrating blue eyes where a little mischief danced at times. A lady of rare charm and accomplishments, modest, humorous, and an excellent mimic, yet easy and graceful in manner, she was free and vivacious in her conversation.

Ruth Butler of Bristol says, "At the Cox home in Bristol, Lorena showed her artistic taste, energy and great sense of beauty. Endowed with these, she transformed the grounds that surrounded their home after their retirement from the gubernatorial home in Nashville into a beautiful plot with lilies and perennials growing between. Gardens were for growing vegetables but walks were edged with flowers."

Lorena Butler and Governor Cox were the parents of a son, Mathew Cox and a daughter Mary Butler Fleming, who lives in Bristol, Tennessee.

Mary, a bright, vivacious schoolgirl, accompanied her parents on a trip that was long remembered:

"On December 15, 1906, there occurred the coincidence of presenting magnificent silver services to three armored cruisers named for three Southern States — Louisiana, Virginia, and Tennessee, the latter at Hampton Roads.

A splendid tug carried the Governor of Tennessee, his staff, Senator James B. Frazier, their wives, and a daughter of each, together with forty invited guests from Tennessee. Captain Berry of Tennessee was commander of the *Tennessee*, with over seven hundred men to serve guests in every way. The $6,000 silver service was placed on deck in the foreground. Governor Cox, attending his daughter Mary who had been chosen to make the presentation address, said:

'Captain Berry, officers, and men of the cruiser *Tennessee*, we are here as the representatives of all Tennesseans in recognition and appreciation of the honor conferred upon our people by the Navy Department in giving to this splendid war vessel the name of our great state.

I assure you that we are delighted to find our namesake commanded by a worthy son of Tennessee. We shall claim of all who command and man the ship as sons and adopted sons of noble. Tennessee, who in every conflict our nation has had with a foreign foe have given to the defense of our common country such devotion, fidelity, courage, and patriotism as to win for our commonwealth the proud and undisputed appellation, *The Volunteer State.*' "

THE FAIR SPONSOR'S WORDS

Miss Mary Cox, sponsor of the occasion, and a winsome young woman said, in formally presenting the beautiful silverware:

"From the land of our ancestral sires, from the old Volunteer State, made memorable by their march to King's Mountain and the victory that turned the tide of the American Revolution; from the gathering place of the clan at Sycamore Shoals, on the beautiful Watauga, we come with greetings and a momento to respect, love, and confidence, in and for those who are in command and man this, our noble namesake, 'The Tennessee.'

Socrates was devoted to his philosophy, Wolsey to his early master, Calvin to his creed, and we to old Tennessee—but not more than to Virginia State and this historic spot; this gateway to the home of Washington, to Lee, and Jackson; this 'open sesame' to all the nations of the world; this landing place of our forefathers.

Brave men, may you ever be foremost in the fight, and last to surrender, if surrender you must."

The proud parents of this remarkable girl lived in Bristol intil their life ended; Governor Cox died in 1946; Lorena Cox died in 1951.

For this or that, Lorena will be remembered for her outstanding sense of humor. She could see the silver lining of any cloud, bring laughter in any social gathering. John I. Cox's good angel, who sometimes mimicked his best friends, was his good adviser in difficulties, a sympathetic companion and the bright spot of his life and as a First Lady.

FORUM OF THE PEOPLE

Nashville Banner, April 14, 1905

A GOVERNOR'S MANSION

To the Editor of the *Banner:*

A Governor's mansion is one thing that I do not think Tennessee needs for a good many years yet. The country is just emerging from a great financial crisis. The Civil War impoverished the wealthiest people and the greatest majority of citizens of the State. The people who have made money and accumulated property since having been heavily taxed to support our charitable institutions, our public school and to pay off our state debt, and I can see no reason to saddle this useless expense on the taxpayers. Our hotels heretofore have been considered good enough for such men as Governors Bate, Turney, Buchanan, Johnson, Taylor, McMillin, and Frazier; and at least I haven't heard any complaint that a candidate for the office couldn't be found because we did not have a Governor's mansion for him to live in. Suppose the present Legislature should appropriate $30,000 to buy a home. It will have to be furnished for every new Governor that is elected. No Governor's wife is going to live in a house that the former Governor's family have worn out the carpets and scarred up the furniture, when she knows she will be expected to entertain all the dis tinguished people who come here, besides Nashville's 400. Most of our Governors since the Civil War have been men of limited means and large families and their salaries have been barely enough to defray their expenses. None of them have got rich that I have heard of. I think it would be much more sensible to pay the Governor enough to enable him to rent a comfortable house that will be his as long as he rents it, and not the State's property, nor his family the servants of the public.

A TENNESSEE WOMAN

Governor Malcolm R. Patterson Home, Clarksville, Tenn.

Mary Russell Gardner Patterson.

courtesy of
Mrs. Charles Phillips, Memphis, Tenn.

Mary Russell Gardner

First First Lady in the Mansion

Wife of Governor Malcolm R. Patterson

Up to the year 1907, the governors of Tennessee had to live, while in office, in hotels, boarding houses, or rented houses, if they did not own a house of their own in Nashville, the Capital City.

After one hundred and ten years as a state, it was considered unworthy of the dignity of a great state that its Governor should have no official residence.

The General Assembly of 1907, with the approval of Governor Malcolm R. Patterson, made a suitable appropriation and bought the house that was called "the Official Mansion."

Here Mary Russell Gardner Patterson came as a young bride, the first First Lady to reside in the Mansion.

She was born in Union City, Obion County, the daughter of Jennie Sutherlan, and a granddaughter of John and Virginia Sutherlan. Her father, Mayor William Gardner, was the son of Ann and Alfred Gardner, both natives of Tennessee.

The Gardners were a large family. Mayor William Gardner was a graduate of the University of Virginia. Fred Gardner was Governor of Missouri and owner of Banner Buggies Manufacturing Company. The other brother was prominent in the New York Stock Exchange and President of St. Louis Coffee Company.

Mary's two sisters were Mrs. Clyde Fitzpatrick of Helena, Arkansas, and Nora, who married Judge Ben Capel of Memphis, Tennessee.

As a child Mary attended grade school in Union City; she also was a student at a girl's school in Cincinnati. She was a graduate of Fairmount College in Washington, D.C.

Returning home from a house party with some college friends, the gay and attractive Mary made the acquaintance of the future Tennessee Governor.

On the train was a friend of her father, Mayor Gardner of Union City, who came down the aisle and stopped to talk to Mary. He said, "Mary, there is a very good-looking man in the rear of the coach, Malcolm R. Patterson, who is going to be our next governor of Tennessee. I want you to meet him."

Mary tossed her pretty head and replied, "Thank you; I am not old enough to vote. I do not care to meet the good-looking man."

Enjoying her solitude as the telephone poles raced past her window, a shadow appeared at her side. As she looked up, she saw the good-looking young man, introducing himself and asking permission to sit beside her — They discussed social and political questions of the day.

The train was nearing the Union City Depot. Mr. Patterson informed Mary that he was to speak in Union City the next evening. As they parted he said, "I hope to see you again."

She replied, "I have enjoyed our talk on the train. Do you really think you will see me again?"

Mary had just entered the front door of her home when she was greeted by her father. "Out of a Clear Blue Sky" he said, "Oh, Mary, the ladies of the city have arranged a bouquet for the speaker, Mr. Patterson, tomorrow night; and they have asked that you make the presentation."

"Oh, papa, please don't ask me to do that; men abhor flowers!"

Her sister Nora said, "Papa insisted. Mary presented the flowers. After the speaking was over, Mr. Patterson walked home with Mary; and for the next six months, he was a week-end guest at our home. On December 7, 1909, they were married with a home wedding. I never dreamed of Mary as a governor's wife!"

> Lord, my heart is not haughty,
> Nor mine eyes lofty;
> Neither do I exercise myself
> in great matters or
> In things too high for me.
> Psalms 131-1

Mary Gardner, the first First Lady in the Mansion, was also the first to give birth to the first child born in the Governor's Mansion, Mary Gardner Patterson, who became Mrs. Charles Phillips of Memphis, Tennessee.

After they left Nashville to live in Memphis, a son, Ham Patterson, was born. They built a home in 1927 out from Memphis, "Mary-Ham," where they lived until the death of Governor Patterson in 1935, and the children were married. Mary Patterson died in Memphis September 12, 1956.

Although she was much younger than the Governor, they were a very congenial and loving couple—always joking about Mary giving him the flowers at Union City. She would tease him and say, "I know you think I am beautiful. You said, 'I want to thank this *beautiful* young lady for these flowers.'"

He would say, "No, I said 'I want to thank this young lady for these *beautiful* flowers.'"

Malcolm Patterson was born in Summerville, Alabama, June 7, 1861. His father, Colonel Josiah Patterson, born April 14, 1837, was a foremost lawyer in Tennessee, and a Confederate soldier in command of the Fifth Alabama Cavalry.

His mother was Josephine Rice, the youngest daughter of Ann Eliza Turner and Judge Green P. Rice. She was educated at the Female Academy in Sommerville, Alabama, and was noted for her modest, retiring ways. She was from a distinguished Virginia family—connected with the Blount, Sykes, and Bynum families of Tennessee, Alabama, and Mississippi.

Besides Malcolm, there were two daughters, Mary Lou, educated at Sayre Institute in Lexington, Ky., and Ann Eliza.

After the close of the War, they moved to Memphis, where Malcolm attended Memphis schools and later went to Vanderbilt; he studied law in his father's office, and he began practice in Memphis.

He first married Lucile Coe Johnson, daughter of Sarah Coe and Malcolm Johnson of Memphis. They were the parents of Malcolm, Jr., Coe, Josiah, and Sarah Patterson, who lived with her father in the Mansion and was later presented at a Chickasaw Guards Ball in Memphis. She became the wife of Thomas Hooker and the mother of a daughter and two sons: Colonel Malcolm P. Hooker, who received the Legion of Merit, one of the nation's highest peacetime decorations as Chief Project Officer at Tactical Air Command Headquarters, at Tan San, Nhut A. V. Vietnam in 1967.

The other son is a Chattanooga businessman, Thomas, Jr., who lives on Lookout Mountain with his wife and three children.

Mrs. Hooker, Sr. died in July, 1967, in Memphis.

Governor Patterson served from 1907 until 1911. He was an able and forceful governor. He created a State Highway Commission and a constructive legislation for Tennessee schools, yet his administration was blurred by the hot political squabble over the question of Prohibition in Tennessee.

In 1894, Malcolm Patterson was made General of Criminal Courts in Memphis until 1900. He served two terms in the U. S. Congress in Washington, D. C. He married the second time, Sybil Hodges of Philadelphia, who became the mother of Elizabeth Patterson; she lived with Mary at the mansion.

In her elevated, conspicious situation, the stateliness of Mary's bearing was very becoming and appropriate. She was happy among kin and friends, conferring happiness on those about her; she was also interested in her religion and the church.

The Pattersons were Presbyterians, as were all the generations before them. The grandfather, Malcolm, Sr., was an elder in the Presbyterian Church for forty-five years. He was born in Abbeville, S. C., of Scotch Irish parentage. As a farmer, he emigrated to North Alabama in 1817 and lived there as an honored citizen until his death in 1859 at the age of seventy.

Governor Patterson's great-grandfather, Alexander Patterson, was a Patriot Soldier in the Revolutionary War and was wounded at Cow Pens. As a farmer, he was married to Mary Deloache, born in 1802, the daughter of John Deloache on Stone River, Rutherford County. They emigrated to Jefferson County, Alabama, where Mary grew to young womanhood. Her brother William was with General Jackson throughout the Indian Wars.

John Deloache was a wealthy, highly respected farmer; he died in 1820 on the farm where the city of Birmingham is now located.

The First Lady, Mary Gardner Patterson, will be remembered as a handsome lady, for she had very dark brown hair, large blue eyes, and a beautiful complexion. She was well educated and had a talent for conversation that left her listeners pondering her well-stated remarks; her excellent taste in dress was a notable characteristic of hers. Her receptions at the Mansion were largely attended and made agreeable to everyone by her wit and spirit of liveliness, as well as courtesy. Mrs. Patterson was an intelligent and sensible lady of outstanding charm, warmth, and humor.

Ann Bell Jones Hooper, Newport, Tenn.

courtesy of
Mrs. E. Hurd

Anna Bell Jones Hooper

B. 1875 — M. 1901 — D. 1967

Wife of Governor Ben Walter Hooper

One of the first things greeting young Captain Ben Walter Hooper on his arriving home from the Spanish American War was an invitation from Anna Bell Jones to a big party at her home in Newport, Tennessee. She was no longer a little girl with brown braided hair, but an accomplished young lady who had just completed her education under Madame Capioni in New York.

In the big brick mansion on the high hill overlooking the town, the Reverend John M. Anderson, the Baptist minister, performed the ceremony. Anna and Ben were married on September 25, 1901. Such a wedding, perhaps in all East Tennessee, had never had a greater gathering of friends and kin on such an occasion of this kind in Newport, Tennessee.

Ben W. Hooper said, "As a young wedded couple, they stepped into life together, having no prevision of the immense variety of experiences that would be theirs, radiant joy and poignant grief, thrilling triumph and depressing defeat, new young lives, and sudden terrible death.

They went gladly and bravely on their way, sharing, co-operating without cessation or deviation, considering their marriage a life partnership and not a temporary convenience, something to be ended at the brink of the grave and not at the bar of the courtroom."

Robert Burns describes such a life as:

> "To make a happy fireside clime;
> To weans and wife,
> That's the rue pathos and subline
> Of human life."

Anna Bell Jones was born August 3, 1875. Her parents were Townsella Randolph and Benjamin Dickinson Jones, Newport's first merchant and first President of Merchant's Bank; he was the son of Isabel Wilson and Samuel Chandler Jones.

Mrs. Hooper's mother, Townsella Jane, was the daughter of Jane Mathilda Robinson and James Henry Randolph; he was a Circuit Judge, State Senator, and United States Congressman from the first District. The Randolphs came from one of the most aristocratic families of the county and on line from Virginia Randolphs and Pocahontas.

One of seven children, her brothers were James Randolph, Benjamin Dickinson, Rolfe, who died in childhood, and Wilson Jones. The sisters were Jane Mae Jones and Townsella Jane Fields. Jane married a Stokley.

The Jones family were wealthy and vert active in social life. Anna Bell, the blue-eyed, brown-haired girl, had a very happy childhood.

Anna Bell and Ben Hooper went together to children's parties now and then; Once, when she was about eleven years old, her mother put a doll on the Sunday School Christmas tree for her, and she was mortified because Ben walked home with her and carried the doll.

Her mother's home was one of hospitality to all the young people of Newport. Anna Bell was a very popular young lady.

She possessed a pleasing personality to all who came in contact with her.

After she graduated from Carson Newman College at Jefferson City, she was a student for four years at Virginia Intermont, where she majored in Music; but she did not write her final theme, which prevented her from graduating there. She went to New York, where she studied voice under Madame Capioni. She was also an accomplished pianist.

She was very active in the Baptist Church of Newport. She directed the choir for a number of years and sang in the church choir until she was eighty years old.

Ben W. Hooper's father, Doctor L. W. Hooper, died in 1899, a few months after Ben returned from the Spanish American War.

As a young fellow Ben Hooper said, "My stepmother knew how to make the most of a boy. I did all manner of work. I fed and watered the horse, fed and milked the cow, raised a hundred chickens, cultivated the garden, cared for the lawn, washed the dishes, churned, and carried in all the wood for a stove and a big fireplace."

"I was permitted to play with other children but not allowed to wander on the streets and went nowhere without permission. I went to church every Sunday morning, rain or shine."

"Once I received fifty cents a month as janitor," he stated. "This was probably a fair index to the large hearted generosity of the old-time Baptists."

He had nothing to do but open the church doors in the early morning and nights, fire two big stoves, sweep out, dust, light, and keep the kerosene lamps cleaned, the wicks trimmed, climb several hundred yards up a steep hill to ring the Academy Bell, that was all for fifty cents.

In 1887, Ben entered Carson Newman College; not twenty years of age, he graduated in 1890.

On his return home he shocked his father by telling him he did not want to study medicine, but that he planned to practice law. Politics always had had a well-nigh irresistible fascination for Ben. He was elected to the Tennessee Legislature in 1892. He introduced the four-mile Law to small incorporated towns, although the bill was not made state-wide until 1909.

"Governor Ben W. Hooper's administration was unquestionably the most turbulent period in the history of Tennessee, not excepting even the period of reconstruction."

It was described as a time of restlessness and dissatisfaction in some social, political, and industrial matters, which at times bade fair to lead to conditions akin to chaos.

Tired and worn, Governor Hooper retired in 1915 to the glories of mountain life in his beloved mountains of East Tennessee. He said, "It is no wonder the Prophet Elijah never heard the still small voice of God until he had fled from the clamor of the multitude into the quiet of the mountains."

It was a cold January morning; they watched their home and its contents burn to the ground. They thought then that was the worst calamity of their married life. They moved into a little stone bungalow that was empty on their place as soon as they could run into Newport for some clothing and food. They built a home of field stone and logs—a house that fits beautifully into the mountainside at Carson Springs.

Governor Hooper later said, "At Christmas they all come home, that is, all but two. Ben Jones was killed in an auto wreck in May, 1931, and Randolph was killed in an auto wreck four years later in 1935.

Th e Republican Ben W. Hooper was elected Governor, November, 1910. He said, "My campaign for the Governorship had many aspects of a religious campaign, both on my own part and on the part of the masses of supporters. In so far as I personally was concerned, I felt most profoundly that I was a mere instrumentality in the hands of an aroused people for the restoration of clean democratic processes in Tennessee. Although I have never been a pious man in the strict sense of the term, I did not make a speech in that campaign that I did not precede by a silent prayer. This may sound like 'can't,' but is a simple statement of fact."

The January inauguration was to take place in the Hall of Representatives; Patterson's friends wanted to see him step out and Hooper's friends wanted to see him step in, all on one platform. So for the first time since 1865, the inauguration was not held at the Hall of Representatives, but was held at the Ryman

Auditorium, where there were gathered about seven thousand people.

The entire family of the Governor soon arrived in Nashville, where they took up their abode in the Governor's Mansion; there were Anna B., age nine; Ben Jones, seven; James Randolph, five; and Margaret Janella, age two.

The Mansion was near the Capitol. It had been purchased during Malcolm Patterson's administration. It had been constructed on a rather expensive scale inside and out and wisely unloaded on the State for an executive mansion.

The two young Hooper boys soon joined the seventh Avenue gang and became skilled warriors in battle wherein limestone macadam was the recognized ammunition.

With the small children, Anna Bell Hooper did little entertaining in the Mansion. She entertained the National Southern Baptist Convention where she gave the Welcome Address.

She gave birth to Lemuel Washington Hooper on August 6, 1911, while living in the Mansion. He was the second child of a Governor to be born in the Tennessee Mansion.

Little Anna B. made a suffrage speech in the Capitol at the age of nine; she marched into the legislative halls in 1912 and announced, "I expect to know as much as my brothers know when we are grown, and I will know as well how to vote as they will."

She was her father's secretary while he was on the Railway Labor Board which was located in Chicago; he joined the Board in 1921. The family lived in Chicago at the time.

Newel Sanders Hooper, who became the wife of Attorney Edward Hurd in Newport, was born after the family had moved from the Governor's Mansion in 1916.

From holocaust and sudden death, the Hoopers turned for mental relief to their flower gardens. Mrs. Hooper was the landscape artist using her natural artistic taste, nature and the surrounding rocks, trees, shrubs, vines, hills, pools, terraces, flowerbeds, streams, and fruit trees, using whatever the nurseries and nature made available.

Governor Hooper, active in Veterans of Foreign wars and Baptist Church, died at Carson Springs in 1957 at the age of eighty-seven.

Mrs. Hooper was the founder of Newport's Twentieth Century Club. Mrs. Elizabeth Stokley Jones says, "I wish you could see and know Mrs. Hooper. She is an inspiration, always happy, walks with a spirited gait, and goes everywhere. She loves to play bridge, winning high score at Benefit Bridge in 1965."

Mrs. Hooper at age ninety-one was still active in the Baptist Church. She was the mother of six children, four living; she had eleven grand children and six great grandchildren.

Betty Arnold Rye.

Betty Arnold Rye

B. 1870 — M. 1888 — D. 1961

Wife of Governor Thomas C. Rye

World War I began in 1914, but not until a German submarine attacked United States ships and forced the United States to declare War against Germany on April 16, 1917, did Tennessee's eighty thousand join the armed Forces.

In the Governor's Mansion was Governor Thomas C. Rye and his First Lady Betty Arnold. They had resided there since January 17, 1915, when he was inaugurated. He served two terms and was later Chancellor of the Eighth Chancery Division.

Tom Rye had been chosen because of his good reputation as an officer, and as Attorney General from 1908 until 1912. He was stern and unbending in his treatment of bootleggers and had been firm in enforcing the law. This struggle had been going on in Tennessee over prohibition for almost seven years.

Governor Tom Rye was born 1863 in a log cabin about one half mile north of Camden. He grew up on his father's farm, attending public schools of Camden. He went to Charlotte, North Carolina where he studied law with an uncle. On returning to Camden later, he hung out his shingle·on his own office door.

He was seven years the senior of Betty Arnold whom he married January 17, 1888 in her home. Her mother was Josephine Hawley, her father was Aaron Arnold. The blue-eyed blonde Betty was the grand daughter of Mary Ann Bussey and Royal Morehead Hawley of Camden, Tennessee.

For twenty-five years they lived in Camden where he was a lawyer and judge. The petite, fair Betty was a happy and domesticated little homemaker going about the business of raising her two children Nell and Paul Rye.

They were active in the Cumberland Presbyterian Church and other civic activities in Camden.

Betty had spent her early days with her three sisters Dora, Della and Pearl Arnold, where they and her brother, George Wiley Arnold attended schools of Benton County.

The Ryes moved to Paris, Tennessee before he became Governor of Tennessee, where they led a happy, wholesome life. Betty was always interested in helping the Governor; at no time in her life did Betty Rye exist for herself, but only for her family who were near and dear to her.

259

While living in the Governor's Mansion they entertained frequently many notable men and women who visited the Capital city.

She was very attractive with a pleasing personality. She was a person who mingled with ease and charm in the society of Nashville.

In 1920, she turned her title over to Nora Bowden Roberts who had much rather have taught music at Alpine than cope with Mansion.

Governor Rye returned to his law practice at Paris, Tennessee where they again attended Cumberland Presbyterian Church. He died on September 12, 1953 and was buried in Paris, Tennessee.

Nell Rye had married John J. Nolan who had been Comptroller during Governor Rye's administration and also after.

The Nolans resided on Richland Avenue in the late fifties. A neighbor and good friend says, "I never knew Mrs. Tom Rye until I was a neighbor. She was living with her daughter Nell. Mrs. Rye was a lovely lady and always looked the part. She was up in years, but always beautifully groomed and still handsome. She was quiet, but one was always conscious of her presence—still Queen of a situation."

"All her possessions were handsome and in good taste—the loveliest furniture, silver, and exquisite china —Everything— When she went out, it was in a shining Cadillac with a uniformed chauffeur at the wheel. Never a pushy person but one felt her to be a real First Lady of Tennessee."

Mrs. Rye lived in Nashville until her death October 1, 1961. She had passed her ninety-first birthday.

It has been written that they are blessed who have a gift for making friends, for it is one of God's best gifts. "Truth makes life a noble thing, and courage makes it strong; but grace and tact must set them off, as music does a song."

Nora Dean Bowden Roberts

B. 1868 — M. 1889 — D. 1932

Wife of Governor Albert H. Roberts

Ten years have elapsed since the first child, Mary Gardner Patterson, was born in the Governor's Mansion. World War I had ended November 11, 1918. A new Governor, Albert H. Roberts, and his First Lady Nora Dean Bowden now joined the stream of Tennessee History. It seemed peculiarly fitting that to Tennessee, whose soldiers turned the tide of the American Revolution at King's Mountain and which has maintained in every crisis the proud Volunteer State, should have fallen the honor of producing the romantic example of Alvin C. York of Fentress County, who had made himself famous in the Argonne Forest where he 'teched off' single handed twenty Germans and captured a hundred thirty-two prisioners including three German officers. He received a hero's welcome, and friends in Tennessee gave to him a farm and home.

Governor Roberts and Nora Bowden gave the Hero and his Gracie a wedding in the Governor's Mansion. This was the first wedding in the Tennessee Mansion. Governor Roberts and Nora Bowden had been reared in adjoining counties to Alvin C. York.

Professor Bailey Owen Bowden was a native of Fentress County, Tennessee. He married the teacher Miss Molly Sproul of the Fentress County schools. They became the parents of Nora Dean, born February 6, 1868. He was an Instructor of Latin at Hiwassee College, Madisonville, Tennessee.

The parents were exceptional people in character and educational circles of West Tennessee. Mrs. Bowden was the daughter of James and Sallie Sproul. They were on their way to Missouri with a stop over in Overton county. Miss Helen Qualls of Livingston says, "My grandfather persuaded the Sprouls to stay in Overton county and teach school, which they did."

Living in a Southern county during the War Between the States, Mary Sproul Bowden wrote an interesting manuscript of her experience as a Union Sympathizer. She was a beloved teacher in Fentress County.

They moved to Madisonville after their marriage and were very active on the Hiwassee Campus. Their son John Sproul and Nora Dean attended Hiwassee College where Nora majored in music; she later taught music at Alpine Private School where Albert H. Roberts was Principal for five years.

Albert Roberts was born in 1868 in Overton County near Nettle Carrier Creek Bridge. He was educated in the Overton schools. A graduate of Hiwassee College in 1889, he evidently was interested in more than an academic college course. He married the Professor of Latin's daughter, Nora Dean, on May 16, 1889.

Albert was the son of Sarah Carlock and John Roberts. He was the grandson of Jesse and Mahalia Morelock Roberts. His mother Sarah was the daughter of B. L. and Eliza Hayter Carlock.

About the time Albert was ready for high school, John and Sarah Carlock Roberts moved to Kansas City, Missouri, where he finished high school. He came back to Tennessee. The old home of the Roberts family at Alpine had burned, leaving only the slave quarters.

The Roberts family lived in Livingston, Tennessee where the grammar school now stands. Mr. Roberts was a member of the I.O.O.F. Lodge, a democrat, President of the Farmer's Bank. He resigned after five years upon his election as Chancellor.

They were active in the Methodist Church of Livingston, where the four children grew up. Mrs. Roberts was pianist, and an active worker of the church.

Maurice Roberts married Miss Hattie Smith of Livingston. He was quite a joker and prankster when a young fellow growing up. The youngest son was Albert, Jr. who became a lawyer in Nashville. Helen was a very attractive young lady; she attended Peabody College and married Dr. Horace C. Gayden of Nashville. She was the mother of two daughters, Helen Gaile and Anna Bell Gayden. One of the Roberts' sons, Allen, died young. Sadie Dean Roberts married Attorney Paul Capp of Nashville; they were the parents of Paul, Jr., and Elizabeth Capp Uffleman.

Nora Dean Roberts as a girl fell in the fire causing a face-scar; even so she was a very attractive and talented lady. She was quiet, loved music, had a keen sense of humor, and was quick to defend her friends. Mrs. Roberts died May 14, 1932, and was buried on her forty-third wedding aniversary.

During the Roberts' administration, a compulsory school term was adopted. Another first for Tennessee, the General Assembly in 1919, gave women the right to vote for President and Vice President of the United States. The first Southern State to pass such an act, Tennessee was the thirty-sixth state to ratify Woman Suffrage of the United States Constitution.

During Albert H. Roberts' Administration, Hamilton and James Counties were consolidated. This was the first county consolidation in the United States.

When his term expired the family moved to 724 Benton Avenue, Nashville in 1921. They later moved to a farm on McGovac Lane in Nashville. Still later, Governor Roberts had a stroke and fell in Livingston while he was conducting court; he died on his Nashvillle farm June 25, 1946, and was buried in Langston, Tennessee.

The Mother of Governor Alf and Bob Taylor.

courtesy of
James Hannah

courtesy of
Mrs. Oscar Brown

Taylor Home, Happy Valley.

Jenny Anderson Taylor.

courtesy of
Bur Harrison, Johnson City, Tenn.

Frances Jean Anderson Taylor

B. 1866 — M. 1882 — D. 1943

Wife of Governor Alfred A. Taylor

Frances Jean Anderson Taylor, lovingly called Jennie by her father, Mr. Anderson, who was a farmer and owner of fine horses in Carter Valley, was born July 10, 1866. From earliest girlhood growing up with her two brothers, among the green hills and towering mountains with the purple and blue sunny skies o'er head, among the crags and peaks near the Buffalo river, bending through the hills into the Holston, in the Anderson's green meadows, she could sit on the grass, listening to the love notes of the birds, the doves, the cradlesong of the robins hopping at her feet, the blue bird and blue jay, the sweet chirp of the red bird's call, while the bullfrog on the bank answered with his deep bass croak as she dreamed on summer days.

It was from these scenes of majesty and beauty that she grew into a young woman of gentleness and charm with affection for friends, kindred and family.

She attended Buffalo Academy (now Milligan College) as a girl riding to and from school on the best of her father's spirited horses. Her education was reading, writing, and Davies' Arithmetic along with other subjects.

Along with this was combined the arts of housewifery that mothers taught their daughters in the sixties. Jennie learned to sew her samplers, even though she sometimes pricked her fingers with the needle. She also helped her mother at the big quilting frame where they stitched the Wedding Wheel quilt for Jennie's hope chest.

In the years that Jennie was growing up, she was an unknown figure to her future husband Alfred A. Taylor, she little dreaming that she would one day be a First Lady in the Tennessee Mansion.

At this time Alfred was eighteen years her senior, helping to develop his brother Bob's oratorical genius, by bringing on a debate by mounting a stump in a cornfield, a lumber pile, or a feed box on the barn floor and making a speech from the Republican standpoint while Bob would arise to the occasion and take up the Democratic standpoint.

Alfred A. Taylor was the son of Nathaniel Green and Emiline Haynes Taylor, Grandson of James and Mary Carter, Great grandson of Mary Patton and General Nathaniel Taylor of West Point, which he built in 1815. The great, great grandfather was Andrew Taylor who came in the second wave of settlers, from Rockbridge County, Virginia, raised his rooftree in the Watauga Valley, afterward popularly known as Happy Valley.

Nathaniel Taylor, the father of Governor Alfred and Bob Taylor, graduated from Princeton in the same class as John C. Breckenridge. He was a prominent politician of the State. In 1860 he took his stand for the preservation of the Union. By 1863 he was forced by deadly pressure of events to leave his home and take refuge within the Federal lines in the city of Knoxville.

In 1860, Reverend Taylor had moved back to the old home in Happy Valley and sold his Buffalo Farm for he foresaw the War Between the States would prevent his paying off a debt he owed.

In 1864 he moved to New Jersey. He was serving as Commissioner of Indian Affairs under President Johnson. They moved to Laurel, Maryland, an hour's train ride to Washington. Here Alfred worked in the Indian Office until 1869; then the family moved back to Happy Valley, and still little Jennie was just three years old.

The family again moved to Athens, Tennessee in 1871. The older children went to East Tennessee Wesleyan University and the younger ones to Preparatory Department, again in 1874 they returned to Happy Valley.

In late 1878, Alfred had not left the parental roof and was a Republican nominee for Congress; his brother Bob's name was also placed before the Convention. From 1875 to 1876 Alfred had been a member of United States Congress. When they asked Bob in his law office to consent for his name to be placed, he said, "What! Me for Congress, just a mountain boy?" But Alfred with his good heart and love for Bob, loaned him his prized Bay and white stallion to ride in his campaign.

Alfred Taylor was thirty-four when he married Jennie Anderson, one month before her sixteenth birthday. They had been married four years when the brothers Alf and Bob were waging the War of Roses (for Governor) in 1886.

The Canvass was one of the most remarkable in the history of the State—brothers running against each other, traveling together. Their mother Emiline had made them promise to stay together, so all along their trail they roomed together.

In that memorable campaign, they crossed swords and clashed shields on many a political stump, but to the Lyceum world, in after years they went as joint lecturers Yankee Doodle (Alf) and Dixie (Bob) together behind the footlights in a role as charmingly original as have been the lives and careers of the two men.

Many years later Afred Taylor became Governor in 1922. As a Republican he had troubles aplenty with the Legislature, but he was a model of equal treatment and a good chief executive. He made an especially fair inquiry, his records show, into extremely difficult labor disputes in 1922.

Governor and Mrs. Taylor were the parents of ten children. Their son John died in infancy, Nathaniel Green, Benjamin Harrison, who married Lelia Ramsey, a daughter of Letia Conner and Reverend Sam Ramsey of Cleveland, Tennessee, a Cumberland Presbyterian minister. The Ben Taylors have three children, Ben Jr., Thad Cox, and Jennie. The other children were David Haynes, James Blaine, Alfred Jr., Robert Love, Mary, Katherine, and Frank who lived with his brother Ben in Johnson City while the family lived in the Governor's Mansion in Nashville.

Mrs. Taylor was known to her friends as Miss Jennie. She like Cornelia, the mother of the Gracchi, considered her children her jewels, representing the greatest glory and crown of womanhood. She was no t only their mother but their queen, whose lightest wish and most trivial request were honored and obeyed as royal commands. Her heart was as young at seventy as a bride's of sixteen, overflowing with sunshine and flowers. She was a close at home mother, cooking, canning, quilting, and entertaining friends, family and relatives who received a most gracious welcome at all times, though the visits be a day or weeks.

The Taylor home was a rendevous for society at large. The Governor was a public man of wide acquaintance, the children's many friends were always welcome. Miss Jennie was always well prepared for unexpected company or invited in her home, with shelves full of canned vegetables, fruits, dried apples, peaches, crocks full of meat and sausage, the smoke house loft hung with Tennessee Country hams. No wonder the Governor's wishes for his favorite dishes could be available on short notice.

The author remembers a visit at the Ben Taylor home while Mr. Taylor was Governor. He was also a visitor in the home and wanted mush for his supper. The daughter-in-law asked if I knew how to make it. We had no black pot but found a large skillet; he ate the mush with two kinds of milk: sweet and buttermilk.

Mrs. Taylor was interested in his political friends and continuously entertained them graciously in their Happy Valley home which adjoins Milligan College.

Robert Taylor said, "No woman ever cooked for or entertained more political friends of her husband than did my mother Jennie."

Mrs. Taylor lived until February 13, 1943; she was buried beside Governor Taylor, who preceded her in death November 24, 1931, and the son Ben Taylor who died in 1930.

Miss Jennie will be remembered for this or that, "She earned a place among women who are truly great by encouraging culture, refinement, and was eager to give of her time and talents to her large family. She will continue to live in the hearts of her children, because she gave them faith in their own powers and possibilities."

Sallie Hurst Peay, 1924.

Sallie Hurst Peay

Wife of Governor Austin Peay

Sallie Hurst, the daughter of Amaryllis Smith and John Hurst of Clarksville, Tennessee, was born November 21, 1876. She grew up in the city of Clarksville, attending the public schools there. She also attended Ward's Seminary, a Junior College for women in Nashville, Tennessee.

At the age of nineteen she married Austin Peay on September 19, 1895. Mr. Hurst called him "The Boy."

He was the son of Cornelia Frances Leavell and Austin Peay, Sr. of Hopkinsville, Christian County, Kentucky. They were well-to-do farmers, sending Austin, Jr. to Hopkinsville elementary and high school. He attended Washington and Lee College and later graduated from Center College, Danville, Kentucky.

Austin Peay studied law. When he went to get his marriage license, he had first to go to the bank and borrow seventy-five dollars to start life as a married man. He gave a good portion of the sum to Rev. A. V. Boone. He began practicing law in Clarksville in 1896, where he made his home the rest of his life.

He gave his time to his legal practice and entered politics as a Democrat. In 1910 he was elected to Tennessee House of Representatives, an office he held for two years.

He became Governor, January 16, 1923, defeating the Republican incumbent Alfred A. Taylor.

It was during his administration that he signed the "Anti-evolution Law," and started the fireworks in Dayton, Tennessee, bringing into Tennessee reporters, cameramen, newspapermen from all over the U. S. —even the religious William Jennings Bryan, the three times defeated candidate for President. The famous attorney, Clarence Darrow, came to uphold John T. Scopes for teaching his biology class "The Theory of Evolution."

Governor Peay combined the sixty-four Bureaus, Boards, Commissioners, and Officers into eight departments—the most radical change in the one hundred seven years of Tennessee Government.

County school consolidation began in Tennessee, highways were expanded, old roads rebuilt and new and improved roads constructed for automobile travel because transportation by wagon began to sidestep for trucks. The state property tax was lowered, the state debt reduced and the Health Department organized.

In January, 1927, Governor Peay became ill with influenza and pneumonia, an illness he was unable to overcome. He lived until October 27, 1927. He had been elected to his third term, one of Tennessee's great men and the only Governor to die while in office.

After his death Mrs. Austin Peay published a book on the Life and Papers of Governor Austin Peay.

The Peays were the parents of Austin Peay III and Amaryllis Peay Armstrong, of Clarksville, Tennessee and the grandparents of Mrs. Paul Rudolph of Clarksville, Tennessee. Mrs. Peay's grandparents were Sallie Carroll Perkins and Joel Watkins Smith. She was a member of the Baptist Church in Clarksville where she was very active in Missionary work and other activities of the Church.

Mrs. Peay was a Democrat and quite a politician, a very civic-minded woman. She was President of Tennessee Federation of Women's Club, Art Study Club, and Student Clubs at Austin Peay College, established in 1927 as a Normal School and Junior College, located at the junction of Cumberland and Red Rivers.

Miss Mable Meacham, Dean of Women at Austin Peay College says, "I had the privilege of knowing Mrs. Peay for many years. I was often a visitor in her home. She was a loveable person, a good conversationalist, a member of the Hermitage Association, entertaining many visitors and friends in the Mansion as First Lady in a most gracious manner. An atmosphere of pleasant social life was felt by all who had the pleasure of being a guest at the Executive Mansion of Tennessee."

273

Anne Adeline Wilhoite Home, Wilhoite, Tenn., now Horton State Park.

Anne Adeline Wilhoit Horton.

courtesy of
Mrs. John Horton, Vanderbilt, Nashville

Ann Adeline Wilhoite Horton

B. 1878 — M. 1896 — D. 1960

Wife of Governor Henry Horton

A Tribute paid to the First Lady of Governor Horton while he was Chief Administrator of Tennessee from 1927 until 1933 was:

"Whenever a man has accomplished much in life somewhere along the road there has been a woman to inspire him—it may be his mother, sister, sweetheart or his wife. People who knew Ann Adeline Wilhoite Horton never doubted or questioned the source of the inspiration of Henry Horton's life. Mrs. Horton was a beautiful woman, of whom any Tennessean could point with pride and say she is the First Lady of my State."

Mrs. Horton had that real beauty of soul which is the only kind that endures. She endeavored always to look at life with the right perspective and to put first things first. She knew with the knowledge born of experience that "he who would be greatest among you must be servant of all." So unselfish was she that when most would think they had done enough, her services had only begun.

She was the daughter of John Benton Wilhoite and Elizabeth Bullock Wilhoite, born March 28, 1878, at "Wilhoite" the family home in Marshall County, Tennessee. Her grandmother bought this place in 1845 and built the dam and mill at old Fishing Ford in 1846. This farm, the mill, and the mill village bore the name Wilhoite.

Her father was descended from Jacob Wilhoite of old "Plantation" in North Carolina and later from Bedford County, Tennessee.

Jacob Wilhoite owned a convoy line for pioneers and had one of the earliest mills on Duck River. His son William Wilhoite married Anna Adeline Warner. He died at the age of twenty seven, leaving her with two small sons.

From this grandmother Mrs. Horton derived her name Ann Adeline Wilhoite. Left a widow at twenty five she early learned to assume responsibility and management. During the War Between the States one of the sons was killed. This grandmother Anna took her wagon and went for her son's body, bringing him dauntlessly through the enemy infested territory back to Wilhoite for burial in the family plot.

Mrs. Horton's mother, Elizabeth Thompkins Bullock Wilhoite, born in Franklin County, was a beloved teacher, a gentle, charming lady, brilliant in the art of conversation and a gracious hostess as the wife of John B. Wilhoite.

The late Governor Jim Nance McCord wrote in his *Marshall Gazette*, "This Wilhoite home became known as one of the most hospitable in Marshall, County." The two older children were Mary who married Walter W. Phillips and Jacob who died a bachelor.

As a young lady growing up Ann Adeline enjoyed the outdoors, boating, fishing on the river which ran through their farm. Horse back riding and hunting were sports she also enjoyed.

She attended early school in Marshall County, Tennessee and a school for young ladies in Franklin, Tennessee. She graduated from Belmont College in Nashville.

Soon after graduation she met Henry Horton, the son of Elizabeth Moore and Reverend Henry H. Horton, born on the paternal acres in Alabama. His mother was a descendent of Carey Moore and the beloved Irish poet Thomas Moore.

Governor Horton attended native schools in Jackson County, Alabama. He entered Scott Academy, Scottsboro, Alabama. He worked on his father's farm. He was a graduate of Winchester Academy and attended the University of the South in Sewanee.

He became a lawyer in partnership with Attorney General N. W. Whitaker and later Judge Frank Lynch in Chattanooga.

After graduation at Sewanee he joined the faculty at Winchester College. Soon after Ann Adeline graduated from Belmont, she was attending an associational meeting in Smyrna Baptist Church adjoining their place as was Professor Horton.

It has been told that Henry Horton especially noticed the small eighteen year old Miss Wilhoite with the laughing brown eyes, wearing a big hat.

When she observed the very dignified Professor, twelve years her senior, who was repeatedly looking at her, she responded with a saucy wink. The romance flourished and they were married November 25, 1896 in the same house in which she had been born.

They lived in Winchester, Tennessee where her husband was Treasurer and also a member of the faculty of Winchester College.

Mrs. Horton had the rare gift of enjoying a joke on herself, "In company with her sedate husband and his older brothers, on whom she had hoped to make a favorable impression, attended church in Winchester, she was trousseau dressed and carried a beautiful umbrella. In self conscious confusion she carried the lifted parasol into church and down the aisle never noticing that it was raised until she sat down."

One son, John Wilhoite Horton, was born to this union October, 1897. While in Winchester she studied art and became a talented artist. In 1905 they moved to Chattanooga until 1911, when he gave up law practice and moved back to Wilhoite. In 1907, he had represented Franklin County in the Lower House.

Mrs. Horton was interested in antiques. Here at Wilhoite she lived among her collections until her husband became Governor in 1927 on the death of Governor Peay. In 1926 Mr. Horton had re-entered the "political Arena", being elected State Senator from Marshall and Lincoln Counties. During the session he was elected Speaker of the Senate and succeeded to the Governor's office.

In October 1927 son John Horton married Miss Josephine Adams and brought her as a bride to live at "Wilhoite" while his parents moved on to the Governor's Mansion in Nashville.

The gown worn by the new First Lady at the Inaugural Ball was described in an article by Jo Sherman in the Magazine "Nashville". "She matched her silver-bugle beaded tunic over-black-net ball gown with black slippers featuring baby Louis heel, and ankle straps tied in front."

"While they entertained many interesting and delightful guests in the Governor's Mansion," says Mrs. Josephine Adams Horton. "Mother Horton especially enjoyed entertaining cousin Grace Moore. She also enjoyed a visit to her and was in New York when Grace Moore made her operatic debut at the Metropolitan."

"She accompanied Governor Horton to Washington when Andrew Jackson's Statue was presented by Governor Horton and placed in the Hall of Fame. They dined with President Coolidge, Alice Roosevelt Longworth and other notables."

During her husband's administration she filled her position as First Lady with graciousness, warmth, energy, loyalty and charm. Most people think holidays belong to themselves and their families. Mrs. Horton was interested in the improvement of conditions in the prison and gave her time to the unfortunate in the Nashville Prison. With much sympathy and fine fairness, she never spoke of them as prisoners, but as the boys."

Her work was done without show, known only to her most personal friends. She showed great interest to working girls who were ill and without funds and to all who were in need. She was a fine Christian woman and clung to the worthwhile things of life.

She took great pleasure and actively participated in Governor Horton's campaigns across the state.

In her later years when she was recalling her yesterdays

she remarked to Elmer Hinton of the Nashville *Tennessean*, "Meeting and knowing all the fine people who were so nice to Henry Horton was the greatest joy of public life."

She served during the depression and often reached out a helping hand. Mr. Henton wrote of Mrs. Horton in the Magazine section, "Somewhere we are told a record is kept of deeds we do in this life good or bad. If there is, I'm certain this entry has been made again and again, on Mrs. Horton's ledger sheet. "I was a stranger and you took me in, hungry and ye fed me."

Mrs. Horton was a member of the Eastern Star, a Baptist, and for many years an inspiring Sunday School teacher.

Putman County Herald in Cookville, wrote an article of her composure on a hectic ride. "She had this same adventurous spirit when she rode over the farm with the grandsons, Henry and Chase Adams Horton. Her grandchildren were her great delight, whom she often entertained as she was a gifted story teller, kind, generous, witty with a radiant personality."

During her last years her days were brightened by the lovely great granddaughters, Mary and Margaret Beasley, daughters of her granddaughter Ann Adeline Horton Beasley, a beloved teacher in the Nashville schools.

From the pen of Coleman Harwell at the time of her death, April 26, 1960 were these words, "I thought of many other days in the time of her husband's tribulations when that same dignity and composure must have been put to even sterner tests. And I was grateful for the memory of one who was the First Lady of her State."

Belle Meade Mansion, Nashville, Tenn. Home of Mrs. Hill McAlister.

Governor Hill and Louise Jackson McAlister Inaugural Ball.

Louise Jackson McAlister.

Louise Jackson McAlister

B. 1879 — M. 1901 — D. 1955

Wife of Governor Hill McAlister

An outstanding social event at the Belle Mead Plantation, on November 1, 1901, guests arriving through the ancient vine covered, cedar bordered driveway to the stone pillared portico of the Mansion—Justice Howell E. Jackson of the United States Supreme Court, recently deceased, and Mary Harding Jackson's daughter Louise, was to become the wife of Nashville, Tennessee's City Attorney Hill McAlister, who was later to be Governor of the state.

Louise Jackson was born at Belle Meade Mansion September 1, 1879. Her mother Mary Harding, before her, was born at Belle Meade, her grand father, General William Giles Harding who married Elizabeth McGovoch, was born here in 1808 in a double log cabin occupied by his father, John Harding of Hugenot ancestory, who with his brother came from Virginia in 1805.

It is said, "The land was acquired from the Indians in exchange for a Shetland pony and a shot gun per acre. It would seem they had a gun factory in Virginia. The state consisted of 1,400 acres and later 5000 were added to it."

Here John Harding laid the "Queen of the Southern Estates" and developed the first thoroughbred breeding establishment in America.

He cleared, fenced his Tennessee land and began the erection of the Mansion, the material and stone pillars quarried by the slaves on the place, living in the meantime in the double log cabin, which still stands on the adjoining lot.

After his death his son, General William Harding carried on, his daughter Mary married Howell Jackson, at that time a distinguished Statesman and Jurist.

He was born in Paris, Tennessee in 1832, educated in Paris, West Tennessee College and University of Virginia, graduated from Lebanon Law School, practicing at Jackson, Tenn. They were the parents of three children, Elizabeth Jackson Buckner, Harding Jackson, and Louise Jackson McAllister.

A story is told of Uncle Bob, one of the slaves of the old school. He had never been farther away from the plantation than to Nashville, a six mile journey. He was greatly upset over taking some colts to New York. The night before he left on a special train he called a prayer meeting at the slave quarters, where he prayed for a safe journey, and ended his prayer with, "Well, Good bye, Lord, I'm going to New York."

The Belle Meade negro quarters were houses of two rooms, with gardens, and built to face the four sides of an open Court, a playground for the negro children, and served as a place for open religious meetings. A church was near for rains and cold weather, in the center of the court was a well with two oaken buckets to supply water, and beside the well stood a tower, which housed a farm bell; it once hung in the belfry of a French Chapel. This mellowed tone bell rang each morning to awaken the hands and each afternoon to announce the day's work done.

Those who heard the sweet musical bell at dusk and the soft singing voices of the negroes as they plodded homeward at the end of the day felt as did Charles Summers who, when visiting at Belle Meade, witnessing the living conditions of slaves remarked to Louise Jackson's grandfather, "General, if what I see is typical of the South, then I must retract much that I have written against slavery."

Here Louise grew to young womanhood with her sister Elizabeth and brother Harding. There were the magnificent lynn trees shading the garden gate to the walk to the mausoleum, bordered on each side with large flower beds. They enjoyed watching deer hunts and fox hunts at Belle Meade.

One expression of hospitality that was handed down from one generation to the next was the custom of keeping the dining table stretched to its full length with places for unexpected guests with the beautiful flower arrangements and exquisite china.

Louise learned from her mother Mary Harding to move with grace among noted guests, which was the lavish entertainment and genuine hospitality which she later bestowed on her distinguished guests in the Governor's Mansion. As First Lady one of her guests was President Franklin D. Roosevelt in 1934.

Hill McAlister descended from a long line of outstanding ancestry in the Tennessee country, one was Joseph Rhea a minister graduated from Glasgow University, Scotland in 1749 and came to America in 1769. He first came to Blountville in 1771 and bought land in 1775. He built "Old Ireland Mansion" a log house of twelve rooms.

His son, Joseph and Frances Brenden Rhea reared a large family and from them decended Hill McAlister.

In 1880 Joseph built a home in Sullivan County and across from their home they had a "cocoonery lot." The Rhea sisters made their dresses of silk. This was said to be the first silk in Tennessee.

His father William King McAlister, a Tennessee Supreme

Court Justice for twenty seven years and later taught law at Vanderbilt, married Laura Brown Dortch, a daughter of Medora Brown and Wylie Blount Dortch.

He was born in Nashville in 1875, attended Vanderbilt receiving his law degree in 1897, Nashville City Attorney 1901 until 1909 and served as State Senator until 1911. Chairman of Democratic Committee in 1918 and elected State Treasurer from 1919 until 1931. He was elected Governor of Tennessee in 1932, and was reelected in 1934.

He was the great, great grandson of Lucinda Baker and Governor Wylie_ Blount (1809-1815), the great grandson of Sarah Burrus and Governor Aaron V. Brown (1845-47), great, great grandnephew of Governor William Blount of South West Territory and his great, great grandfather Joseph Burrus was a member of the House of Burgess in Virginia. So he grew up in a family with an extended record of public service.

During his administration, it is said that, with the possible exception of Governor Isham G. Harris, no governor was ever called upon to take over the control of government at a more critical period, with a State debt of eighty million dollars.

A period when the nation and world was in the worst part of a world wide depression. The greatest financial panic that ever swept our country.

Hill McAlister was a keen student of finance, having served from 1919 until 1927--1931. He was also State Treasurer, so the State Credit was maintained under his guidance.

The State flower, the Iris and the State bird, the Mockingbird were adopted. State expenditures were cut so deep, school house doors stayed open with the wolves chewing on the door knobs.

He was a friend of Public Education--appointing a Tennessee Education Commission to make a study of education conditions in the State, the first such study of the sort to be made in Tennessee. (I was one of three Bradley Countians that worked with that state commission on state Curriculum).

After retiring from Governor's office, Louise and her husband moved back to Nashville to their Nashville residence.

They had two daughters, Laura, Mrs. Donald Bathrick, and Louise (Mrs. Hamilton Love) the three grand children are Donald Bathrick Jr., Lt. Hamilton Love Jr., and Mrs. Harry Davis.

Laura Bathrick says, "Mother was fair, blue eyes, and petite. She attended Ward Seminary, Nashville, and Miss Summer's School in Washington, D.C. She was a leader in Nashville and Middle Tennessee civic and social life. She was very popular and well loved and highly respected by all who knew her. She did exquisite handwork. She belonged and was always in the Vine Street Christian Church.

While her husband was Governor she was interested and active in all social and official affairs of the State and entertained with charm and grace as she had been accustomed to all her life at Belle Meade, and continued so in the Mansion.

She passed away in Nashville, March 3, 1955. Governor McAlister lived until 1960. He was eighty five at the time of his death.

Governor Gordon and Ida Leach Browning.

Ida Leach Browning

Wife of Governor Gordon Browning

If the charms of nature, grand scenery, pleasant views and ever varying harmony of beautiful skies, could add to the growth and development of childhood, Ida Leach was blessed completely. The years of the brown eyed, auburn haired little girl were spent in Huntingdon, Tennessee in the home of her parents Madonna Baird and William Edward Leach. In this happy home circle were her two sisters: Mary Leach who resides in the Leach home in Huntingdon, and a younger sister Mrs. Raymond Ralls of Nashville who died leaving a son Raymond who lives in Jackson, Tennessee.

She grew to young womanhood in Huntingdon, attending the schools of that place, often spending some of her time with the two sets of grandparents, Julia McCollum and William Foster Leach and Mary P. Moore and William Baird.

In the early home of quiet and refinement she acquired the habits of order and truthfulness which characterized her conduct in after years of modesty, refinement and her quiet ways while First Lady of the State of Tennessee.

Governor Gordon Browning, the young lawyer, who had set up his law office in Huntingdon was much attracted by the gentle modest manners of Ida Leach when he first saw her in 1915. They were married in her parent's home in 1920.

Gordon Browning was born in 1895, the youngest of four children of Malissia Brock and James Browning of Carroll County. His father was a farmer, and justice of the peace of Gibson County, where he lived for many years at Milan, Tennessee.

As a boy, Gordon Browning attended grade school and graduated from Milan High School in 1906. He received his B.S. B.P. in 1913 at Valparaiso, Indiana. He studied law at Cumberland University, graduating in 1915.

He was Captain in First Tennessee Field Artillery in 1918, in World War I; he was overseas ten months. He saw action in the Battle of St. Michel, Argonne, and the battle of Woenie. He returned home in 1919.

He resumed his law practice in Huntingdon and on the secondary anniversary of the signing of the Armistice, being held at the tomb of the Unknown Soldier in Arlington National

Cemetery and a legal holiday in Tennessee, the Brownings were united in wedlock, November 11, 1920.

Ida Leach Browning says her happiest days have been spent in Huntingdon. They resided in Washington, D.C. while Gordon Browning served his District in Congress from 1923-1936.

In 1937, the forceful and intelligent Mr. Browning became Governor of Tennessee. They moved back to Tennessee and the vivacious, brown eyed Ida Leach Browning became a First Lady in the Governor's Mansion.

As Governor Mr. Browning's attitude of independence and ignoring being dictated to, mispleased Memphis Boss Crump. Yet under his administration, Tennessee State debt was reduced more than eighteen million dollars. He approved the eight point program for the improvement of public education, a department of Conservation was established, also the renovation and improvement of prisons and hospitals.

Mrs. Browning rendered her husband most efficient help in his struggle for eminence in Tennessee and was the wings by which he soared so high.

The receptions and dinners during his two terms 1937-1939 and 1949-1953 administrations were many. They entertained small groups for dinners—which was their preference for parties. But at times there were affairs for two and three hundred guests over which Mrs. Browning presided with grace and charm as hostess in the Mansion.

Some of the notables entertained during their sojourn in the capitol city of Nashville, were Lord Marley of England, Mr. Sam Rayburn of Texas, Senator Long of Louisiana and Governor Happy Chandler of Kentucky.

Mrs. Browning said, "The one thing I tried hardest to do while Gordon was Governor was to stay out of the limelight because my personal feelings have always been for women to stay in the background."

At the close of his administration they returned to their home in Huntingdon. The interior of each room has a different kind of wood panelling.

Here Mrs. Browning works in her flower gardens, spending many leisure hours. Her friends say she has the green thumb. She attends the Garden Club, Woman's Club and church.

The Brownings are members of the Methodist Episcopal Church, South; are well known for their cordial hospitality in Huntingdon and are esteemed for their personal and political interest o f Huntingdon Community Affairs. They have no children.

The William P. Cooper Home, Shelbyville, Tenn., where Mrs. Prentice Cooper and sons reside since the death

Hortense Powell Cooper, Tennessee 1st State Vice Regent, D.A.R.

Governor Prentice and Hortense Cooper and sons in London.

courtesy of
Mrs. Prentice Cooper

Mrs. Argie Shofner Cooper, Ambassadress to Peru.

Hortense Hayes Powell
Argie Shofner Cooper

Governor Cooper's Mother as First Lady

Hortense Powell Cooper is the wife of ex-Governor Prentice Cooper at Shelbyville, Tennessee. Their home is interesting and attractive, filled with interesting family antiques. This is where she takes care of her ex-Governor husband and their three sons, William Prentice, sixteen years old, who attended Groton School, Groton, Massachusettes, James Hayes, age fourteen, and John Norment, age eleven.

Hortense Hayes Powell was born in Nashville, April 28, 1919. She is the daughter of Margaret McGavock Hayes and Ferdinand Powell of Johnson City. Mrs. Powell was a descendent of Oliver Bliss and Emily McGavock Hayes. He was the first of the Hayes to come to Nashville; he owned Rockeby, Clara Shields inherited Rockeby, Corne Hayes Lawrence, Hillside, and Henry Martin Hayes owned Ensworth.

Dr. J. L. Crabb in his very interesting and informative Historical Novel, takes you to "dinner at Belmont" and the people, prominent in the building of early Nashville come alive in their notable entertainment and way of life during the War Between the States—with Sarah Polk, Adelicia Hayes Acklen, a great aunt of Hortense Powell Cooper and also her great grandfather, Oliver Bliss Hayes.

Many streets of Nashville bear the name of her Mother's people; Adelica Acklen, Hayes, Belmont, McGavock Lane and Rockeby.

Rockeby had a long history of notable entertaining in the early social life of Nashville. During the War Between the States, the soldiers thought Rockeby was haunted; its doors had a way of flying open on their own accord, even when bolted fast, and strange faces appeared in mirrors over one's shoulder. Footsteps of no visible form ran up and down the stairway and halls at different times of the day.

The Federal soldiers who occupied Nashville after its capture during the sixties adopted the ghostly superstition and left the Mansion unsacked when other homes were ransacked and the silver and valuables taken. Mrs. Hayes and her family fled to seek safety during the Battle of Nashville, but no guard was needed for the Rockeby valuables; "A bodyless Man stood guard."

Margaret McGavock Hayes of Rockeby graduated from Ward Belmont in Nashville and Horace Mann School in New York City. After her marriage to Mr. Powell, the family lived in Johnson City, Tennessee. Mr. Powell is an insurance, lumber, and real estate man of many interests. He graduated from U. P. I. in Blacksburg, Pennsylvania, and is a brother to Dr. John Powell of Richmond, Virginia. The Powells trace their ancestry back to Captain William and Nathaniel Powell, whose names are on the momument at Jamestown, Virginia, 1607.

Mrs. Cooper's brother is Ferdinand Powell, Jr., a lawyer in Johnson City; her sister is Mrs. Jerre Whitson Lowe of Cookeville, Tennessee. Hortense grew up in Johnson City, a graduate of Sweet Briar, Virginia; she taught school for a while.

She was attending the World's Fair in New York when she first met Prentice Cooper who was then Governor of Tennessee.

She was Administrative Assistant of the United Nations in 1946, when everyone had great hope for the U. N. Mrs. Cooper says, "I worked as A. A. four years. This was fascinating, especially as my work took me to Paris Assembly of 1948, and to Trade Conference in Havana in 1947. I met many famous people, and interesting people from all over the world."

Governor Cooper was born in Shelbyville in 1895. He was the son of Argie Shofner and William Prentice Cooper, who was a lawyer; he served as Speaker of the House in 1915, and was a Trustee of the University of Tennessee for forty years.

He was a grandson of Mr. and Mrs. J. M. Shofner and the great-grandson of Mr. and Mrs. Ab Landis of "Beach Hall," Bedford County.

Governor Cooper attended schools of Shelbyville; attended Princeton and Vanderbilt in Nashville, graduating from Princeton in 1917. He studied law at Harvard. In 1922 he began his career as a private lawyer and served as Attorney General of the Eighth Judicial District, City Attorney of Shelbyville, and Lewisburg. In 1923 he was Representative of Tennessee House and Representative of Senate in 1937.

He was inaugurated January 16, 1937 serving until 1945. At the Inaugural Ball Jeanie Blackburn of Pulaski, led the grand march with the bachelor Governor Cooper.

His administration was one of economy and good business administration. Funds were appropriated for free text books for elementary schools, another first of things in Tennessee.

Governor Cooper accepted one of the greatest responsibilities that ever comes to a Governor of a state: That of mobilizing a state and it s resources from peace time to a war-time basis.

Life in Tennessee changed after the December 7, 1941, attack of the Japanese on the U. S. Naval Fleet at Pearl Harbor. It was days of rationing sugar, food and gasoline. The man power and woman power entered Wartime activities.

The first Atomic Bomb was dropped on Hiroshima, Japan, with a loss of over 100,000 people. Tennessee, the Volunteer State, furnished 308,000 Tennesseans in the Second World War. Also, the Bomb was manufactured at Oak Ridge, Tennessee.

Mrs. Argie Shofner Cooper, a descendent of Martin Shofner, a distinguished Revolutionary soldier, was Tennessee's First Lady during these years from 1939 until 1945.

She attended Price's School in Nashville, married William Prentice Cooper in 1894, a practicing lawyer for nearly sixty years in Shelbyville. Mrs. Cooper, interested in political and civic life, often accompanied her husband to the Nashville Capitol when he was Speaker of the House.

She was Regent of Shelby Chapter D. A. R. for sixteen years. She gave her time and devotion to the American Cause of Freedom. Her home was always a welcome gathering place for the Organization.

A charming Dresden doll-type of lady, Mrs. Cooper filled the place of First Lady with charm, grace and distinction during the three terms of her son as Governor.

When Governor Cooper was appointed United States Ambassador to Peru, his mother again went with him as his Hostess. She charmed the Peruvians while enjoying the many attractions and made a marvelous Ambassadress from 1946-48. Hortense Powell and Governor Cooper had known each other for ten years, before they were married in 1950, in the chapel of St. Bartholemews Church in New York City. An aunt and uncle living in New York entertained with a wedding breakfast in their apartment.

Mrs. Cooper belongs to the American Legion Auxiliary, A. P. T. A., Colonial Dames, P. T. A. Garden Club. She enjoys gardening, music and reading. She is interested in all phases of the Episcopal Church. She has served twice as D. A. R. Regent, District Director, State Historian and is now Vice Regent of Tennessee.

Governor Jim Nance and Vera Kercheval McCord.

courtesy of
Conservation

Vera Kercheval McCord

B. 1879 — M. 1901 — D. 1953

First Lady 1945-1949

Vera Kercheval McCord affectionately called, "Bebe," was probably the most loved and admired woman of Lewisburg, Tennessee, a trait she won by service and loving deeds; she was born June 30, 1879, to Mollie McKenny and William Kennedy Kercheval. Mr. Kercheval was editor of the Marshall Gazette. Vera grew up in a political environment and liked the excitement and thrill of keeping in touch with politics, the news both State and National.

She grew up with her sister Elaine who married Doctor G. H. Galloway, and her two brothers Fred and Howard Kercheval; they often spent time with the two sets of grandparents, Colonel and Mrs. C. C. McKenney and the B. K. Kerchevals.

The family were Presbyterians; Miss Vera, as she was often called, worked in all phases of the Sunday School and Church. She had a lovely, warm contralto voice, was a member of the choir and graciously used her talent for funerals, weddings, and other special occasions.

She had an enthusiasm for living and loving and in return was loved. She married Jim Nance McCord May 21, 1901. He was then a traveling salesman. She spent her first years traveling with him, returning to make Lewisburg, Tennessee, "The best little town in the world," their home.

Jim Nance McCord was born March 17, 1879, in Bedford County, where he grew up on a farm and attended public schools. At seventeen, he became a traveling soap salesman and later developed an intense love of animals and auctioneering. He once said, "I have sold every important Jersey animal that has been sold in either the United States or Canada at auction since 1925.

At an early age he plunged into politics and served 13 terms of Mayor of Lewisburg. He was a member of the Marshall County quarterly court 25 years. Voters of his rural, 11-county district elected him to Congress in 1942 and two years later he was elected to the first of his two consecutive terms as Governor.

In 1944 he was the first Democratic candidate for Governor to run without opposition in his party primary. During that first term, his administration established the Departments of Veterans Affairs and Employment Security.

Trying to raise funds to increase teachers' salaries, McCord got the legislature in 1947 to impose the State's first sales tax—at the rate of two cents per $1.

Unknown to his political associates, he flew to Columbus, Ohio, during his gubernatorial campaign and conducted a sale for the American Jersey Cattle Breeders Association.

He was active many years in the operation of the Marshall County Gazette of which he became owner and publisher, and he served one year as president of the Tennessee Press Association.

Jim Nance McCord's love for Tennessee people was exemplified throughout his career and in turn the people revealed their respect and affection for him; this was shown each time he attended a gathering.

The McCords had no children, but loved and helped many. All the nieces adored and loved the sparkling eyed, brown-haired Aunt Vera.

On the occasion of inauguration, as First Lady of Tennessee in 1945, her aide was James Marion Hawkins of Lewisburg, who had just returned from service to his country in the South Pacific. At the second inauguration in 1947, her aide was Edward Ennis Murrey Jr., who had just returned from service overseas.

Mrs. McCord, a charming hostess, meeting every responsibility as First Lady with grace and charm with her touch of antiques to the beauty of the Governor's Mansion. She loved parties, teas, and her Bridge Club.

She was a member of the James K. Polk Auxiliary, The Hermitage Society, the Centennial Club, the Colonial Dames, and the Daughters of the American Revolution. Her ancestor was Captain William Edmiston; he was born in Virginia in 1734, was an officer in the Virginia Rangers during the American Revolution. He was killed in performance of his duties at the Battle of King's Mountain in 1780, leaving a wife and three children. There were eight Edmistons in that engagement, three of whom lost their lives.

Mrs. McCord loved her home, to cook the foods the Governor liked — her favorite was homemade bread. She landscaped the three homes in which she lived; under a large beech tree were large fern beds and wild flowers, which she had retrieved from the woodlands. There were lilies, Dutch iris, and a border of bulbs and perennials to pick for arrangements in her home, and always a rare rose garden near her back terrace.

In 1951 the McCords celebrated their Golden Wedding anniversary. She died two years later in 1953.

When she was in Washington she was a member of the Ladies Congressional Club. She enjoyed the many social activities there and her trip to Canada.

On her stone the Governor placed this motto: "Hers was a Radiant Life." A niece, Mrs. Ernest Irwin of Mount Pleasant, Tennessee, says the little poem by James Whitcomb Riley, portrays the life of Aunt Vera Kercheval McCord;

"Whatever the weather may be, says he,
Whatever the weather may be,
Its the song you sing,
And the smiles ye wear,
That's making the sunshine everywhere."

Wedding in the Governor's Mansion, Ex Gov. McCord and Sula Sheeley.

Sula Sheeley McCord.

Sula Sheeley McCord

B. 1891 — M. 1954 — D. 1968

2nd Wife of Ex-Governor James Nance McCord

"I've seen yesterday, I've lived today and I am not afraid of tomorrow."

A favorite quotation of Sula Sheeley whose marriage on November 3, 1954, made history in a number of ways. It was the first time a governor of Tennessee had served as best man for a former Governor; a number of marriages have been performed in the Governor's Mansion, but never between a Cabinet member and a close relative of a Cabinet member.

Former Governor Jim Nance McCord and Mrs. John Arthur Sheeley were married in a quiet ceremony at the Governor's Mansion in Nashville. Governor Frank Clement served as best man and Mrs. Herman Reynolds, Commissioner of State Welfare, and daughter of Mrs. Sheeley, was her mother's matron of honor.

Reverend Will Henry Atkins of Oakwood Methodist Church in Knoxville, Tennessee, solemnized the rites. He was a Colonel on Governor Clement's staff. A program of nuptial music was given by Miss Ann Powers, a niece of the bride.

Mrs. McCord wore a black French cashmere costume suit and a black velvet hat lined with aqua satin and a purple orchid. Mrs. Reynolds wore brown tweed, and a brown orchid. Only members of both families and close friends, including Captain Toby Lewis, Governor and Mrs. Clement, attended the ceremony. Mr. and Mrs. Leonard Sheeley and Mr. and Mrs. Herman Reynolds were host at a wedding breakfast at the Governor's Mansion.

Mrs. Sula McCord was born in Dickson County in 1891, the daughter of Green Leonard and Elizabeth Johnson Tatum. Her maternal grandparents were David W. and Elizabeth McEthorney Johnston and her paternal grandfather and mother were George Washington and Martha D. Bowen Tatum.

Mrs. Leonard Tatum died in 1905 leaving Sula, fourteen, her two sisters, Effie, eleven, and Elizabeth, eight.

Sula with her golden brown hair, hazel eyes and fair skin, the other sisters a real brunette and a blond were three unusual sisters. They were educated in public and private schools of Dickson County. Sula took special piano and voice training.

In 1908, Sula married H. K. Meadows of Nashville, Tennessee. In 1909, she became the mother of Christine Meadows (Reynolds) who became the first woman to serve as a Commissioner in a Tennessee Governor's Cabinet.

In 1910, Sula was left a widow — Mr. Meadows died of T.B. She took her baby Christine and lived with her father until she married John Arthur Sheeley in 1913, a conductor on the L. & N. Railroad. They lived in Paris, Tennessee where Sula was active in the Methodist Church, singing in the choir for over thirty years. She served as President of Matinee Music Club, organized the McDowell Jr. Music Club and also started an annual piano Ensemble (16 players) giving concerts in the Paris auditorium. In the church she served on the membership committee, President of W.S.C. in which she was given life membership.

She became the mother of two boys, Leonard Jr. and Hartwell Sheeley; with the three children she was active in serving as President of all P.T.A. in Paris, the Robert E. Lee, Arthur Porter and E. W. Grove high school.

While the sons served in the Air Force during World War II, she served as Gray Lady at near-by Camp Tyson. She opened her home for visiting wives whose husbands were stationed at Camp Tyson.

Christine Meadows Reynolds says, "Our home was one of love, Mr. Sheeley was a great person, quiet, reserved but had great dignity. I adored him, Dad Sheeley loved me as he did the boys; we were encouraged to bring our friends home for overnight or a week. He died in 1950, and Hartwell met an untimely death in an auto accident the same year."

Julia Williams and husband Bryant who is owner and publisher of The Paris Post Intelligencer of Paris, Tennessee were old friends of ex-governor Jim Nance McCord who was Commissioner of Conservation in Governor Frank Clement's Cabinet and soon after Christine Reynolds, daughter of Mrs. Sheeley, was named first Woman Commissioner of Welfare, Governor and Mrs. Clement held open house at the Mansion for friends of all Cabinet members. The Williams took Mrs. Sheeley to Nashville with them and introduced her to Governor McCord, playing cupid to the romance that soon developed.

Mrs. William says, "Sula was not a stranger to tragedy — yet never imposed her grief on others — soon after the death of her son Hartwell, I met her on the street. I told her I had never seen her look lovlier, she was glowing," I was amazed. With her sweet smile she answered, "My heart was near breaking this morning, I could not sleep last night and felt I could not go on, any longer, but Julia, honey, I went into my room, closed the door and fell on my knees. I don't remember praying but I must have. I know now there must have been a reason for Hartwell's death and that God will see me through. Joy will come in the morning. And joy did come through her marriage to Gov. McCord.

"I met her again one bright spring morning; knowing her financial status was not good, I exclaimed over her band box appearance, she held up her mended snow white gloves! She wore a bouquet of violets pinned to her shoulder—walked away with a spring in her walk. Her inner qualities reacted to friends in trouble. I once received a card from her:

"I heard a bird sing in the darkness of December;
A magical thing, sweet to remember.
We are nearer to spring than we were in November
     Because
I heard a bird sing in the dark of December."

Mrs. Sheeley often spent time with Mrs. Reynolds in her Nashville apartment. And after meeting Governor McCord, they often met at social functions. On Easter Sunday, 1954, Sula Sheeley received an orchid from Jim Nance McCord, then an invitation to a special movie. After several lunch invitations, there were two-some engagements. Cupid had shot his dart.

They were persuaded by Governor and Lucile Clement to be married in the Governor's Mansion.

They lived in a Nashville apartment, moving to Lewisburg in 1959. Sula was interested in government; in 1939 she was co-chairman of the Democratic Women for Prentice Cooper and served on the State Committee with the late Mrs. Albert Hill. She was an able public speaker with depth and wit. People frequently remarked at her beautiful and youthful countenance: "She glows."

She was a member of Nashborough Chapter of the Daughters of American Revolution. Her hobbies were her home and books—she was an avid reader of history, poetry, classics and a continuing Bible student. A lover of birds, keeping bird feeders and bath in her garden where she grew flowers for home and friends.

Elizabeth McGowan of Colliersville, Tennessee was also a close friend of Sula and Jim Nance McCord. She says, "A wonderful friend whom I first met at the Methodist Church in Paris, I looked at her one sabbath day and thought, 'The most beautiful woman I have ever seen, we smiled and met. She knew how to meet people and was sincere, and loved people; her attire was always appropriate and artistic as the occasion demanded. She often wore off-white, and black; for formal wear

305

her favorite color was American beauty. She was fond of pearls and emeralds. Her home was always in order, her family came first with church the foundation. I loved her in life and her memory is sacred above all friendships.' "

While living in Lewisburg, Mrs. McCord delighted in small dinner parties for their numerous friends and also Miss Vera's former friends and family. Governor McCord often remarked, "he was lucky, a real family of his own." His name for Sula was "Miss Gorgeous."

She played the organ as well as the piano. Most every day she played at dusk and she and Mr. Jim would sing his favorite, "How Great Thou Art," also "Brahms Lullaby," and "Moonlight Sonata."

After a major coronary, they moved to Nashville to the Continental Apts. to be nearer her Doctor and ex-Governor close to the center of government, which he loved. Few knew her health was impaired; she continued their public and social engagements, her charity and sharing with others.

Sula McCord lived a rich full life — on the night of March 3, 1966, she kissed Christine good night, then leaned over saying, "Good night sweet Prince," and laid down beside the Governor and gasped her last breath.

She was laid to rest under a pall of plumoss ferns.

Frank Clement and Wife Lucille

Lucile Christenson Clement

B. 1920 — M. 1940 — D.

Wife of Governor Frank Clement

Lucile Christenson Clement spent ten years as Tennessee First Lady. At the time of Frank Clement's first inauguration, she was one of the youngest First Ladies in the Nation in 1953. Governor Clement had campaigned for honesty, decency, and morality in State affairs and for government in a "Gold Fish Bowl," winning 57,000 vote plurality over the incumbent Browning. In 1954 he was elected to his first four year term.

Again in 1963, Lucile Christenson came back to receive the list of guest towels and silver in the Mansion from Mrs. Ellington.

Lucile, the beautiful, brown-eyed blonde, reflecting her Swedish ancestry, was born June 20, 1929 at Erin, Tennessee in Houston County. Her parents were Mr. and Mrs. Nelson Christenson. Her paternal grandparents emigrated to America from Sweden - the grandfather from Stockholm and the grandmother from Lynn. The maternal grandparents were of Irish descent.

Lucile spent her childhood in Erin, where her father was Mayor and Judge of Houston County and a very active Democratic politician for over forty years. She attended the Elementary and High Schools, winning several honors on the girl's basketball team. She graduated from Houston High School, where she first met Frank Clement of Dickson County at a basketball game.

While in school, the popular blonde Lucile entertained civic groups in Houston and surrounding counties by giving readings at which she was quite talented, and like her mother she was endowed with musical talent. She sang in all the churches of Erin.

Her mother, Mrs. Christenson, was a musician. She played the violin, and taught music. She was also a gifted artist and sculptress.

Lucile was chosen Queen of the Senior Class, being selected the prettiest girl in Erin High School.

She attended Cumberland University. She married Governor Clement while he was a law student at Vanderbilt University, on January 25, 1940. She was nineteen years old at the time.

While he finished his law course at the University, Lucile worked as receptionist in Radio Station, W.L.A.C. in Nashville to help augment the family income.

Frank Clement went from law school to the F.B.I. as special

agent. Lucile was his secret confidante. After years he waived military deferment and entered the army as a private, later he became company commander.

He left the army as lieutenant. In 1950 he was recalled to the army; he spent sixteen months at Camp Gordon, Georgia as an instructor and was discharged as a first lieutenant.

The Clements were the parents of three sons, Robert born in 1943 married Marilyn LaJean Wims during Christmas vacation in 1966 in the executive Mansion in Nashville. Frank Jr. was born in 1949 and James Gary was born in 1952.

Frank Clement attracted state-wide attention at the early age of twenty-six, a young lawyer of Nashville, when he won some notable phone rate victories as General Counsel for the Railroad and Public Commission saving phone users millions.

He assumed state-wide leadership in the March of Dimes, the Red Cross, and the Young Democratic Clubs, and was State commander of the American Legion.

In 1954, Frank G. Clement was again elected Governor over Browing with 286,000 votes, carrying ninety-four counties of Tennessee. He received personal recognition as Chairman of Southern Governor's Conference, Chairman of Southern Regional Education Board, and Chairman of Cordell Hull Foundation for International Education. He was named by the Junior Chamber of Commerce as one of the "Ten Outstanding Men" of the United States.

His grandfather James Clement, born in 1865 in Henry County, had been a State Senator. His great grandparents Christian Buchanan and Aaron Clement were natives of Virginia.

James Clement was one of eight children, reared on his father's farm. He was a wagon maker; he studied law and was admitted to the Bar in 1890. In 1903 Robert Clement moved to Dickson, Tennessee; he had married Sallie Stockdale of Benton County in 1898.

Governor Clement grew up with four sisters, Agnes Ship Dixon died in 1913, Luetta married J. A. Allen, and Martha Caroline married W. H. Lashlee of Camden, Anna Bell was Secretary for her brother during his Administrations, and was Secretary of Capitol Chevrolet Co., and also Secretary to Buford Ellington, when Commissioner of Agriculture. She is now Mrs. O'Brian of Clarksville, Tennessee. All the women in the Clement family are Baptist; all the men are Methodist.

During Governor Clement's Administration, Tennessee achieved its highest status in education, the public schools receiving around seventy million dollars annually.

Mentally retarded and mental hospitals were given a Commissioner of Mental Health.

The Tennessee Constitution of 1870, stated "No public school shall allow white and negro children to be together in the same school." In 1954, the Supreme Court of the United States, stated it unconstitutional for separate education of whites and negroes in public schools.

During the Clement Administration, desegregation of white and colored schools went peacefully except for one John Kasper, who came down from New Jersey to play "John Brown" in Tennessee. He received a sentence term in prison for his two bombings, and since then Tennessee has gone peacefully on with its desegregation.

In June 1966, in a brief ceremony following a Cabinet meeting Governor Clement made former heavyweight boxing champion Joe Louis an "honorary citizen" of Tennessee.

Louis, in Nashville for a golf tournament at the time, was cited by the Governor as "one of America's sons who has grown greater with passing years."

"By his (Louis') example and his patriotism," Clement said, "he has become an even bigger man out of the ring where he won worldwide acclaim."

In January 1965, the Clements celebrated their Silver Wedding Anniversary, and January 1967, Lucile again gave back her Mansion list of towels and silver to Catherine Cheek Ellington.

Lucile, an avid and excellent golf player, continues on the field in both Richland and Blue Grass Country clubs and gives of her time to the Ladies Hermitage Association.

Mrs. Buford Ellington in the Mansion.

Catherine Cheek Ellington.   *courtesy of*
                                                  Conservation

Catherine Cheek Ellington

Excited but Not Awed as Tennessee's First Lady

The gracious tribute accorded Mrs. Buford Ellington on March 15, 1961 by the General Assembly expressed an admiration earned not only as Tennessee's First Lady — the role she has honored — but as help mate and homemaker, her life work nobly filled through a longer tenure.

The resolution stated, "Mrs. Catherine Cheek Ellington has brought to the Executive Mansion grace and charm in the highest tradition of southern womanhood, unsurpassed in the history of our state."

The text of that homage was the spirit of flowers to the living — richly deserved; an acknowledgement of character wrought in the design of beauty. It could be added that Tennessee in the aggregate shares the appreciation thus formally expressed—its heart, if not all its names upon that scroll".

Presenting her with a silver tray, and a copy of the resolution.

"This is just almost too much", said Mrs. Ellington as she fought back the tears; sitting by the Governor, she also said, "The experience that we have had during the past few years has been wonderful and we are proud and thankful for the many friends that we have made.

A CHRISTMAS ENCOUNTER

Catherine Cheek was a nineteen year old Tennessean when Buford Ellington first crossed her path at Durant High School in Mississippi. She with other teachers were working on a Christmas play just before Christmas holidays in 1928.

Buford was the editor of a newspaper in Durant in search of news for his paper. It was a brief introduction, a mild exchange of courtesies and a chat about the play in progress as he went on his way to write up his notes for publication.

Soon there was more than the Black River flowing through the town of Durant, as Neptune was in transit, a fascinating thing was happening to the future Governor of Tennessee, his world, amazing and miraculous was a burst of love for the slim, shapely, brunette Commercial Arts Teacher, moving with grace and freedom. Her dark hair glossy and thick framed a long face. smooth in contour, firm in its planes.

Catherine's large eyes were the feature people remembered full dark under heavy brows, eyes that could smile without the movement of lips. A vivacious, intelligent girl, sympathetic to the burst of Ellington's love.

They were married January 19th, 1929.

Buford Ellington, the son of Mr. and Mrs. A. E. Ellington of rural Lexington, Holmes County, Mississippi, attended elementary Bethesada school and graduated from Holmes County Agricultural School. After high school at Goodman, he attended Milsap College at Jackson, Mississippi.

A young editor of the weekly newspaper at Durant, the reporter editor, and young married man and not twenty-two until June, yet old enough to vote, the future Governor not knowing what the stars predicted, brought the wife Catherine to Tennessee to visit her parents, Fannie Bell and James Cheek at Caney Creek Farm in Marshall County and to show off the four year old son John Earl.

They stopped at a General Store in Verona, Tennessee, marvelling at the pace of life of the young owner, Governor Ellington said, "With $11.20 in his pocket, he took up the man's "Store for Sale" after a little visit to the Bank in Lewisburg, the store changed names to Ellington's General Store." So the year 1939 in December, he became a citizen of Tennessee.

Catherine was happy to be near her family. Now Verona was home. The Governor's political life begin in 1941, interested in Marshall County politics, helping in the local elections and in 1946 he was chosen as campaign manager for Joe L. Evins in his first race for Congress.

Working with the Tennessee Farm Bureau, setting up its insurance program in the state, meeting people in all walks of life, in all the counties of the state, won for him political success.

His first political office came in 1948 as a represenative of Marshall County, he was elected to the General Assembly of Tennessee.

Anna Bell Ellington was now ready for the second grade at Verona; John in elementary school, later graduating from Marshall High School, Ann graduated from Hillsboro High in Nashville, both children graduating from Tennessee Middle State College in Murfreesboro.

Governor Frank Clement appointed Buford Ellington as Commissioner of Agriculture in 1952. The Ellingtons moved to Nashville in 1953.

The highlights of the Ellington's tenure as Commissioner of Agriculture included the eradication of brucellosis in Tennessee and the founding of Ellington Agriculture Center, an agricultural diagnostic laboratory in Nashville.

Like the Black River in Durant Mississippi, time glides along. The slender thread of light that now breaks upon Catherine Cheek Ellington's senses is like unto the dull burning of her Grandmother Cheek's old brass lamp wick, flickering feebly, of little consequence as yet, attending P.T.A., playing a little golf, singing in the Glendale Methodist Church choir, however on the stage of Tennessee, she does not in her wildest moments of waking, not yet in the dawn cobwebs of her dreams, think once to herself, "Someday I shall go as First Lady to the Governor's Mansion; someday she would be the head of social life, an industrial factor and preadventure a political factor twice removed in the Governor's Mansion in Tennessee.

In 1958 Governor Ellington waged a successful campaign for Governor and was inaugurated on January 19, 1959, a most unusual way of celebrating their Thirtieth Wedding Anniversary, with father and mother Ellington and Mrs. Fannie Bell Cheek of Lewisburg sharing the inaugural reception.

Catherine had told some friends that part of being Tennessee's First Lady after January 19th, "just leaves me cold." "Entertaining hundreds of the States great and near great at a time is going to be a far cry from having the members of Verona, Tennessee Home Demonstration Club drop by for coffee."

"The first year will be hard, but with experience and adequate help I think we will do all right." Most of all, she said, "I'm hoping this will be one of the best administrations the State has ever had, and I am going to be helping Buford all I can."

Wednesday January 21, 1959 at ten o'clock a.m. the First Lady of Tennessee, Mrs. Buford Ellington, was at home, poised and ready to meet radio and press in the Executive Mansion, Far Hills on Curtiswood Lane, wearing a seafoam silk shantung dress with tropical orange chiffon scarf and matching bracelet.

Tuesday was her first day, adding her touch to the furnishing with an original flower arrangement for their living quarters on the second floor.

Anna Bell had the third floor for her very own, where she could receive her many friends, one of the fifteen rooms and seven baths of the rambling Italian Renaissance Mansion.

Mrs. Ellington has an office, where Miss Lily Clemons takes over as Secretary, giving the First Lady time to play golf, work with flowers, sew for Ann—she said when she first moved in she must find a spot for her sewing machine, also her organ and piano which she admitted she played for her own pleasure.

One guest room, she had furnished in provincial decor against wedgewood blue walls and draperies.

Catherine Cheek Ellington was excited but not awed as First Lady in The Mansion.

Governor Ellington's first administration was marked by an unprecedented growth of industry in the State. He reorganized State government in a way that gave taxpayers a great savings. There was no increase in taxes for his four year term.

A Youth Center was founded at Jolton, a 4-H Camp at Milan, updating camps in other counties, opening the pardoning and parole hearings to the press and public, also urging additional industry to move to Tennessee and adopting the Kerr Mills Medical Act, which was the forerunner of Medicare.

Catherine Cheek Ellington now turns back to Lucile Clement the responsibility for all the State property in the Residence, just as the Commissioners are responsible for their State Departments, including everything from the guest towels to the $6,000 silver service from the Battleship U.S.S. Tennessee which was presented to the armored cruiser Tennessee at Hampton Roads in Virginia, December, 1906.

Governor Ellington unable to succeed himself after serving four year term, re-entered private life as Vice-President of Louisville and Nashville Railroad and in charge of bringing new industry and new jobs to Tennessee.

This venture into private enterprise did not last long, for the former Governor was chosen by President Johnson to serve with the Community Relations Service. Working closely with the President and Vice President Humphrey, he visited thirty-four states in regard to implementing the Civil Rights Act.

In 1965 he was tapped by the President for the job of Director of the Office of Civil and Defense mobilization, the National Security Reserve Board, and the War Manpower Board.

In this post Ellington directed the efforts of other Federal Government Agencies in alleviating the effort of disasters and coordinating plans for war time mobilization. He served as a member of the National Security Council; regularly sat in on Cabinet meetings and was especially assigned with Vice President Humphrey as the administration's point of contact between Federal, State, and local governments. He served as liaison between the White House and the Nation's Governors.

The Governor served four years as Chairman of Cordell Hull Foundation and was awarded the Legion of Merit by the Federation for his contribution to education in South America. The Foundation was established to foster understanding between Latin America and the United States through the exchange of teachers and students.

He served as Chairman of the Southern Governor's Conference and was a member of the executive committee of the

National Governor's conference, serving two years on Southern Regional Education Board. He has served on the Board of Trustees, University of Tennessee, Rust College, Holly Springs Miss., George Peabody College, Nashville, and a member of Board of Directors of Milsaps College Alumni Association, Jackson, Miss., also an Honary member of National Council of Boy Scouts of America.

A Sunday school teacher of Men's Class and member of the Board of Stewards at Glendale Methodist Church in Nashville. He is the only 33rd degree Mason of the Scottish Rite, presently serving as Governor in the United States.

On January 16, 1967, Governor Ellington was inaugurated as Governor for the second time, thereby becoming the forty-second man to serve as Governor of the Volunteer State.

Betty Pritchard Dunn.

Betty Pritchard Dunn

Wife of Governor Winfield Dunn

After fifty years of solid Democratic family men in the Tennessee Mansion, the voters in 1970 decided to try Doctor Winfield Dunn a Republican, who is the first of Tennessee's six Republican governors from 1796 to 1970, since the Inauguration of Governor Alfred A. Taylor in 1920.

In his inaugural address he said, "I have never known the pleasure or perhaps the pain of elected office...........'' He asked the citizenship to "support me when you can--------oppose me if you must."

The new Governor takes over at a time when there are great problems to be made and agonizing choices ahead. As he noted, he must work with legislative majorities of another party, if the problems are formable, so are the opportunities in the next four years of vital importance.

It was a grand old party for Democrats and Republicans with the men in their tuxedos, many with bright colored formal shirts and ladies in ball gowns who attended the $100 plate pre-inaugural dinner at the magnificent room of Nashville Auditorium. The room was beautifully decorated by hundreds of candles glowing in silver candelabrum filled with orchids, on the tables and twinkling lights on trees added to the elegant decor of the buffet tables with Boots Randolph and his band opening the entertainment show.

The new First Lady Mrs. Dunn, gracious and charming dressed in a gown of white silk chiffon with jewling and white orchids, greeted old and new friends who crowded around her.

There were daughters Julie and Gayle also son Charles known as Chuck who hovered near mother as she conversed with Mrs. Robert Stack in her pink, gold and black brocade pant suit.

Mrs. Dunn said, of the inauguration, "I would not have believed this time last year that I would be working on plans to make the Governor's Mansion available to the people of Tennessee, to whom it really belongs.

"I hope to have open house one day a week to the public and have knowledgeable people act as guides to tell visitors about the house and a little about Tennessee history."

Her husband Governor Winfield Dunn said that there will

be understanding, compassion, interest and enthusiasm for people, from every walk of life in his administration.

At historical McKendree United Methodist Church in downtown Nashville, Governor Winfield Dunn began his inauguration day with his family on January 16, 1971.

Dr. J. Howard Beaty of Memphis, Bishop A. Durick of Roman Catholic Diocese of Nashville read scriptures and Rabbi Matthew Derby of Knoxville delivered the prayer of supplication. The Rev. Wallace Chappell, McKendree pastor gave the closing prayer.

Dr. Beaty's topic, "What can one man do?"

"One person can always pray, one can serve where he is, one person can stand firmly for truth, justice and liberty and all other intrinsic religious and democratic values.

"One person can wholeheartedly support dedicated leaders and sound government."

At 12:39, on Saturday Bryant Winfield Culbertson Dunn turned to Ross Dyer, Chief Justice of Tennessee Supreme Court and said in a firm voice, "Mr. Chief Justice, I am ready to take the oath."

His breath frosting in 29 degree weather the new 43rd governor pledged to bring a "New era of citizens participation", and acknowledgement that the government faced a financial crisis.

Several thousand people jammed into Memorial Square watched the transfer of power in a colorful, festive ceremony, roared in applause.

A National Guard Artillery battery boomed out a 19 gun salute to the new governor, and a flight of Air National Guard jets, zoomed overhead in a tribute.

After the inaugural parade went by Governor Dunn returned to the Capitol where his Cabinet members took oath of office.

Tennesseans stood in line in the lobby of the Municipal Auditorium — a line reaching out into James Robertson Boulevard for a full half hour before the doors of the Inaugural Ball opened at seven p.m.

They were clad in tuxedo, gown clad, pant suit clad. Governor and Mrs. Dunn in a floor length A line white dress, a sleeveless bodice completely embroidered with silver beads, pearls and rhinestones, lead off the dancers to the strains of "The Tennessee Waltz". They soon went on to the second Ball at the National Armory and the third at Sheraton Motor Inn to the young people's Ball where Julie was seen in her gown of rosebud embroidered white moire and pink velvet.

Sister Gayle was wearing an empire gown of ice blue organza and satin with blue beading at the waistline and cuffs.

320

The three day inaugural festivities heralding the advent of the administration of the new governor Dunn and First Lady in Tennessee closed with more than 5000 persons from every county in the state attending the reception at the Mansion which stands on a hill overlooking Curtiswood Lane.

An orderly line moved through the entrance off the gardens in front into the foyer, and down the hallway to the South, where Betty Pritchard Dunn so sweet, and gracious in her apple green dress stood beside the Governor greeting guests.

Standing in the receiving line is hard work, even though Julie, Gayle and Chuck now and then came to help their parents but this offered no relief because all these Tennesseans from Memphis to Mountain City were not leaving until they held the hand of the First Lady and Winfield Dunn's the one . . .

During the campaign the soft spoken, silvery blond First Lady made it clear by the look in her twinkling eyes and tone of voice she had recognized twenty years ago the "Charisma" of Governor Dunn. . . "He has the real feel for the fine and right thing to do."

Betty Dunn often laughed and said, "If my hair looks nice I can face anything."

She did her first political activities in Shelby County when she put Julie in a stroller and went from door to door, campaigning for Republican candidates after she and her husband joined the Republican party and "became active at the grass roots level."

Governor Dunn was born and reared in Mississippi (Meridian). He was called Win by his boyhood chums, was closely connected to politics as a boy.

He and a young friend who was to help him in Coffee County were sitting on some steps in a dry dusty Mississippi town one summer while his father Albert Dunn, campaigned for United States Congressman.

Out of boredom the boys latched on to some firecrackers and the expected happened, with the firecrackers popping all over the street. His father ran toward him and his friend, screamed, "You'll have me beaten."

They did not, his father served one term in Congress, an experience which gave Winfield an insatiable taste for politics.

Young Win began a life of work and schooling, with ambitions of being a lawyer like his father.

His critics in his gubernatorial campaign took every opportunity to denote his Mississippi birthright. "Dunn who takes over from another Mississippi born, Buford Ellington" was quick to answer, "I have no apologies about where I was born, On that day I was born, I had to be pretty close to my mother."

Winfield Dunn learned the dignity of work, the worth of people and the value of a dollar during high school and college years, during which he worked as a car hop at a local drive in restaurant, as a laborer on Mississippi highways during the hot summer months and a loader of 100 pound feed bags in a feed mill.

He worked as a railway mail clerk and later as a mailman on foot. He has sold women's shoes, worked in a blood bank and sold insurance. He also has distinguished himself in his chosen career, Dentistry.

When Bryant Winfield Culbertson Dunn finished high school at the age of seventeen, he volunteered and served in the Navy during World War II.

After the war ended he entered the University of Mississippi and worked on his degree in banking and commerce. He became president of the school of Commerce and Business.

He was a cadet in the Air Force R.O.T.C. and was commissioned second lieutenant in the Air Force Reserve upon graduation.

Dr. Frank Pritchard of Memphis, Tennessee had sent his beautiful, soft spoken blond Betty to Ole Miss to complete her "Book Learnin".

Cupid always lurking in the least expected places, shot the dart that pierced the two hearts of Betty Pritchard and Win Dunn making them one in 1950.

They began housekeeping in a garage apartment at Bay, St. Louis, Mississippi. Winfield was engaged in the insurance business and was away from home so much that his father-in-law encouraged him to enter his profession of dentistry.

That would bring Betty and the baby Charles (Chuck) back to Memphis.

After they returned to Memphis Betty taught school while her husband attended the University of Tennessee Medical Units in Memphis.

After graduation he entered the practice of his father-in-law Dr. Pritchard, in the meantime he became one of Memphis' most active young men. They became the parents of Gayle and Julia, who was lost for a short time during inauguration day. She finally rushed upon the platform, kissing her daddy and saying, "Oh! I finally got the autograph of Robert Stack."

Winfield Dunn was chairman of the Republican party in Shelby County for four years. He was a delegate to the 1968 Republican National Convention.

He has kept active in Boys Clubs, the Hospital Board, Junior Chamber of Commerce and Civic Clubs.

He has been a Bible teacher in Christ United Methodist

Church and vice chairman of administration of the church.

The new First Lady Betty Pritchard Dunn, who lives in Tennessee's busiest home, the Governor's Mansion on Curtiswood Lane in Nashville has again brought out the $6,000 silver service that was presented on December 15, 1906 to the U.S.S. Tennessee at Hampton Roads while Governor John I. Cox was Tennessee's chief magistrate.

On this memorable occasion ex-Governor and Mrs. J.B. Frazier and family, and the governor's family and Cabinet represented the state of Tennessee.

Mary Cox the fair daughter (now Mrs. Fleming of Bristol) gave the sponsor's words in formally presenting the beautiful silver service to the U.S.S. Tennessee.

It now adorns the Mansion dining room where you will see the pedestal table and its eighteen Chippendale chairs presented to Tennessee by the late General Charles De Gaulle. One other feature in this room is the portrait of General George Washington.

Mrs. Winfield Dunn has added the portrait of General Andrew Jackson, the only portrait of him painted from real life in 1819 by Samuel Lovet Waldo.

The Dunns take their meals in the family dining room with its provincial furniture, just off the blue tile and stainless steel kitchen where Ida Leach Browning had a wood range when she went as First Lady to this Mansion.

The large affairs are served in the Mansion dining room by a catering service while the cooks serve family meals and for small parties of twenty-five or less.

Betty Dunn loves her lovely new house which she is making it a home to live, love and enjoy. She has brought furniture from their Memphis home she says she won't feel embarassed if the children and their guests spill cokes on her own coffee table. Their bedrooms and sitting room upstairs is a place where friends of the children can feel relaxed and an informal place for living.

The Dunns are a loving family and have good times together. The Governor is a charmer, who brings out the best in people, his zest for friendship was shown at the Mansion reception January 17, 1971 by his spontaneous enthusiasm shaking hands with multitude of Tennesseans, who had shivered for three long hours for their turn to shake his hand and meet the First Lady.

Betty Dunn is a pretty blonde who is intelligent with common sense and her charm is already bringing to her a complimentary personality that proves she was born with taste and talent which fitted her for a First Lady.

She said, "I never dreamed when I became Betty Dunn twenty years ago I would be privileged to be a First Lady. I really pray each day for guidance."

Mrs. Walker's "creative dolls", representing Tennessee Governors and Ladies, 1796-1971.

GOVERNORS
OF
TENNESSEE

Governor William Blount, Territory South of Ohio, 1790-1796

Governor William Blount, S.W.T.
1790-1796

Governor John Sevier
1796-1801, 1803-1809

Governor Archibald Roane
1801-1803

Governor Willie Blount
1809-1815

Governor Joseph McMinn
1815-1821

Governor William Carroll
1821-1827, 1829-1835

Governor Sam Houston
1827-1829

Governor William Hall
1829

Governor Newton Cannon
1835-1839

Governor James Knox Polk
1839-1841

Governor James Chamberlain Jones
1841-1845

Governor Aaron V. Brown
1845-1847

Governor Neil S. Brown
1847-1849

Governor William Trousdale
1849-1851

Governor William B. Campbell
1851-1853

Governor Andrew Johnson
1853-1857, 1862-1865

Governor Isham Green Harris
1857-1862

Robert L. Caruthers
elected 1863, not inaugurated

Governor William G. Brownlow
1865-1869

Governor Dewitt Clinton Senter
1869-1871

Governor John Calvin Brown
1871-1875

Governor James D. Porter
1875-1879

Governor Albert Smith Marks
1879-1881

Governor Alvin Hawkins
1881-1883

Governor William B. Bate
1883-1887

Governor Robert L. Taylor
1887-1891, 1897-1899

Governor John Price Buchanan
1891-1893

Governor Peter Turney
1893-1897

Governor Benton McMillin
1899-1903

Governor James B. Frazier
1903-1905

Governor John I. Cox
1905-1907

Governor Malcolm R. Patterson
1907-1911

Governor Ben W. Hooper
1911-1915

Governor Tom C. Rye
1915-1919

Governor Albert H. Roberts
1919-1921

Governor Alf. A. Taylor
1921-1923

Governor Austin Peay
1923-1927

Governor Henry Hollis Horton
1927-1933

Governor Hill McAlister
1933-1937

Governor Gordon Browning
1937-1939, 1949-1953

Governor Prentice Cooper
1939-1945

Governor Jim Nance McCord
1945-1949

Governor Frank G. Clement
1953-1959, 1963-1967

Governor Buford Ellington
1959-1963, 1967-1971

GOVERNOR'S MANSION, NASHVILLE, TENNESSEE

920 Walker   104217
Out of a clear blue sky